# THE CRISIS OF OUR AGE

## P. A. SOROKIN *has written:*

THE CRISIS OF OUR AGE
MAN AND SOCIETY IN CALAMITY
RUSSIA AND THE UNITED STATES

# THE CRISIS OF OUR AGE

## THE SOCIAL AND CULTURAL OUTLOOK

*By*

PITIRIM A. SOROKIN

*A Dutton* **dep** *Paperback*

*Everyman*

NEW YORK

E. P. DUTTON & CO., INC.

1957

*1941*

PITIRIM A. SOROKIN is a native of Touria, Russia. He studied at the University of St. Petersburg from 1910-1914, and in 1917 became secretary to Alexander Kerensky. From 1919-1922 Dr. Sorokin was Professor of Sociology at the University of St. Petersburg, but was banished by the Soviets in 1922. He came to the United States in 1923 to teach at the University of Minnesota. In 1930 Dr. Sorokin transferred to Harvard University where he organized the Department of Sociology in 1931, was its Chairman for some fifteen years and an active member until his retirement in 1955.

THE CRISIS OF OUR AGE was first published in 1941.

## FOREWORD

Since its publication in 1941 *The Crisis of Our Age* has appeared in Portuguese, German, Spanish, Dutch, Czech, Norwegian, Finnish, and Japanese translations. In this new edition nothing is changed in the original text of the book. Since the historical events have been unfolding according to the diagnosis and prognosis of *The Crisis* there is no need for correction of its main propositions. The only exception, perhaps, is the cautiously expressed hypothesis that, so far as the data up to 1908 indicated, the rate of increase in scientific discoveries and inventions in the twentieth century has tended to slow down. Actually, this rate after 1908 has been increasing rather than decreasing. For this reason the hypothesis needs to be corrected. However, when the movement of scientific discoveries and inventions in the twentieth century is tied up with their trend towards increasing destructiveness, stressed in *The Crisis*, and with the danger of explosion of a new world war, then the "incorrect" hypothesis may turn out to be doubly correct. For a new world war, carried on with all the scientific—nuclear, bacteriological and other—instruments of destruction, will certainly stop for a long time scientific as well as other creativity of mankind. So much for the "correction" of this point.

In accordance with the prognosis of *The Crisis, the central process for the last few decades has consisted in: a) a progressive decay of sensate culture, society, and man, and b) in an emergence and slow growth of the first components of the new—ideational or idealistic—sociocultural order.*

In *science* this double process has manifested itself in: a) the mentioned increasing destructiveness of the morally irresponsible, sensate scientific achievements, and b) in a transformation of the basic theories of science in a morally responsible, ideational or idealistic direction. This change has already made today's science less materialistic, mechanistic, and deterministic—or less sensate—than it was during the preceding two centuries. For this modern science matter has become but a condensed form of energy which dematerializes into radiation. The material atom is already dissolved into more than thirty non-material, "cryptic, arcane, perplexing, enigmatic, and inscrutable" elementary particles: the electron, the proton, the photon, the mesons, etc., or into "the image of waves which turn out into the waves of probability, waves of consciousness which our thought projects afar . . . These waves like those associated with the propagation of light quanta need no substratum in order to propagate in space-time; they undulate neither in fluid, nor in solid, nor yet in a gas." Around a bend of quantum mechanics and at the foot of the electronic ladder the basic notions of "materialistic and mechanistic science" such as: matter, objective reality, time, space, causality are no longer applicable, and the testimony of our senses largely loses its significance. As to the deterministic causality it is already replaced in the modern science by Heisenberg's principle of uncertainty, by fanciful "quanta jumps," by a mere chance relationship or—in psychosocial phenomena—by "voluntaristic," "free-willing, law of direction" exempt from causality and chance.

Similar transformations have taken place in the new, leading theories of biological, psychological, and social sciences. In contrast to the superannuated, though still intoned, clichés of mechanistic, materialistic, and deter-

*for Philosophy { increasing decline of materialistic "positivistic"
philosophies.
Emergence + growth of Existential & Neo-Thomist
philosophies}*

FOREWORD

ministic biology, psychology, and sociology, the rising, significant theories in these disciplines clearly show that the phenomena of life, organism, personality, mind, and sociocultural processes are irreducible to, and cannot be understood as, purely materialistic, mechanistic, and sensory realities. According to these theories, they have, besides their empirical aspect, the far more important— mindfully-rational and even supersensory and superrational—aspects. In these and other forms the most modern science has already become notably ideational or idealistic in comparison with what it was in the nineteenth century. This means an increasing replacement of the dying sensate elements of science by the new—idealistic or ideational—ones.

*In the field of philosophy* this double process has manifested itself in increasing sterility and decline of recent materialistic, mechanistic, "positivistic," and other sensate philosophies and in the emergence and growth of "the Existential," "the Intuitive," the "Neo-Thomist," "the Integral," "the Neo-Mystical," "the Neo-Vedantist," and other philosophies congenial to the basic principles of Ideationalism or Idealism.

A similar double process has been going on in *all fields of fine arts*.

*In the realm of religion* it has shown itself in the simultaneous growth of: a) militant atheism and b) religious revival.

In *ethics* it has called forth: a) utter bestiality and horrible demoralization shown in the Second World War, bloody revolutions, and increasing criminality, and b) growth of moral heroism, sublime altruism, and organized movements for abolition of war, bloody strife, and injustice.

In *politics* the double process has resulted: a) in proliferation of all kinds of tyrannical dictatorships, and b) in the slowly swelling grass-roots movements for establishment of a competent, honest, and morally responsible government of the people, by the people, and for the people.

This struggle between the forces of the previously creative but now largely outworn sensate order and the emerging, creative forces of a new—ideational or idealistic—order is proceeding relentlessly in all fields of social and cultural life. The final outcome of this epochal struggle will largely depend upon whether mankind can avoid a new world war. If the forces of the decaying sensate order start such a war, then, dissipating their remaining energy, these forces can end or greatly impede the creative progress of mankind. If this Apocalyptic catastrophe can be avoided, then the emerging creative forces will usher humanity into a new magnificent era of its history. Which of these alternative courses is going to take place depends tangibly upon every one of us.

PITIRIM A. SOROKIN

Winchester, May, 1957.

cf. outline on page 341

# PREFACE AND ACKNOWLEDGMENT

The book represents in a modified form my public lectures on *The Twilight of Sensate Culture* given at the Lowell Institute in February, 1941. It is based upon four volumes of my *Social and Cultural Dynamics*. In these volumes the reader can find an ampler evidence for the conclusions reached, a more detailed analysis of the problems discussed, and a vast body of the literature concerning each problem.

For the privilege of giving the Lowell lectures I am indebted to A. Lawrence Lowell, the trustee of the Lowell Institute, and W. H. Lawrence, its curator. Without their kind invitation this book would hardly have been written. For the permission to use some of the plates, diagrams and text of my *Social and Cultural Dynamics* I bring my thanks to the American Book Company. I am indebted to the Duke University Press for the permission to reproduce a part of my address, "Socio-cultural Trends in Euro-American Culture," given at the Duke University Centennial Celebration and published by this Press in a volume, *A Century of Social Thought;* to the Georgetown University and the American Catholic Sociological Society for a similar permission to use my addresses given at the Sesquicentennial Celebration of the Georgetown University in 1939 and at the annual meeting of the Catholic Sociological Society, in December, 1940. Finally, I thank the Harvard Committee for the Research in the Social Sciences for a financial help in typing and typographical preparation of the manuscript.

# CONTENTS

PAGE

*Preface and Acknowledgment*     5

CHAPTER

I. THE DIAGNOSIS OF THE CRISIS     13

Three Diagnoses: Criticism of the views regarding the crisis as ordinary and as the death agony of Western culture and society     13

II. THE CRISIS OF THE FINE ARTS     30

1. The Ideational, Idealistic, and Sensate Forms of the Fine Arts     30

2. Notable Shifts in the Forms of the Fine Arts     36

3. The Contemporary Crisis in the Western Fine Arts: its achievements and maladies; the revolt against sensate art     52

III. THE CRISIS IN THE SYSTEM OF TRUTH: SCIENCE, PHILOSOPHY, AND RELIGION     80

1. Three Systems of Truth: Ideational, Idealistic, and Sensate     80

2. The Rhythm of Domination of Systems of Truth in History, and Its Reason. Importance of intuitional cognition     102

3. The Crisis of the Contemporary Sensate System of Truth     116

| CHAPTER | PAGE |
|---|---|

IV. THE CRISIS IN ETHICS AND LAW — 133

1. Ideational, Idealistic, and Sensate Systems of Ethics — 133

2. Ideational, Idealistic, and Sensate Systems of Law — 146

3. Shifts in the Domination of Ideational, Idealistic, and Sensate Law — 154

4. The Disintegration of Sensate Ethics and Law — 157

V. THE CRISIS OF CONTRACTUAL FAMILY, GOVERNMENT, ECONOMIC ORGANIZATION, LIBERTY, AND INTERNATIONAL RELATIONS — 167

1. Familistic, Contractual, and Compulsory Relationships — 167

2. The Rise of Contractualism in Modern Society — 169

3. The Crisis of Contractualism — 176

4. Roots of the Crisis — 195

VI. CRIMINALITY, WAR, REVOLUTION, SUICIDE, MENTAL DISEASE, AND IMPOVERISHMENT IN THE CRISIS PERIOD — 205

1. Criminality, War, Revolution, Suicide, Mental Disease and Impoverishment as the Symptoms and Consequences of the Crisis — 205

2. The Bloodiest Crisis of the Bloodiest Century — 212

CHAPTER                                                              PAGE

VII. TRAGIC DUALISM, CHAOTIC SYNCRETISM, QUANTITA-
TIVE COLOSSALISM, AND DIMINISHING CREATIVENESS
OF THE CONTEMPORARY SENSATE CULTURE                          241

  1. The Culture of Man's Glorification and Deg-
     radation                                                241

  2. Culture of Chaotic Syncretism                           247

  3. The Culture of Quantitative Colossalism                 252

  4. Decline of Creativeness of our Overripe Sen-
     sate Culture                                            256

VIII. THE PRESENT PHASE OF AMERICAN CULTURE                  272

  1. Similarity of European and American Social
     Trends                                                  272

  2. Similarity of European and American Cultural
     Trends                                                  280

  3. Conclusions and Diagnosis                               294

IX. THE DISINTEGRATION OF SENSATE CULTURE; THE
ROOTS OF THE CRISIS AND THE WAY OUT                          298

  1. The Meaning of the Disintegration of Sensate
     Culture and Society                                     298

  2. The Roots of the Crisis                                 308

  3. The Way Out and Beyond                                  315

  4. Crisis—Ordeal—Catharsis—Charisma—Resur-
     rection                                                 321

# THE CRISIS OF OUR AGE

# CHAPTER I

# THE DIAGNOSIS OF THE CRISIS

## THREE DIAGNOSES

A number of years ago, in several of my works and particularly in my *Social and Cultural Dynamics*, I stated clearly, on the basis of a vast body of evidence, that

> every important aspect of the life, organization, and the culture of Western society is in the extraordinary crisis. . . . Its body and mind are sick and there is hardly a spot on its body which is not sore, nor any nervous fiber which functions soundly. . . . We are seemingly between two epochs: the dying Sensate culture of our magnificent yesterday and the coming Ideational culture of the creative tomorrow. We are living, thinking, and acting at the end of a brilliant six-hundred-year-long Sensate day. The oblique rays of the sun still illumine the glory of the passing epoch. But the light is fading, and in the deepening shadows it becomes more and more difficult to see clearly and to orient ourselves safely in the confusions of the twilight. The night of the transitory period begins to loom before us, with its nightmares, frightening shadows, and heartrending horrors. Beyond it, however, the dawn of a new great Ideational culture is probably waiting to greet the men of the future.[1]

Contrary to the prevalent opinion at that time, in the same works I indicated that wars and revolutions were not disappearing but would grow in the twentieth century to

[1] P. Sorokin, *Social and Cultural Dynamics* (New York, 1937), Vol. III, p. 535. Similar statements were made in several of my articles and books, such as *Social Mobility* (New York, 1926) and *Contemporary Sociological Theories* (New York, 1928).

an absolutely unprecedented height, looming more imminent and more formidable than ever before; that democ-
racies were declining, giving place to various kinds of
despotisms; that the creative forces of Western culture
were withering and drying up; and so on.

When these statements were written, there was no war,
no revolution—not even an economic depression of 1929.
The horizon of the socio-cultural life looked clear and
unclouded. Everything on the surface seemed to be excellent and hopeful. For this reason the prevalent opinion
of the leaders of thought as well as of the masses was
optimistic. They believed in a "bigger and better" prosperity and the disappearance of war and bloodshed; in
international good will and cooperation led by the League
of Nations; in the economic, mental, and moral improvement of mankind and in "streamlined" progress. In such
a mental atmosphere my statements and warnings were
naturally a voice crying in the wilderness. They were
either sharply criticized or disdainfully dismissed. A legion
of supposedly competent scholars and critics showered
upon me the term "Cassandra" and other *epitheta
opprobria*.

A decade or so elapsed. What then appeared to be impossible to many is, at the present moment, already a fact
as solid as a fact can be. The "sweet" theories of my
supposedly competent critics are pitilessly thrown by history into its ash can. The prevalent optimism of that time
has evaporated. The crisis is here in all its stark and unquestionable reality. We are in the midst of an enormous conflagration burning everything into ashes. In a few weeks
millions of human lives are uprooted; in a few hours cen-

Theory I — Sharp form of economic or political crisis, Prescribe readjustment of economic conditions or modification of political conditions

Probably most prevalent

THE DIAGNOSIS OF THE CRISIS 15

tury-old cities are demolished; in a few days kingdoms are erased. Red human blood flows in broad streams from one end of the earth to the other. Ever-expanding misery spreads its gloomy shadow over larger and larger areas. The fortunes, happiness, and comfort of untold millions have disappeared. Peace, security, and safety have vanished. Prosperity and well-being have become in many countries but a memory; freedom, a mere myth. Western culture is covered by a blackout. A great tornado sweeps over the whole of mankind.

If the explosion of the crisis is thus undeniable, its nature, its causes, and consequences, are much less certain. We read and hear daily a dozen different opinions and diagnoses. Among these, two opposite views seem to be prevalent. Many so-called experts seemingly still think that it is an ordinary crisis, similar to many through which Western society has passed several times in every century. Most of them view it as a sharp form of either economic or political crisis. Its main issue they see, respectively, in a conflict of democracy versus totalitarianism, or capitalism versus communism, or nationalism versus internationalism, or despotism versus liberty, or Great Britain versus Germany. There are among these diagnosticians even such "experts" as reduce the issue to a mere conflict of "wicked men," like Hitler or Stalin or Mussolini, and "good fellows," like Churchill or Roosevelt. Viewing the crisis in this light, these diagnosticians accordingly prescribe as the cure such medicine as a slight or substantial readjustment of economic conditions, from a rearrangement of money, or banking, or social security to the elimination of private property; or a modification of political conditions—national and international—in this or that way; or the elimination of Hitler and other "wicked men." Through these and similar measures they hope to correct the maladjustment, to eradicate the evil, and to return to the bliss of "bigger and better" prosperity, to the sunshine of secure peace, to the boons of "streamlined" progress. Such is one—probably the most prevalent—diagnosis of the crisis, its roots, and its cure.

The other diagnosis is much more pessimistic, though less prevalent, especially in the United States. It views the crisis as the death agony of Western society and culture. Its partisans, led recently by Oswald Spengler, assure us that each culture is mortal. Having reached maturity, it begins to decline. The end of the decline is the irretrievable collapse of the culture and society in question. Western culture and society have already passed their zenith; at the present time they are in the last stage of decline. The present crisis is but the beginning of the end of their historical existence. No remedy can avert this destiny; no cure can prevent the death of Western culture. Such is the essence of the second diagnosis of our crisis. In this acute form it is voiced by only a few thinkers. In the diluted form of "a mortal danger facing Western culture," of its possible disintegration and decay if the forces of an enemy should prove victorious, it is noisily proclaimed every day by college presidents and professors, by ministers and journalists, by statesmen and politicians, by members of men's and women's clubs. In this diluted form it has become a stock feature of our leading dailies.

In my opinion both these diagnoses are grossly inaccurate. Contrary to the optimistic diagnosis, the present crisis is not ordinary but extraordinary. It is not merely an economic or political maladjustment, but involves simultaneously almost the whole of Western culture and society, in all their main sectors. It is a crisis in their art and science, philosophy and religion, law and morals, manners and mores; in the forms of social, political, and economic organization, including the nature of the family and marriage—in brief, it is a crisis involving almost the whole way of life, thought, and conduct of Western society. More precisely, it consists in a disintegration of a fundamental form of Western culture and society dominant for the last four centuries.

Any great culture, instead of being a mere dumping place of a multitude of diverse cultural phenomena, existing side by side and unrelated to one another, represents a unity or individuality whose parts are permeated by the same fundamental principle and articulate the same basic value. The dominant part of the fine arts and science of such a unified culture, of its philosophy and religion, of its ethics and law, of its main forms of social, economic, and political organization, of most of its mores and manners, of its ways of life and mentality, all articulate, each in its own way, this basic principle and value. This value serves as its major premise and foundation. For this reason the important parts of such an integrated culture are also interdependent causally: if one important part changes, the rest of its important parts are bound to be similarly transformed.

Take, for instance, Western medieval culture. Its major principle or value was God, the true-reality value. All the important sectors of medieval culture articulated this fundamental principle-value as formulated in the Christian Credo. In all its integrated compartments medieval culture articulated:

> *Credo in unum Deum, Patrem omnipotentem, factorem coeli et terrae, visibilium omnium et invisibilium; et in unum Dominum Jesum Christum, filium Dei unigenitum, et ex Patre natum ante omnia saecula, Deum de Deo,* and so on, up to *Confiteor unum baptisma in remissionem peccatorum, et expecto resurrectionem mortuorum, et vitam venturi saeculi.*
>
> *Amen.*

Its architecture and sculpture were the "Bible in stone." Its literature, again, was religious and Christian through and through. Its painting articulated the same Bible in line and color. Its music was almost exclusively religious: *Alleluia, Gloria, Kyrie eleison, Credo, Agnus Dei, Mass, Requiem,* and so on. Its philosophy was almost identical with religion and theology and was centered around the same basic value-principle: God. Its science was a mere handmaid of Christian religion. Its ethics and law were but an elaboration of the absolute commandments of Christian ethics. Its political organization, its spiritual and secular powers, were predominantly theocratic and based upon God and religion. Its family, as a sacred religious union, was indissoluble and articulated the same fundamental value. Even its economic organization was controlled by a religion prohibiting many forms of economic relationships, otherwise expedient and profitable, and stimulating many forms of economic activity, otherwise inexpedient from a purely utilitarian standpoint. Its dominant mores, ways of life, and mentality stressed the union with God as the only supreme end, and a negative or indifferent attitude toward this sensory world, with all its wealth, pleasures, and values. The sensory world was considered a mere temporary "city of man" in which a Christian was but a pilgrim aspiring to reach the eternal City of God and seeking to render himself worthy to enter it. In brief, the integrated part of medieval culture was not a conglomeration of various cultural objects, phenomena, and values, but a unified system—a whole whose parts articulated the same supreme principle of true reality and value: an infinite, supersensory, and superrational God, omnipresent, omnipotent, omniscient, absolutely just, good, and beautiful, creator of the world and of man. Such a unified system of culture based upon the principle of a supersensory and superrational God as the only true reality and value may be called *ideational*. A basically similar major premise respecting the superrational and supersensory reality of God, though differently perceived in its properties, underlay also the integrated culture of Brahmanic India, the Buddhist and Taoist cultures, Greek culture from the eighth to the end of the sixth century B.C., and some other cultures. They have all been predominantly ideational.

The decline of medieval culture consisted precisely in the disintegration of this ideational system of culture. It began at the end of the twelfth century, when there emerged the germ of a new—and profoundly different—major principle, namely, that *the true reality and value is sensory*. Only what we see, hear, smell, touch, and otherwise perceive through our sense organs is real and has

"Seeds of Renaissance; Rationalism soon to follow."

"Rationalism has been the legacy of the humanism of the Renaissance"

From Beowulf to Thomas Hardy.
Robert Schafer    Vol II P. 4

value. Beyond such a sensory reality, either there is nothing, or, if there is something, we cannot sense it; therefore it is equivalent to the nonreal and the nonexistent. As such it may be neglected. Such was this new principle—one entirely different from the major principle of the ideational system of culture.

This slowly rising new principle met with the declining principle of ideational culture, and their blending into one organic whole produced an essentially new form of culture in the thirteenth and fourteenth centuries. Its major premise was that *the true reality is partly supersensory and partly sensory*—that it embraces the supersensory and superrational aspect, plus the rational aspect and, finally, the sensory aspect, all blended into one unity, that of the infinite manifold, God. The cultural system embodying this premise may be called *idealistic*. The culture of the thirteenth and fourteenth centuries in Europe, like the Greek culture of the fifth and fourth centuries B. C., was predominantly idealistic, based upon this synthesizing major premise.

The process, however, did not stop at this point. The ideational culture of the Middle Ages continued to decline, whereas the culture based upon the premise that true reality and value are sensory continued to gather momentum during the subsequent centuries. Beginning roughly with the sixteenth century, the new principle became dominant; and with it the new form of culture that was based upon it. In this way the modern form of our culture emerged—the sensory, empirical, secular, and "this-worldly" culture. It may be called *sensate*. It is based upon, and is integrated around, this new principle-value:

*the true reality and value is sensory*. It is precisely this principle that is articulated by our modern sensate culture in all its main compartments: in its arts and sciences, philosophy and pseudo-religion, ethics and law; in its social, economic, and political organization; in its dominant ways of life and mentality. This will be developed in subsequent chapters. Thus the major principle of medieval culture made it predominantly otherworldly and religious, oriented toward the supersensory reality of God and permeated by this value. The major principle of the idealistic culture was partly supersensory and religious and partly "this-worldly" and secular. Finally, the major principle of our modern sensate culture is predominately "this-worldly," secular, and utilitarian. All these types—ideational, idealistic, and sensate—are exemplified in the history of Egyptian and Babylonian, Greco-Roman, Hindu, Chinese, and other great cultures.

After this digression we may return to our thesis and state more closely the fact that the present crisis of our culture and society consist exactly in the disintegration of the dominant sensate system of modern Euro-American culture. Having been dominant for several centuries, the sensate form has impressed itself on all the main compartments of Western culture and society and made them also predominantly sensate. As the sensate form disintegrates, so all these compartments of our society and culture likewise disintegrate. For this reason the crisis is not a maladjustment of this or that single compartment, but rather the disintegration of the overwhelmingly greater part of these sectors, integrated in and around the sensate form. Being "totalitarian," or integral, in its nature, the crisis is in-

3 Major Principles of Distinctive Western Cultures

1. Ideational – supersensory + superrational God is only true reality + value (eg. middle Ages)

2. Idealistic – mixture of supersensory + sensory (eg. 13th + 14th centuries)

3. Sensate – predominantly secular + utilitarian (eg. 16th cent. to present)

comparably deeper and more profound than any ordinary crisis. It is so far-reaching that during the last thirty centuries there have been only four crises in the history of Greco-Roman and Western cultures comparable to the present one. Even these four were on a smaller scale than that with which we are faced. We are living and acting at one of the epoch-making turning points of human history, when *one fundamental form of culture and society— sensate—is declining and a different form is emerging.* The crisis is also extraordinary in the sense that, like its predecessors, it is marked by an extraordinary explosion of wars, revolutions, anarchy, and bloodshed; by social, moral, economic, political, and intellectual chaos; by a resurgence of revolting cruelty and animality, and a temporary destruction of the great and small values of mankind; by misery and suffering on the part of millions—a convulsion far in excess of the chaos and disorganization of the ordinary crises. Such transitional periods have always been the veritable *dies irae, dies illa.*

This means that the main issue of our times is not democracy versus totalitarianism, nor liberty versus despotism; neither is it capitalism versus communism, nor pacifism versus militarism, nor internationalism versus nationalism, nor any of the current popular issues daily proclaimed by statesmen and politicians, professors and ministers, journalists and soapbox orators. All these popular issues are but small side issues—mere by-products of the main issue, namely, the sensate form of culture and way of life versus another, different form. Still more insignificant are such issues as Hitler versus Churchill, or England versus Germany, or Japan versus the United States, and the like. We have heard such slogans before, during the war of 1914-1918. Then, also, innumerable voices proclaimed certain persons, like Emperor Wilhelm Hohenzollern, and certain countries, like Germany, as the root of the evil and viewed their elimination or defeat as the main issue of the war and as a radical cure of the evil. The Kaiser was eliminated and Germany was defeated; yet this neither prevented nor weakened the subsequent development of crises nor forestalled the present catastrophe. It was not the Hitlers, Stalins, and Mussolinis who created the present crisis: the already existing crisis made them what they are—its instrumentalities and puppets. They may be removed, but this removal will not eliminate the crisis nor even appreciably diminish it. It will merely create new super-Hitlers and Stalins, Churchills and Roosevelts, as long as the crisis lasts.

In all these respects the first diagnosis is fallacious. No less faulty are its prescriptions. They can neither cure the crisis nor even stop its further development. At best, these medicines are useless; more often than not they are harmful. Even if the Anglo-Saxon bloc is victorious in the present war, its victory will neither arrest nor decrease the tragedy of the crisis until, as we shall see, the sensate premise of our culture is replaced by a more adequate foundation. *( How true this has proved itself ) /*

No less sharply do I disagree with the other—the pessimistic—diagnosis. Contrary to its claim, the present crisis is not the death agony of Western culture and society, nor does it mean their irretrievable disintegration or the end of their historical existence. Based mainly on a biological analogy, all such theories are groundless. There is no uniform law requiring that every culture and society should pass through the stages of childhood, maturity, senility, and death. None of the partisans of these very old theories has shown what is meant by either the childhood of society or the senility of culture; what are the typical characteristics of each age; when one age ends and the next begins; when and how a given society dies, and what the death of society or culture means. In all these respects the theories in question are mere analogies, consisting of undefined terms, of nonexisting uniformities, of undemonstrated claims. Still less convincing are they in their contention that Western society and culture have reached the last stage of senility and are now in their death agony. Not only is the meaning of the death of Western culture not clearly elucidated, but no evidence for it is really given.

A careful study of the situation accordingly shows that the present crisis represents only a disintegration of the sensate form of Western society and culture, to be followed by a new integration as notable in its own way as was the sensate form in the days of its glory and climax. Just as the substitution of one mode of living for another by an individual does not mean his death, so also the substitution of one fundamental form of culture for another is not equivalent to the death of the society and culture that undergo such a transformation. Western society and culture at the end of the Middle Ages underwent a similar shift from one fundamental socio-cultural form to another—from the ideational to the sensate form. And yet such a change neither put an end to their existence nor paralyzed their creative forces. After the chaos of the transition period, at the end of the Middle Ages, Western society and culture displayed magnificent creative forces for five centuries and recorded one of the most brilliant pages in the history of human culture. The same is true of the Greco-Roman and other great cultures, which experienced during their historical existence several such shifts. Similarly, the present disintegration of the sensate form is in no way identical with the end of Western society and culture. The tragedy and chaos, the horrors and sorrow of the transition period being over, they will evolve a new creative life, in a new integrated form, as magnificent in its own way as the five centuries of the sensate era.

Moreover, such a change, however painful, seems to be the necessary condition for any culture and society to remain creative throughout their historical existence. No fundamental form of culture is infinite in its creative possibilities, but is limited. Otherwise it would be not one of several forms but an absolute, embracing all of them. When their creative forces are exhausted, and all their limited potentialities are realized, the respective culture and society either become petrified and uncreative (if they retain their already exhausted form) or else shift to a new form which opens new creative possibilities and new values. All the great cultures, indeed, that remained creative underwent just such shifts. On the other hand, the cultures and societies that became stagnant, petrified, and uncreative were precisely the cultures and societies that did not change their form and could not find new wine and new vessels for it. Sterility and an uncreative, vegetative existence have been the nemesis of such societies and cultures. Thus, contrary to the diagnosis of the Spenglerians, their alleged death agony has been but the birth pangs of a new form of culture, the travail attending the release of new creative forces.

The complete disintegration of our culture and society, claimed by the pessimists, is impossible, also, for the reason that the *total sum* of social and cultural phenomena of Western society and culture has never been integrated into one unified system. What has not been integrated cannot, it is evident, disintegrate.

Though most of the important compartments of medieval culture were dominated by the ideational form, side by side with this there existed sensate and unintegrated—eclectic—varieties of the medieval fine arts and science, philosophy and religion, ethics and ways of life, as minor currents. Although the dominant pattern of modern culture in all its compartments has been sensate for the last four centuries, side by side with it there have existed, as minor currents, ideational and other forms of the fine arts, religion, philosophy, law, ethics, and modes of living and thinking. Hardly any culture in the history of mankind has been totally and completely integrated. The term, "dominant form of integration," does not mean an absolutely monopolistic domination, to the complete exclusion of all other patterns of culture.

This means that only those cultural and social phenomena which have been integrated into one sensate sociocultural form can disintegrate, as they are indeed doing. But though these phenomena compose the major part of the total culture of the West, nevertheless they do not embrace all the socio-cultural phenomena that make up this culture. Its other part, unintegrated into the sensate form, can continue to exist and function without any disintegration. Since these phenomena are not a part of the sinking sensate ship, they need not go down with it.

Still more ridiculous are the daily cries of politicians, journalists, and the press about the end of civilization and progress if they are defeated and if their opponents are victorious. During every political campaign we hear a petty politician threatening his listeners with "the end of civilization" if he is not elected. Who is not familiar with "the fight for progress and culture" of the leaders of warring cliques? Who does not know the slogan, "The world is coming to an end," uttered by an ambitious person unable to attain his Lilliputian objective? Almost daily we hear a familiar variation on this theme from a crowd of highbrow and low-brow seekers after certain objectives, often utterly insignificant and egotistic. If we are to believe these pseudo-prophets, then civilization and culture must have died long ago or must be about to perish any minute! Fortunately, culture and civilization are infinitely tougher than these clowns of the historical circus assure us. Political and other parties, cliques, factions, and armies come and go; yet culture persists, in spite of all their funeral orations. Thousands of petty aspirants are incessantly balked in their rightful or wrongful ambitions. And yet, contrary to their "requiem" to civilization, it continues to exist. Many a country has been defeated in war; and still civilization has not perished. As has been said, it is made of a much tougher stuff and has a much greater vitality than these "undertakers of culture" assure us.

Moreover, they hardly ever stop to ask whether the culture they stand for is really *worth* saving—whether, on the contrary, it would not be better for it to perish. As we shall see, many of the values of the contemporary culture they advocate hardly deserve being fought for. A large portion of these are already dead and await only a decent burial. Their disappearance is a benefit to humanity rather than a loss—a liberation from poison rather than an impoverishment of culture. With these remarks we shall leave these "undertakers of culture" to their own devices. Neither ethically nor scientifically are their lamentations worth a moment's thought.

The foregoing criticism is sufficient to reject both prevalent diagnoses as grossly misleading. Their dismissal carries with it, as well, the rejection of their proposed remedies. More valid seems to be the third diagnosis. It was developed by the author in great detail several years before the present catastrophe, and in a preliminary form it is restated here without any change. It declares that the present trouble represents the disintegration of the sensate form of Western culture and society, which emerged at the end of the twelfth century and gradually replaced the declining ideational form of medieval culture. For the past four centuries it has been dominant. In the period of its ascendancy and climax it created the most magnificent cultural values in most of the compartments of Western culture. During these centuries it wrote one of the most brilliant pages in human history. However, no finite form, either ideational or sensate, is eternal. Sooner or later it is bound to exhaust its creative abilities. When this moment comes, it begins to disintegrate and decline. So it has happened several times before, in the history of a number of the leading cultures of the past; and so it is happening now with our sensate form, which has apparently entered its decadent stage. Hence the magnitude of the crisis of our time. Even if it does not mean the extinction of Western culture and society, it nevertheless signifies one of the greatest possible revolutions in our culture and social life. As such, it is infinitely deeper and more significant than the partisans of the "ordinary crisis" imagine. A change from a monarchy to a republic or from capitalism to communism is utterly insignificant in comparison with the substitution of one fundamental form of culture and society for another—ideational for sensate, or vice versa. Such shifts are very rare phenomena. As we have seen, during the thirty centuries of Greco-Roman and Western history they occurred only four times. But when they do take place, they produce a fundamental and epoch-making revolution in human culture and society. We have the rare privilege of living, observing, thinking, and acting in the conflagration of such an ordeal. If we cannot stop it, we can at least try to understand its nature, its causes, and its consequences. If we do this, we may be able, to some extent, to shorten its tragic period and to mitigate its ravages. To help in these crucial tasks by unfolding and substantiating the meaning of the third diagnosis is the purpose of the subsequent chapters. Let us pass, then, to an analysis of the crisis in various fields of our cultural and social life.

*Purpose of Book*

# CHAPTER II

# THE CRISIS OF THE FINE ARTS

## I. THE IDEATIONAL, IDEALISTIC, AND SENSATE FORMS OF THE FINE ARTS

We shall begin our anatomy of the crisis with the compartment of the fine arts. The fine arts are one of the most sensitive mirrors of the society and culture of which they are an important part. What the society and culture are, such will their fine arts be. If the culture is predominantly sensate, sensate also will be its dominant fine arts. If the culture is unintegrated, chaotic and eclectic also will be its fine arts. Since contemporary Western culture is predominantly sensate, and since the crisis consists in the disintegration of its dominant supersystem, so the contemporary crisis in the fine arts must also exhibit a disintegration of the sensate form of our painting and sculpture, music, literature, drama, and architecture. Let us see just what are the sensate forms of the fine arts in general and the contemporary sensate art forms in particular; also what are the symptoms of, and the reasons for, this disintegration.

In Chapter I, I stated briefly that each of the three main forms of culture—ideational, idealistic, and sensate—has its own form of the fine arts, and that these differ profoundly from one another in their external style as well as in their internal content. The essential traits of each of the three forms of the fine arts follow from the major premise of each of these systems of culture. Let us give a concise preliminary portrait of the ideational, idealistic, and sensate types of art.

*Ideational Art.* In its content as well as in its type, ideational art articulates the major premise of ideational culture that the true reality-value is God. Therefore *the topic of ideational art is the supersensory kingdom of God*. Its "heroes" are God and other deities, angels, saints and sinners, and the soul, as well as the mysteries of Creation, Incarnation, Redemption, Crucifixion, and Salvation, and other transcendental events. It is religious through and through. It pays little attention to the persons, objects, and events of the sensory empirical world. Therefore neither *paysage*, nor *genre*, nor portraiture of empirical persons can be found in it in any tangible degree. Its objective is not to amuse, entertain, or give pleasure, but to bring the believer into a closer union with God. It is a part of religion, and functions as religious service. It is a communion of the human soul with itself and with God. As such it is sacred in its content and form. As such it does not admit any sensualism, eroticism, satire, comedy, caricature, farce, or anything extraneous to its nature. Its emotional tone is pious, ethereal, and ascetic.

*Its style is and must be symbolic.* It is a mere visible or sensory sign of the invisible or supersensóry world of values. Since God and supersensory phenomena do not have any material forms, they cannot be perceived and depicted naturalistically, as they appear to our senses. They can only be denoted symbolically. Hence the transcendental symbolism of ideational art. The signs of the dove, anchor, and olive branch in the early Christian catacombs were mere visible symbols of the values of the invisible kingdom of God, as distinct from the empirical dove or olive branch. Wholly immersed in an eternal supersensory world, such an art is *static* in its character and in its adherence to the sanctified, hieratic forms of tradition. It is wholly internal and therefore looks externally simple, archaic, devoid of sensory trimmings, pomp, and ostentation. It suggests a marvelous soul dressed in shabby clothes. Its significance is not in its external appearance but in the inner values it symbolizes. It is not an art of the professional individual artist but the creation of the anonymous collectivity of believers conversing with God and with their own soul. Such a communication does not need any professional mediators or any beautifying externalities. Such in black and white are the essential traits of ideational art, whenever and wherever it is found. It is clearly but a derivation from, and articulation of, the major premise of ideational culture.

*Sensate Art.* Its typical characteristics are almost opposite to those of ideational art, because the major premise of sensate culture is opposite to the ideational premise. Sensate art lives and moves entirely in the empirical world of the senses. Empirical *paysage*, empirical man, empirical events and adventures, empirical portraiture—such are its topics. Farmers, workers, housewives, girls, stenographers, teachers, and other human beings are its personages. At its overripe stage, prostitutes, criminals, street urchins, the insane, hypocrites, rogues, and other subsocial types are its favorite "heroes." Its aim is to afford a refined sensual enjoyment: relaxation, excitation of tired nerves, amusement, pleasure, entertainment. For this reason it must be sensational, passionate, pathetic, sensual, and incessantly new. It is marked by voluptuous nudity and concupiscence. It is divorced from religion, morals, and other values, and styles itself "art for art's sake." Since it must amuse and entertain, it makes wide use of caricature, satire, comedy, farce, debunking, ridiculing, and similar means.

*Its style is naturalistic, visual, even illusionistic, free from any supersensory symbolism.* It reproduces empirical phenomena as they look, sound, smell, or otherwise appear to our sense organs. It is dynamic in its very nature: in its emotionality, in the violence of the passions and actions which it portrays, and in its incessant modernity and change. It has to be eternally changing, presenting a constant succession of fads and fashions, because otherwise it will be boring, uninteresting, unenjoyable. For the same reason it is the art of external show, dressed up for an exhibition. Since it does not symbolize any supersensory value, it stands and falls by its external appearance. Like a pretty but stupid glamour girl, it succeeds only as long as it is trigged out and retains its superficial beauty. To retain its charm, it has to make lavish use of pomp and circumstance, colossality, stunning technique, and other means of external adornment. Furthermore, it is an art of professional artists catering to a passive public. The more it develops, the more pronounced become these characteristics.

*Idealistic Art.* Idealistic art is an intermediary between the ideational and sensate forms of art. Its world is partly supersensory and partly sensory, but only in the sublimest and noblest aspects of sensory reality. Its heroes are partly gods and other transcendental creatures; partly the empirical man, but in his noblest aspects only. It is an art intentionally blind to everything debasing, vulgar, ugly, and negative in the empirical world of the senses. Its style is partly symbolic and allegoric, partly realistic and naturalistic. Its emotional tone is serene, calm, and imperturbable. The artist is merely the *primus inter pares* of the community of which he is a member. In a word, it represents a marvelous synthesis of the ideational and the noblest forms of sensate art.

*Eclectic Art.* Finally, there is a pseudo-art which is not integrated in any serious manner, representing a purely mechanical mixture of anything and everything. It has no internal or external unity, no individual and consistent style, and represents no system of unified values. It is the art of a bazaar, a miscellany of different patterns, forms, subjects, and ideas. Such an art is a pseudo-art rather than a genuine art.

*Historical Examples.* As ideational, idealistic, and sensate systems of culture are perennial and universal forms exemplified in the past and the present, among both primitive and civilized peoples, so all three integrated forms of the fine arts are also found in the past and in the present, among both primitive tribes and complex civilizations. Ideational fine arts in an impure form occur among many primitive peoples, such as the Zuñi Indians, the Negro tribes of Africa, and certain Australian tribes. Likewise the geometric art of Neolithic man, when it is symbolic, was typically ideational. In the so-called historical cultures, ideational art dominated at certain periods the art of Taoist China, Tibet, and Brahmanic India, Buddhist culture, and ancient Egypt; that of Greece from the ninth to the end of the sixth century B.C.; that of the early and medieval Christian West; and so on. The sensate form of the fine arts, in turn, has been scattered everywhere and at all times. It is the prevailing form of the art of early Paleolithic man; of many a primitive tribe, such as the Bushmen of Africa; of many an Indian and Scythian tribe; and the like. It pervaded the fine arts of Assyria, at least during some periods of its history; and those of ancient Egypt in the later stages of the Old Kingdom, Middle Kingdom, and New Empire, and especially during its latest periods—the Saite, Ptolemaic, and Roman epochs. It definitely characterized the later known era of the Creto-Mycenaean culture and the Greco-Roman culture from the third century B.C. to the fourth century A.D. Finally, it has been dominant in Western culture during the last five centuries. The idealistic form of art has not been so widespread as the other two, but has occurred many times. Its best examples are furnished by the Greek fine arts of the fifth century B.C. and by the Western art of the thirteenth century.

However different in many respects are the fine arts, for instance, of primitive and civilized peoples, they all exhibit a series of similar internal and external characteristics when they belong to the same type. Among other things, these facts mean that the domination of this or that form in the fine arts is not a matter of the presence or absence of artistic skill, but is the result, rather, of the ideational, sensate, idealistic, or mixed mentality of the respective peoples and cultures. Living in a sensate age, we are prone to interpret ideational art as more primitive than the sensate, and the ideational artist as less skillful and masterly than the sensate artist. Such an interpretation is, however, without foundation. Paleolithic man or the man of the early Stone Age was a sensate artist, highly skillful in the visual *not a question of artistic skill but of cultural value.*

reproduction of the empirical objects he was interested in, such as animals, hunting scenes, and the like. Neolithic man or the man of the more highly developed culture of the late Stone Age was essentially an ideational artist, and his work revealed little traces of sensate art. Thus the later and more developed stage of culture produced ideational art, rather than the sensate art which had preceded it. Likewise, the perfect sensate art of the Creto-Mycenaen Age was replaced after the ninth century B.C. by the ideational art of early Greece. Similar shifts from one form of art to another we observe in the fine arts of ancient Egypt, China, and several other countries. Finally, the perfect sensate art of Greco-Roman culture from the third century B.C. to the fourth century A.D. was replaced by the ideational art of the medieval Christian West.

All this means, as we have seen, that the preeminence of each form of the fine arts is not a question of the presence or absence of artistic skill but of the nature of the dominant supersystem of culture. In a culture marked by the ideational supersystem, its fine arts will be prevailingly ideational; and a similar generalization holds true for the cultures dominated, respectively, by the sensate, idealistic, or mixed supersystem. (*Dynamics*, Vol. I, chaps. 5-7)

ct 3 #3 my
Summary

## 2. NOTABLE SHIFTS IN THE FORMS OF THE FINE ARTS

When in a given total culture the dominant supersystem changes, the dominant form of the fine arts changes in the same direction. If the sensate supersystem is superseded by the ideational, sensate art gives way to ideational art; and vice versa. An example of this phenomenon is furnished by the shifts of the Greco-Roman and the Western fine arts from one dominant form to another. Let us glance at these shifts, not only for their own sake but also for an understanding of the nature of the contemporary crisis in the Western fine arts.

The story begins with the Creto-Mycenean art, which, exemplified by the famous Vaphio cup, is a perfect visual art, showing an unexcelled sensate mastery on the part of the artist. It gives us a superlative impressionistic rendition of the taming of a bull. We know also that the late period of the Creto-Mycenean culture was decadently sensate.

When we come to the Greek art of the eighth century to the end of the sixth century B.C., we encounter the realm of so-called archaic or, more exactly, ideational art, with all the characteristics proper to such an art. It is symbolic, religious, and otherworldly. It does not depict things as they appear to the eye; instead, it employs geometric and other visible symbols of the invisible world of predominantly religious values.

Beginning with the end of the sixth century B.C., we note a decline of ideational art in all its aspects and the emergence of an idealistic art which reaches its climax in the fifth century B.C. with Phidias, Aeschylus, Sophocles, and Pindar. It is probably the example *par excellence* of idealistic art. Exemplified by the Parthenon, it is half religious and half empirical. From the sensory world it derives only its noble types and positive values. It is an idealizing, typological art. Its portraits are beautified types—not realistic representations of a given individual. It is marred by nothing low, vulgar, or debasing. It is serene, calm, and sublime. Its idealism manifests itself in the artists's excellent knowledge of human anatomy and of the means of rendering it in an ideal or perfect form; in the type of persons represented; in their postures; in the abstract treatment of the human type. There are no concrete portraits, no ugliness, no defective traits. We are introduced to immortals or idealized mortals; the aged are rejuvenated; infants are depicted as grown up; the women reveal few traits that are specifically womanish, and appear in the guise of athletes. There is no concrete landscape. The postures and expressions are free from anything violent, from excessive emotion and distorting passion. They are calm and imperturbable, like the gods. Even the dead reflect the same serene beauty. These characteristics are the result not of technical limitations but, rather, of the artist's desire to avoid anything that might disturb the harmony or ideal order of the idealistic scheme of life. Finally, this art was deeply religious, moralizing, instructive, ennobling, and patriotic. It was not just art for art's sake, but an art indissolubly connected with other values, religious, moral, and civic. The artist was self-effacing and merged his identity in that of the community: Phidias, Polycletus, Polygnotus, Sophocles, and other masters were just *primi inter pares* in a collective religious or patriotic enterprise embracing the whole community. They had not yet turned, like the sensate artists, into professionals wholly absorbed in art for art's sake and therefore liberated from civic, moral, religious, and other duties. In brief, it was an art perfectly blending heavenly perfection with the noblest earthly beauty, interfusing religious and other values with those of sublime sensory forms. It may be designated as a "value-laden" art, in contradistinction to the "value-empty" art of the pure aesthetician.

After the fifth century B.C. the sensate wave began to rise, and the ideational wave to decline. As a result the idealistic synthesis was shattered, and sensate art came to dominate the field from approximately the third century B.C. up to, roughly, the fourth century A.D. During the first centuries of our era it entered its overripe phase, marked by realism and by an ever-accelerating tempo of imitation of the archaic, classic, and other styles. This same period witnessed the emergence of Christian ideational art, which kept pace with the growth of Christianity, becoming in the sixth century A.D. the dominant form.

With the advent of the fourth century A.D., the sensate Greco-Roman art underwent a significant change. Though many a historian characterizes this mutation as the decay of classic art, it may be more accurately interpreted as the decay of the sensate form and its eventual replacement by a new dominant form, namely, by the Christian ideational art, which held sway from the sixth century to the end of the twelfth century.

The supreme examples of medieval *architecture* are the great cathedrals and temples—buildings devoted to God. Their external forms—the cruciform foundation, the dome or spire, and almost every architectural and sculptural detail—are symbolic. They are truly the Bible in stone! Medieval *sculpture*, in turn, is religious through and through. It is once again the Old and the New Testament "frozen" in stone, clay, or marble. Medieval *painting* is likewise overwhelmingly religious—a pictorial representation of the Old and New Testaments. It is almost entirely symbolic and otherworldly. There is no attempt to produce in two-dimensional terms the illusion of three-dimensional reality. There is little nudity, and what little there is is ascetic. There is no *paysage, no genre, no realistic portraiture, no satire, caricature, or comedy*. Medieval *literature* is derived mainly from the Bible, certain comments on it, prayers, the lives of the saints, and other religious literature. Literature of a purely secular character occupies scarcely any place in it. If some secular Greco-Roman literature is used, it is so fundamentally transformed and so symbolically interpreted that Homer, Ovid, Virgil, and Horace constitute a mere simulacrum. We have to wait until almost the twelfth century for a genuine secular literature. The entire empirical world is ignored. The medieval *drama and theater* consists of the church service, religious processions, and mystery plays. Medieval *music* is represented by the Ambrosian, Gregorian, and other plain chants, with their *Kyrie eleison, Alleluia, Agnus Dei, Gloria, Requiem, Mass*, and similar purely religious songs.

All this is externally simple and austere, archaic and traditional, and hieratic. Externally, for a sensate person accustomed to the luxurious trimmings of sensate art, it may appear very bleak and unattractive—devoid of technical mastery, of entertainment, of beauty. Nevertheless, when it is understood that ideational art is subjective, immersed in the supersensory world, it is seen to be as impressive in its own way as any known sensate art. The ideational art of these centuries is ethereal, admirably expressive of its supersensory orientation, and eminently consistent. It is the art of the human soul conversing with its God. As such it was not designed for the market, for purposes of profit, for fame, popularity, or other sensate values, or for sensual enjoyment. It was created, as Theophilus has observed, *nec humane laudis amore, nec temporalis premii cupiditate . . . sed in augmentum honoris et gloriae nominis Dei.* Hence its anonymity. The artists were collective. The whole community built a cathedral or church. Individual leaders did not care to affix their name to their creation. With very insignificant exceptions, we do not know even the identity of the creators of the foremost cathedrals, sculptures, or other masterpieces of medieval art. Such were the pre-eminent characteristics of medieval art from the sixth to the end of the twelfth century.

These traits are not derived from superficial impressions, but from a systematic quantitative and qualitative analysis of more than one hundred thousand medieval and modern pictures and sculptures, of most of the medieval literature extant, of the greater part of the surviving medieval music, of the bulk of medieval architecture and drama. Later on, the principal data of this statistical study will be given. They will show clearly the ideational character of the dominant medieval art. For the present, let us continue our brief characterization of the main swings throughout the later centuries.

At the end of the twelfth century we witness the first signs of the decline of the ideational fine arts in most of its fields except that of music, where the decline appears somewhat later. The fine arts pass from the ideational form to the idealistic form of the thirteenth century and of part of the fourteenth century. This is similar in certain respects to the Greek idealistic art of the fifth century B.C. In both cases it is moored to the supersensory world; but in either case it begins to reflect more and more the noblest and most sublime positive values of the empirical world, whether they relate to man and civic institutions or to idealized beauty. In its style it unites the ripest technical mastery of the sensate artist with a pure, noble, and idealistic *Weltanschauung*. It is a highly selective art, so far as the sensory world is concerned, choosing only the positive values, types, and events and ignoring the pathological and negative phenomena. It embellishes even the positive empirical values, never depicting them as they actually look, sound, or otherwise appear to the senses. It is an art of idealized types, and rarely of sharply individualized persons or events. As in the Greek art of the fifth century, its portraiture is not a bald reproduction of the traits of a given person, but an abstract and noble type having remote, if any, resemblance to the real traits. Its *genre* reflects only the noble events. Its heroes are the immortals and semidivine beings—heroic figures, whether in their achievements or in their tragedy. It immortalizes the mortals. Even when it depicts the dead, it often represents them with open eyes, as if they beheld the light inaccessible to us, and free from any symptoms of decomposition and death. It is serene, calm, free from any frivolity, comedy, or satire, violent passions or emotions, anything debasing, *pathétique,* or macabre. It is the art of a pure nun who for the first time notes the beauty of the empirical world—the spring morning, the flowers and trees, the dew, the sunshine, the caressing wind and blue sky. These traits are conspicuous in all the fine arts of these centuries, though in music they are markedly weaker. Music still remains mainly ideational; only about a century later does it come to assume the noble forms of the sensory beauty of idealistic music.

The idealistic period ends with the close of the fifteenth

century. The continued decline of the ideational form and the progressive rise of the sensate form result in the dominance of the sensate form in most of the fine arts. This domination increases, with slight fluctuations, throughout the subsequent centuries, reaching its climax and possible limit in the nineteenth century.

We already know the characteristics of this sumptuous sensate art. It has been overwhelmingly *secular*, aiming to reflect sensory beauty and to provide sensory pleasure and entertainment. As such, it has been an art for art's sake, divorced from religious, moral, and civic values. Its heroes and personages have been common mortals and, in its later stage, preeminently the subsocial and pathological types. Its emotional tone has been passionate, *pathétique*, sensational. It has been marked by voluptuous and sensual nudity. It has been an art of *paysage* and *genre*, of portraiture, of caricature, satire, and comedy, of vaudeville and operetta; an art of show, decked out *à la* "Hollywood"; an art of individualistic, professional artists catering to a passive public. As such it has been made for a market, as a commodity to be bought and sold like any other commodity, depending for success on competition with other commodities.

In its external style it has been *realistic, naturalistic, or visual*. It has depicted empirical reality as it appears to our senses. In music it has presented a combination of sounds that please or displease, as such, through their sheer physical qualities, without any symbolism or transcendental meanings behind them. In this sense it has reflected merely the *surface of empirical phenomena*—their superficial forms, appearances, and sounds—instead of penetrating the three-dimensional depth of the object in painting, and the essence of the reality that lies beneath the surface. Hence its *illusionistic* character. A sensate picture, with its foreshortening and perspective, aims to give an illusion of three-dimensional reality through a two-dimensional medium. Similar illusionistic devices have been abundant in sculpture and even in architecture. They tend to produce a show, reflecting surface appearances rather than the substance itself. In brief, we find all the characteristics of a full-fledged sensate art as indicated above.

In order to perceive the essential differences between this sensate art and the medieval ideational and idealistic art, to obtain a clearer conception of the major shifts of the Western fine arts, and to procure the necessary evidence for the correctness of the foregoing outline, let us glance at some summary statistics taken from my *Dynamics*. The figures are based on a study of more than one hundred thousand pictures and sculptures of the eight principal European countries from the beginning of the Middle Ages up to 1930. This cross section, embracing as it does the overwhelmingly greater part of the pictures and sculptures of these countries known to the art historian, is thus the most representative ever given. While the details may exhibit certain inaccuracies, the essentials are certainly reliable. Likewise the conclusions concerning music, literature, drama, and architecture are based on similarly representative samples of the foremost known musical, literary, dramatic, and architectural creations of the eight countries.

One of the most important characteristics of ideational, idealistic, and sensate art is the nature of their topics, whether in the field of the supersensory-religious or in that of the sensory-empirical. From this standpoint the history of European art is well depicted by the following figures.

Among all the pictures and sculptures studied, the percentages of religious and secular works are as follows for the specified centuries:

| | Before the 10th | 10th-11th | 12th-13th | 14th-15th |
|---|---|---|---|---|
| Religious | 81.9 | 94.7 | 97.0 | 85.0 |
| Secular | 18.1 | 5.3 | 3.0 | 15.0 |
| Total | 100.0 | 100.0 | 100.0 | 100.0 |

| | Before the 16th | 17th | 18th | 19th | 20th |
|---|---|---|---|---|---|
| Religious | 64.7 | 50.2 | 24.1 | 10.0 | 3.9 |
| Secular | 35.3 | 49.8 | 75.9 | 90.0 | 96.1 |
| Total | 100.0 | 100.0 | 100.0 | 100.0 | 100.0 |

The figures show that medieval *painting* and *sculpture* were overwhelmingly religious. This religious factor began to decline after the thirteenth century, becoming quite insignificant in the nineteenth and twentieth centuries, whereas the percentage of secular pictures and sculptures—which were virtually absent in the Middle Ages—has risen since the thirteenth century to approximately 90 to 96 per cent of all the known pictures and sculptures of the countries in question.

A similar situation has prevailed in music, literature, and architecture.

Medieval *music* is represented *par excellence* by the Ambrosian, Gregorian, and other plain chants of religious character. As such, it is almost 100 per cent religious. Between 1090 and 1290 there appears for the first time a secular music—that of the troubadours, trouvères, and minnesingers. Thereafter secular music becomes more and more dominant. Among the leading musical compositions the percentage of religious compositions falls to 42 per cent in the seventeenth and eighteenth centuries, 21 in the nineteenth, and 5 in the twentieth. The percentages of secular compositions rise, respectively, to 58, 58, 79, and 95 per cent.

In *literature* likewise, for the period from the fifth to the tenth century, there is almost no secular masterpiece. The works of the Greco-Roman poets and other writers used are so drastically remodeled and subjected to such rigorous symbolic interpretation that they have little in common with their originals and serve as a mere adjunct of religious literature. In the ninth, tenth, and eleventh centuries and at the beginning of the twelfth there appear a few semi-secular or semireligious works, such as the *Heliand*, the *Hildebrandslied*, *La Chanson de Roland*, and *Le Pèlerinage de Charlemagne;* but we must await the second half of the twelfth century for the emergence of genuinely secular literature. On the other hand, in the literature of the eighteenth to the twentieth century the percentage of secular works rises to 80-90 per cent, according to the country.

In *architecture* virtually almost all the foremost creations of the Middle Ages were cathedrals, churches, monasteries, and abbeys. They dominated the sky line of the cities and villages, embodying the creative genius of medieval architecture. During the last few centuries, on the other hand, the overwhelmingly majority of architectural creations have been secular in character—the palaces of the secular rulers, the mansions of the rich and powerful, town halls, business buildings, railroad stations, museums, concert halls, theaters, opera houses, and the like. Amid such structures as the Empire State and Chrysler Buildings, Radio City, and the towers of the great metropolitan dailies, even the vast cathedrals of our cities are lost.

These unquestionable facts leave no doubt as to the ideational character of the medieval fine arts and the secular nature of those of the last four centuries, especially from the eighteenth to the twentieth. They show how exactly this change proceeded, from century to century. Among other things, they indicate that in the topics treated the art of the thirteenth century was still overwhelmingly religious.

Another important aspect of ideational-idealistic and sensate art is its external style, whether it be formal and symbolic or visually and audibly sensate. The change in this respect is outlined by the following summary data concerning the percentage of each specified style of European pictures and sculptures for the centuries in question.

| Style | Before the 10th | 10th-11th | 12th-13th | 14th-15th |
|---|---|---|---|---|
| Visual (sensate) | 13.4 | 2.3 | 6.0 | 53.6 |
| Ideational formal, symbolic) | 77.0 | 92.2 | 51.1 | 29.2 |
| Expressionistic | .... | .... | .... | .... |
| Mixed | 9.6 | 5.5 | 42.9 | 17.2 |

| Style | Before the 16th | 17th | 18th | 19th | 20th |
|---|---|---|---|---|---|
| Visual (sensate) | 72.0 | 90.6 | 96.4 | 95.5 | 61.5 |
| Ideational (formal, symbolic) | 20.3 | 5.9 | 2.5 | 0.3 | 0.7 |
| Expressionistic | .... | .... | .... | 2.8 | 35.5 |
| Mixed | 7.7 | 3.5 | 1.1 | 1.4 | 2.3 |

[The diagram (*next page*) sums up pictorially the preceding figures showing the rise of the sensate wave from 1200 to 1930. It shows also the movement of other additional characteristics.]

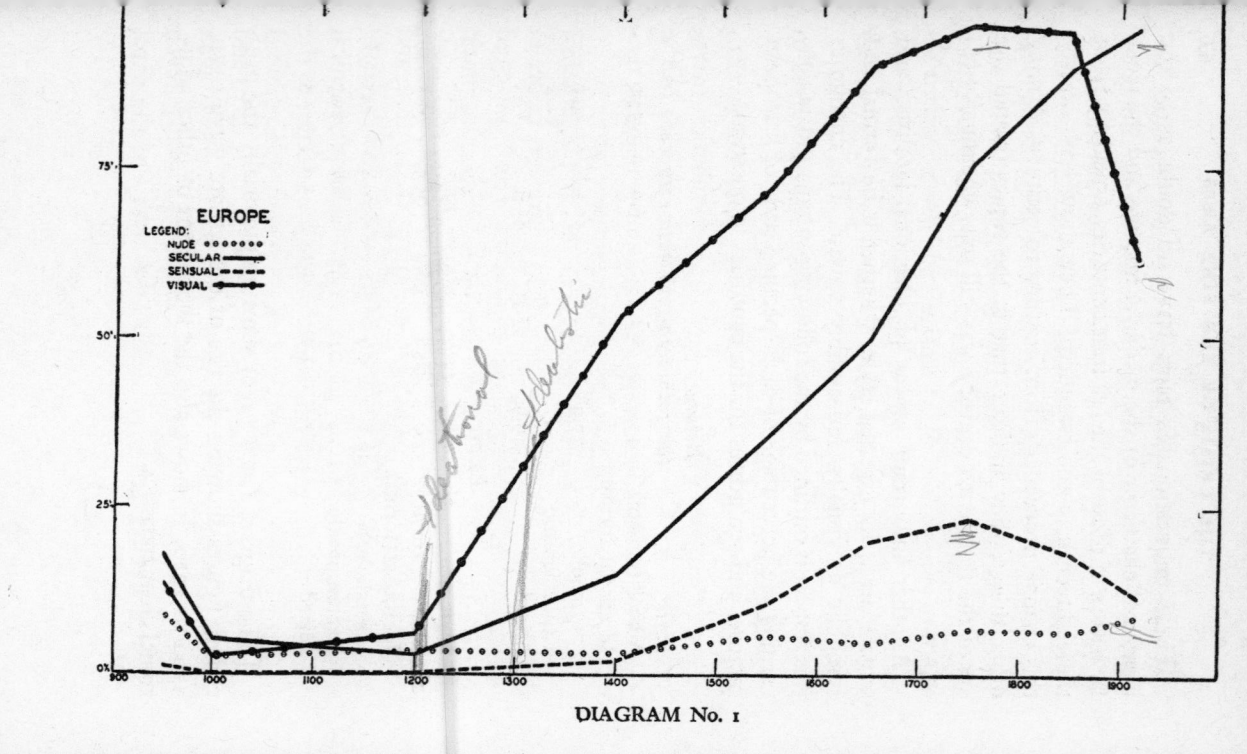

**DIAGRAM No. 1**

The overwhelmingly ideational (symbolic, hieratic, formal) style of the medieval centuries and the preeminently visual, or sensate, style of the last five centuries are now sufficiently clear. The thirteenth and fourteenth centuries mark the first sharp decline in the domination of the ideational style in favor of first the idealistic and then the sensate form. The twentieth century is characterized by a sharp decline in the visual-sensate style and a marked increase in the expressionistic manner, thus breaking the trend that prevailed from the thirteenth to the nineteenth century, inclusive.

In a modified form similar great shifts have occurred in other fine arts.

In literature we witness a decrease, after the twelfth century, in purely religious—and thus symbolic—literature in favor of the essentially allegorical literature of the thirteenth to the fifteenth century and of the realistic, naturalistic manner of the last four centuries.

In music we observe a decrease in the simple, ethereal music of the chants and an increase in music ever richer in its sensory embellishment and trimmings. This manifested itself in a replacement of the unadorned unisonous music of the chants by polyphony, counterpoint, and fugue; by harmony, or monophony; by complicated rhythms and dynamic contrasts; by an increasing number and diversity of instruments; and by all the other elaborate technical means characteristic of the music of the seventeenth to the twentieth century. Finally, the present century introduced such innovations as the whole-note scale, atonality, and cacophony. We must not forget that the famous Roman *Schola*, in the time of Saint Gregory had only seven singers. Even much later, despite the luxury of the papal

*Music – from 7 singers to 100 instruments*

Sistine Chapel, there were hardly more than thirty-seven
singers, and these were reduced in the time of Palestrina
(*ca.* 1565) to twenty-four. There was no orchestra and no
instrumental accompaniment. Then, step by step, the
choruses and instrumental means progressed both in quantity and in quality. Monteverde's *Orpheus* (1607) was
scored for about thirty instruments; the orchestras of Bach,
Lulli, and Stamitz were of the same size. Most of the notable symphonies of the eighteenth century (from Mozart
to Beethoven) were scored for a still larger number of instruments—about sixty. Those of the nineteenth and
twentieth centuries (from Berlioz and Wagner to Mahler,
Richard Strauss, and Stravinsky) are scored for a hundred
or more instruments. Such has been the course of the qualitative and quantitative evolution of music during the sensate centuries.

In architecture the trend, up to the recent years of the
twentieth century, was in the same direction, that of sensateness—from the Romanesque and Gothic to the over-
ornate flamboyant Gothic, the imitative styles of the Renaissance, the showy baroque, the still more puerile rococo,
and finally, in the nineteenth century, the overdecorative,
incoherent Victorian manner and successive waves of imitation of the Gothic, Romanesque, Moorish, and so on.
These styles are marked by displayfulness and ornamenta-
tion, utility, and eclecticism. The twentieth century gives,
as we shall see, the first signs of hope—that of a new integration.

Other relevant characteristics demonstrate the same
shifts of the Western fine arts as are indicated by the
transformation of their topics and style. Take, for instance,
the *otherworldly-ascetic* and the *sensual atmosphere* of

pictures and sculptures. In those of the medieval period from the sixth to the fourteenth century the percentage of sensual works fluctuates between zero and 0.8 per cent. In recent centuries it rises to 20.2 for the seventeenth, 23.6 for the eighteenth, and 18.4 for the nineteenth; and then recedes to 11.9 for the twentieth, as the crisis century. The Middle Ages disclose no picture or sculpture of extremely sensuous or sexual character, and a notable proportion of medieval works are highly spiritual and ascetic. For the last three centuries the percentage of preeminently spiritual paintings and sculptures falls to an insignificant fraction, whereas the percentage of strongly sensual pictures shows a sharp upswing, especially from the eighteenth to the twentieth century. In medieval representations of the nude the percentage of eroticism is zero up to the thirteenth century; in recent centuries it mounts to 21.3 per cent for the seventeenth, 36.4 for the eighteenth, 25.1 for the nineteenth, and 38.1 for the twentieth. Other symptomatic characteristics show the following percentual figures for the pictures and sculptures studied:

| Centuries | Paysage | Portrait | Genre | Love Scenes |
|---|---|---|---|---|
| Before the 10th | 0 | 1.4 | 5.4 | 0 |
| 10th to 11th | 0 | 0.4 | 1.6 | 0 |
| 12th to 13th | 0 | 0.9 | 0.5 | 0 |
| 14th to 15th | 0.1 | 6.6 | 4.1 | 0 |
| 16th | 1.6 | 11.5 | 5.3 | (From 3 to 47 |
| 17th | 2.9 | 17.8 | 14.9 | per cent, de- |
| 18th | 6.6 | 21.8 | 25.3 | pending upon |
| 19th | 15.4 | 18.9 | 35.9 | the country) |
| 20th | 21.6 | 18.0 | 37.4 | |

Those who desire more detailed figures as to these and several additional traits can find them in my *Dynamics*

(Vol. I, chaps. 5-13). For our present purposes the foregoing statistics are sufficient to corroborate the above statements concerning the trend of the Western fine arts from the medieval ideational form to the idealistic form of the thirteenth and fourteenth centuries and to the sensate form characteristic particularly of the period from the seventeenth to the twentieth century.

### 3. THE CONTEMPORARY CRISIS IN THE WESTERN FINE ARTS

This brings us to the contemporary crisis in the fine arts of the West. Wherein does it consist and what are its symptoms? A general answer as to the nature of the crisis has already been given: it consists in the disintegration of the sensate form of the fine arts that has been dominant for the last five centuries. In the second part of the nineteenth and in the twentieth century it reached its overripe stage, and it has subsequently tended to become progressively hollow and self-contradictory. This increasing vacuity makes it more and more sterile and should enlist increasing revolt. Its mounting self-contradictions widen enormously its inner dualism and progressively destroy its unity—indeed, its very nature.

*The Achievements of Our Sensate Art.* Let us, accordingly, survey concisely the achievements of its *Blütezeit* and the growing weakness of its most recent stage—that of its decadence. The achievements of sensate Western art are both prolific and illustrious.

In its technical aspects it is possibly more masterly than the sensate art of any other age or culture. Our art-masters are unequaled in their command of technical resources. They can imitate primitive art, the art of Phidias or Polygnotus, that of the Gothic cathedrals or Egyptian temples, of Raphael or Michelangelo, of Homer or Dante, of Palestrina or Bach, of the Greek or medieval theater. In addition, the fine arts of modern Western culture have achieved *chefs-d'oeuvre* unknown to previous periods.

Quantitatively, our culture has produced art creations *unexampled* either in *volume or in size*. Our buildings dwarf the hugest structures of the past; our orchestras and choruses make those of the past seem actually Lilliputian; and the same is true of our novels and poems. As a result, our art touches the lives of the masses to an extent heretofore unknown. It has penetrated the whole of social life and all the products of civilization, from prosaic tools and instruments (such as knives and forks, tables, and automobiles) to the appointments of the home, dress, and what not. Whereas music, pictures and sculptures, poems and dramas, were formerly accessible only to the select few who were fortunate enough to be in a room where the music was played, the picture or sculpture was exhibited, the poem was read, or the drama was performed, at the present time almost anyone can enjoy symphonies played by the best orchestras; dramas performed by the best actors; literary masterpieces published in thousands, sold for a price available to millions, and accessible in multitudes of public libraries; sculptures and pictures in the original, exhibited in public museums and reproduced in millions of excellent copies; and so on. With the expenditure of the slightest amount of energy almost anyone can be in touch nowadays with almost any object of art. This form of art has entered the daily life of contemporary man, from the color and lines of his car, the color and shape of its tires, the curvature of his shoes or table, to the accessories of his bath. The socio-cultural objects sold even in five-and-ten-cent stores are not merely objects of utility, but incorporate in themselves a great deal of sensate beauty. Such a diffusion of art and beauty throughout society, pervading man's daily life and all the objects of his culture, has hardly occurred before. Instead of being a rare and artificial plant, cultivated in only a few "nurseries," by a small group of artists, and accessible to only a few fortunate persons, art and beauty have become a daily routine accessory of the whole of Western culture, affecting every part of our private dwelling houses, every inch of our streets and highways, our parks, and all the other features of our socio-cultural life. This is certainly an achievement of no small value. It means a total embellishment of man's entire life and culture.

Another significant merit of our art is its *infinite diversity and variety*—a typical characteristic of any sensate art. It is not restricted to any one style or any one field, as was the art of many past epochs. It is so rich in its variety that almost anyone possessed of any degree of taste can find in it something that meets his approval. Primitive, archaic, Egyptian, Oriental, Greek, Roman, medieval, classic and romantic, expressionistic and impressionistic, realistic and idealistic, Renaissance, baroque, rococo, visual and tactile, ideational and sensate, cubistic, futuristic, and old-fashioned, religious and secular, conservative and revolutionary, saintly and erotic—all these styles and patterns, and hosts of others, are present in our art. It is like an encyclopedia or gigantic department store where one can find anything he is looking for. Such diversity, on so vast a scale, has never before been exhibited by any sensate art. It is a unique phenomenon—one meritorious rather than blameworthy.

Finally, respecting the inner value of its foremost creations, Western sensate art requires no apologia. Bach, Mozart, and Beethoven; Wagner, Brahms, and Tschaikowsky, need not apologize to any composer of any previous period. A similar generalization holds good for Shakespeare, Goethe and Schiller; Chateaubriand, Hugo, and Balzac; Dickens, Tolstoi, and Dostoevski; for the builders of the mightiest skyscrapers; for the most eminent actors; or for the most distinguished painters and sculptors from the Renaissance to the present time. Any master of our sensate art is as competent in his own field as almost any master of earlier periods and cultures.

In all these respects contemporary art has enormously enriched man's culture and immensely ennobled man himself.

*Maladies of Our Sensate Art.* But side by side with these superlative achievements, our sensate art contains in itself the germs of its own decay and degeneration. These pathogenic germs are inherent in it. So long as it is still growing and maturing, they are not virulent. But when it has finally exhausted most of its truly creative forces, they become active and turn many a virtue of sensate art into a vice. The process usually leads to the growing aridity and sterility of its decadent stage, and then to its disintegration. More precisely, first, the function of giving enjoyment and pleasure leads any sensate art at its decadent stage to degrade one of its own socio-cultural values to a mere means of sensual enjoyment on the level of "wine, women, and song." Second, in its endeavor to portray reality as it appears to our senses it becomes the art of progressively thinner and more illusory surfaces, instead of reflecting the essence of sensory phenomena. Thus it is destined to become ever more superficial, puerile, empty, and misleading. Third, in its quest for sensory and sensational "hits," for stimulation and excitement as the necessary conditions for sensory enjoyment, it is increasingly and fatally deflected from positive to negative phenomena—from ordinary types and events to those which are pathological, from the fresh air of normal socio-cultural reality to the social sewers, until it becomes a museum of pathology and of negative aspects of sensory reality. Fourth, its charming diversity impels it to seek ever-greater variety, until all harmony, unity, and balance are submerged in an ocean of incoherency and chaos. Fifth, this diversity, together with the effort to give pleasure, and to stimulate, leads to an increasing complication of technical means; and this, in turn, tends to make of these instrumentalities an end in themselves—one which is pursued to the detriment of the inner value and quality of the fine arts. Sixth, sensate art, as we have seen, is the art of professional artists creating for the public. Such specialization, while in itself a distinct advantage, results, in the later phases of sensate culture, in the separation of artists from the community—a factor from which both parties suffer, as well as the fine arts themselves.

Such are the inherent virtues of sensate art which, in the course of its development, turn more and more into vices and eventually lead to its disintegration. Let us examine a little more specifically each of these maladies.

The art of Greece prior to the third century B. C. and that of the Middle Ages was never debased to a mere means of sensual entertainment or utility. By the artist as well as by the public it was regarded as the incarnation either of Plato's ideal of absolute beauty or of the absolute value of God. It was not divorced from religious, moral, cognitive, or social values. It was indissolubly bound up with all the other fundamental values—with God, truth, goodness, and the majesty of absolute beauty itself. As such, it was never the empty shell of an "art for art's sake." Thus it was sublime and serene, instructive and elevating, religious and idealistic, intellectually, morally, and socially inspiring. It almost entirely ignored the negative aspects of man and of his empirical world. Nothing coarse, vulgar, debasing, or pathological found place in it. Its topics were the noblest mysteries of this world or the other world; its heroes and personages, as we have seen, were mainly the gods and demigods or the saints. Hence, without specific intention, it uplifted man and his culture to celestial heights, immortalized the mortals, ennobled the commonplace, embellished the mediocre, and idealized the whole of human life. It was the incarnation of absolute values in a relativistic, empirical world.

And the artist himself created, to quote once more the dictum of the famous Theophilus of the Middle Ages, *nec humane laudis amore, nec temporalis premii cupiditate . . . sed in augmentum honoris et gloriae nominis Dei.* His creation was for him a service rendered to God and mankind, the discharge of his religious, social, moral, and artistic duties.

Such was the spirit of the art of Phidias, as exemplified

by the Parthenon, and of the cathedrals of the Middle Ages. Such it remained, in large measure, up to the eighteenth and nineteenth centuries, as revealed by the works of Bach and Beethoven, and of their confrères in music and in other fields of art.

As we move nearer and nearer to contemporary art, we are well-nigh shocked by the contrast that we encounter. Art becomes increasingly a commodity manufactured primarily for the market; motivated largely by *humane laudis amore* and *temporalis premii cupiditate;* and aimed almost exclusively at utility, relaxation, diversion and amusement, the stimulation of jaded nerves, or sexual excitation. Aside from a handful of old fogies, who cares nowadays for an art that does not amuse, entertain, thrill, or relax, like a circus, the advances of a charming girl, a glass of wine, or a good meal? Since it caters to a market, it cannot ignore the tastes of this market. The bulk of such demands are always vulgar; therefore it cannot itself escape vulgarization. Instead of elevating the masses to its own level, it sinks to the level of the common herd. Since it has to entertain, thrill, or relax, how can it avoid becoming progressively more sensational, "stunning," exotic, and pathological? It has to disregard virtually all religious and moral values, because these are rarely "amusing" and "entertaining" in the same sense as wine and women. Hence it comes to be more and more divorced from truly cultural values and turns into an empty art known euphemistically as "art for art's sake," at once amoral, nonreligious, and nonsocial, and often *antimoral, antireligious* and *antisocial* —a mere gilded shell to toy with in moments of relaxation.

As a commercial amusement commodity, it is more

and more controlled by commercial dealers, commercial motives, and the fashion of the moment. Any market commodity is relatively short-lived. If a contemporary artist does not wish to starve, he cannot create eternal values, independent of the fads and fancies of the moment. He is necessarily a slave of market demands, "manufacturing" his commodities in response to these demands. Such an atmosphere is highly unfavorable to the creation of authentic and permanent values. It leads to the mass production of ephemeral "hits," short-lived "best-sellers," and so forth. It makes commercial dealers the supreme arbiters of beauty, compelling artists to adapt themselves to their requirements, enforced through advertising and similar media. These dealers, imposing their "tastes" upon the public, thus strongly influence the course of art development. However much respect one may have for an honest commercial dealer, one is entitled to skepticism concerning his competency as an art *arbiter elegantiarum*. More often than not, he is thoroughly incompetent in such matters.

As a mere means of amusement, contemporary art naturally degrades itself to this level. From the realm of the absolute it sinks to the level of commodity values. No wonder that it eventually comes to be so regarded both by the public and by the artists themselves! It becomes a mere adjunct of advertisements of coffee, drugs, gasoline, chewing gum, and the like. This is clearly brought out by radio, newspaper, poster, and movie art. Not only the dubious art values of the moment but even the greatest art values of the masters are nowadays degraded to the level of such an adjunct. Any day one may hear a selection from Beethoven or Bach as an appendage to the eloquent advertising of such commodities as oil, banking facilities, automobiles, cereals, and laxatives. Rembrandt's or Praxiteles' creations are used as labels for soap, beer, razor blades, or silk stockings. They become mere "satellites" of the more "solid" enjoyments, such as a bag of popcorn, a glass of beer, a highball, or a pork chop consumed at popular concerts or art exhibitions.

As a result, the divine values of art tend to evaporate in the mind of the public. The boundary between authentic art and mere amusement becomes obliterated, and the very standards of true art tend to disappear and to be increasingly replaced by the counterfeit criteria of a pseudo-art. Such is the first degradation of art, artist, and man himself implicit in the development of sensate art.

*The second malady of sensate art is its tendency to become more and more superficial in its reflection and recreation of the sensory world itself.* As we have seen, it strives to reproduce the world as this appears to our sense organs. It does not posit any supersensory value behind the sensory forms. It stands or falls according to its ability to reflect and reproduce this sensory world as faithfully as possible. Such a function necessarily restricts it chiefly to mere surface phenomena. A painter or sculptor whose aim is to reproduce a given landscape or *genre* or individual with the maximum sense of illusion is an artist dedicated to the surface appearances, rather than to the essence, of the phenomena. Like the Impressionist School of the end of the nineteenth century, he gives us only an illusion of what a concrete object looks like at a given moment, or the impression which its fleeting and changing surface makes upon us. Any visual painting is thus inevitably confined not simply to surface appearances but to those of a given moment, because, through the incessant play of light and shade, the surface aspect constantly changes.

With a corresponding modification the same can be said of the other fine arts of the sensate type. They rarely come to grips with the essences. Sensate music stands or falls in accordance with its surface values, as a combination of sounds. Behind and beyond the sounds there is no super-sensory value to refer to. Sensate literature, again, is simply the "behavioristic reflection" of surface psychology, surface events, surface personages. Everyone of the sensate arts, even at its climax, is thus doomed to portray merely the superficial appearances of the phenomena depicted. In this respect it is a twin sister of snapshot photography. It was no accident that the latter art was invented exactly at the moment when the sensate art of the West had become decadent and impressionistic. Like photography, sensate art can "shoot" any object or phenomenon of the sensory world in its surface aspects. No wonder that photography, being simpler, more mechanical, and cheaper, has success-fully driven many a form of sensate art from the market!

Throughout its growth and even at the moment of maturity, sensate art, being still concerned with the eternal values, is highly discriminating in its choice of the objects and events to be reproduced or re-created. It realizes that not everything in the sensory world deserves to be repro-duced or re-created. It still chooses the more important values and phenomena as its topics. In this sense it is not yet entirely divorced from religion, ethics, civic values, and science. It remembers its divine origin and its great mission. In the earlier stages, though it reflects the surface of sensory phenomena, it selects for the most part those which are important, and those aspects which give an insight into their essence. Hence the sensate art of those stages is not entirely superfluous and superficial. Unfortunately, the fundamental objective of sensate art—namely, to entertain, to give pleasure, to excite or to relax—does not permit it to remain very long at this stage of its development. The basic sensory values, through constant repetition, come to lose the fascination of novelty—to become hackneyed and boring. Without novelty the entertainment value begins to evaporate. In order to retain its appeal, the art is forced, under these conditions, to pass rapidly from one object, event, style, and pattern to another, at an ever-increasing tempo. It finds it increasingly difficult to grasp adequately the essentials of its topics, which tend to become mere fleeting shadows caught up by the lens of a camera cranked at an ever-giddier pace. The product of such an art camera inevitably becomes more and more a matter of surface appearances, an incidental and momentary snapshot of reality. Hence the progressive superficiality of sensate art at its later, decadent stage.

The same impasse is reached by another route. In order to be a successful market commodity, sensate art has to impress, to produce a sensation. At its earlier stages its normal personages, normal, positive events, and normal, well-rounded style possess the fascination of novelty. But as times goes on, its topics, through constant repetition, grow familiar and trite. They lose their power to excite, to stimulate, to thrill. Hence the tendency of such an art to seek the exotic, the unusual, the sensational. Together with the ever-shifting fads of the market, this leads at its later stages to an excessively artificial selection of themes and patterns. Instead of the typical and the significant, it chooses such abnormal or trivial topics as criminals, insane persons, paupers, "cave men," or "glamour girls." This concentration on abnormal, artificial, and incidental phenomena makes the inherent superficiality of sensate art still more superfluous, still more misleading as a reflection of empirical reality, still more empty, and increasingly perverse. This is exactly the stage reached by our sensate art at the present moment. It is a rudderless boat, tossed hither and thither by the shifting winds of fad, market demands, and its own quest for the sensational. It has reached the stage of a disfiguring mirror that reflects only the shadows of evanescent and incidental phenomena. Such is, then, the second malady of our sensate art—one inherent, like the first, in its very nature.

The foregoing malady leads, in turn, to a third: *the morbid concentration of sensate art on pathological types of persons and events*. As has already been pointed out, the heroes and other personages of Greek and medieval art were mainly God, deities and semigods, saints, or the noblest of human heroes—the bearers of the basic positive values. The subjects depicted were the mysteries of God's kingdom; the tragedy of victims of fate, such as Oedipus; the achievements of such semidivine or human heroes, such as Prometheus, Achilles, and Hector, the saints of the Middle Ages, or King Arthur and his followers. In this art the mediocre, and especially the subsocial, types of human beings found almost no place. The prosaic daily events of human life, and particularly its negative and pathological aspects, were ignored. If the devil, monsters, debased types of persons, or negative events were occasionally employed, they served merely to throw into sharper relief the positive values. Both Greek art (before the third century B. C.) and that of the Middle Ages immortalized the mortals, shunned the prosaic and mediocre, as well as the vulgar and the negative and pathological. It was a highly selective art, choosing principally the fundamental values of God's kingdom, of nature, or of man's socio-cultural life. It was an art that glorified man, ennobling him and elevating him to the level either of the child of God or of the immortal or semimortal heroes. It reminded him at once of his divine nature and of the importance of his mission in the world.

As we pass from the Middle Ages to more recent centuries the scene changes. These ennobling and idealizing tendencies tend to disappear, their place being taken increasingly by their opposites. When we come to the art of the present day, the contrast, as has already been observed, is well-nigh shocking. Like contemporary science and philosophy in their debasing aspects (see further, Chapter III), contemporary art mortalizes the immortals, stripping them of everything divine and noble. Likewise, it ignores almost all that is divine and noble in man, in his social life and his culture, sadistically concentrating on the mediocre, and especially on the negative, the pathological, the subsocial and subhuman. In music and literature, painting and sculpture, the theater and drama, it chooses as its "heroes" either the ordinary, prosaic types of human beings or the negative and pathological. The same is true also of the events with which it deals. Housewives, farmers and laborers, businessmen and salesmen, stenographers, politicians, doctors, lawyers, and ministers, and especially detectives, criminals, gangsters, and "double-crossers," the cruel, the disloyal, hypocrites, prostitutes and mistresses, the sexually abnormal, the insane, clowns, street urchins, or adventurers—such are the "heroes" of contemporary art in all its principal fields. God, saints, and real heroes are, as a rule, conspicuous by their absence. Even when—as an exception—a contemporary novel, biography, or historical work chooses a noble or heroic theme (such as George Washington, Byron, or some saint), it proceeds, in accordance with the prevailing psychoanalytical method, thoroughly to "debunk" its hero.

Thus in the realm of music the "heroes" are comedians, clowns, murderers (as in *Pagliacci* and *Petrushka*); smugglers and prostitutes *(Carmen)*; pregnant women and their paramours *(Gurrelieder)*; seduced girls *(Faust)*; urbanized "cave men" and "cave women" *(Le Sacré du Printemps)*; insane persons *(The Emperor Jones)*; romantic brigands *(Robert le Diable)*; and the exotic or erotic types represented by the Manons, the Thaises, the Salomes, the Sapphos, the Islamys, the Tamaras, the Aidas; not to mention the dandies of many an opera, suite, and other musical composition. Still more vulgar, negative, and pathological are the heroes of musical comedy and *opéra bouffe*. The music of the nineteenth and twentieth centuries has turned increasingly from the divine and heroic to the mediocre and pathological. My statistical studies show that from 1600 to 1920, among the leading musical works, the number of satirico-comical and prosaic *genre* compositions increased from 24 in the seventeenth century to 106 in the nineteenth, whereas the number of heroic compositions decreased from 123 to 63.

Still more conspicuous is the pathological bent in literature, painting, and sculpture. In these fields the "heroes" are the Babbitts, the Elmer Gantrys, the warped and morbid characters of Hemingway and Steinbeck, Chekhov and Gorki, D'Annunzio, and the like, consisting of insane and criminal types, hypocrites, the disloyal, the wrecks and derelicts of humanity, interspersed here and there with mediocrities. The criminals and detectives of our "relaxation literature" and "thrillers" only serve to emphasize the point. In the field of drama most of the personages, as in Chekhov's, Gorki's, and O'Neill's works, are morbid, warped derelicts or downright criminals, or at best, sheer mediocrities. Even more striking are the pathology and vulgarity that prevail in our motion pictures. The main prescription of the typical scenario is very simple. A society girl falls in love with a gangster, which demonstrates that he is not a gangster but a hero. Or else the rôles are reversed, a prostitute ensnaring a juvenile society "sucker." In the two cases the "moral" is much the same. Statistical studies show that from 70 to 80 per cent of all cinema offerings concentrate on crime and sexual love.

The same trend is exhibited by contemporary European and American paintings and sculpture. The principal personages are not God, the saints, or real heroes, but miners, farmers, laborers, businessmen, pretty girls with seductive curves, or criminals, prostitutes, street urchins, and so on. The events depicted are either routine incidents of daily life or something exotic and pathological. In the rare instances of a truly noble theme, such as Epstein's "Christ" or "Adam," the subject is debased to the level of a subcaveman. Even in such a specialized field as portraiture, some 88 per cent of the foremost works of the masters of the twentieth century are devoted to the lower classes or the bourgeoisie, whereas in the medieval centuries only 9 per cent of all the portraits dealt with these classes, the rest representing royalty, aristocracy, or the higher clergy.

In addition, all the branches of present-day art exhibit an exaggerated penchant for *satire and caricature*—a mode of treatment little known to the Middle Ages. Everything and everybody, from God to Satan, is ridiculed and degraded. We fairly revel in such debasement, which has become the stock in trade of a variety of debunking magazines and other periodicals. Moreover, our art is sexually unbalanced, perverse, and often sadistic. Sex and love are distorted by mocking refrains—such as the crooners' "We kiss and the angels sing" or "Heaven can wait; this is paradise"—which profane the most cherished moral and religious values.

To sum up, contemporary art is primarily a museum of social and cultural pathology. It centers in the police morgue, the criminal's hide-out, and the sex organs, operating mainly on the level of the social sewers. If we are forced to accept it as a faithful representation of human society, then man and his culture must certainly forfeit our respect and admiration. In so far as it is an art of man's debasement and vilification, it is paving the way for its own downfall as a cultural value.

Fourth, *the diversity of sensate art results eventually in a growing incoherence and disintegration*. What a medley of heterogeneous styles, patterns, and forms it displays, from the imitative archaic, primitive, classic, and romantic styles to the most bizarre modern forms! Taken as a whole, it is an inchoate complex, devoid of unity or harmony. Inasmuch as any art worthy of the name must be integrated, this unintegrated agglomeration is inevitably incoherent. Even more serious is its *internal*, or *inward*, incoherence. A musical composition constituting a medley of passages from the Gregorian chants and from the works of Palestrina, Mozart, Wagner, and Stravinsky, peppered with jazzy rhythms and with the catcalls of the crooners, is necessarily a patchwork, or *potpourri*, devoid of expressive unity. The same is true of a literary piece composed in the style, now of Dante, now of Zola, now of the *Roman de la Rose*, now of Shakespeare. The reason for the patchiness that permeates almost the whole of contemporary art is to be found in the enormous diversity of its patterns and styles. The richer the diversity, the more difficult are its assimilation and its unification in a single consistently expressive pattern. Only a genius is capable of such unification.

The phenomenon is brought out even more clearly by the cubist, futurist, Dadaist, pointillist, and other "supermodern" trends. As we shall see, these trends constitute a revolt against the sensate art of surface appearances, against the emphasis upon mere sensate enjoyment and pleasure—an effort, instead, to present the essence of things in their three-dimensional substantiality and to make art something more fundamental, something that in its discordancy reveals the "center of gravity" of the objects dealt with. Yet how tragically they fail to attain these commendable objectives! A Dadaist picture or cubist sculpture, instead of giving the material substance of the object, exhibits simply a distorted and incoherent chaos of surfaces contradicting our normal visual and tactile perceptions.

We never actually see the subjects of Picasso's *Violin* or *Lute Player* as he depicts them. Likewise, we may sympathize with many a modern composer in his revolt against the debasement of music to the level of a mere pleasurable stimulant of the digestive processes. Yet here again we encounter simply a welter of strident, incoherent, and dissonant sounds, neither pleasant nor stimulating, nor expressive of any basic idea, unity, or value. Instead of the artist's commanding the rich assortment of technical means at his disposal, these means dominate the artist, rendering him incapable of properly mastering them. And so it is in the other branches of the fine arts, with the possible exception of architecture, which is now beginning to shake off the bonds of nineteenth-century Victorian tastelessness and formlessness.

This incoherence is still further accentuated by the waves of imitation which have uniformly emerged during the later stages of sensate art. The more decadent it becomes, the more imitative it grows and the swifter becomes the tempo of the successive phases of the process. Its creative potentialities being exhausted, sensate art relies increasingly upon a sophisticated imitation of earlier styles and patterns, beginning with primitive and archaic art and ending with the classical, ideational, idealistic, romantic, neo-classic, or neo-romantic style, according to the preference of the artist and the demands of the market. So it was in the Greco-Roman period of the first to the fourth century A. D., and so it is with the decadent art of the present day. We imitated and still imitate the Egyptian, Chinese, Greek and Roman, Moorish, Romanesque, and Gothic architecture. We imitate the art of the primitive tribes of

Australia and Africa, and the archaisms of the Egyptian, Chinese, Persian, Mayan, and many other styles. We imitate in particular the art of the Negro, and that of the peasantry of all countries; the heraldic art of the medieval nobility; the hieratic art of ancient Egypt; the classical art of Greece; and the art of the Renaissance. Such a flux, together with the sophistication infused into the imitated styles, turns contemporary art into a kind of cosmopolitan museum representing the utmost diversity of styles and patterns. This incoherence, as we have already remarked, is in itself a symptom of the disintegration of contemporary sensate art.

Finally, the disintegration manifests itself in *an increasing subordination of quality to quantity, of inner content and genius to means and techniques*. Since sensate art has to be sensational, it can achieve its effects either through its qualitative or through its quantitative aspects. When it cannot rely on its qualitative superiority, it resorts to a quantitative appeal. Hence the *disease of colossality*, typical of the decadent sensate phase of Greco-Roman and present-day art. We construct the tallest buildings, and boast that they are the best precisely *because* they are the biggest. We maintain huge choruses and orchestras—the bigger the better. A book sold *en masse* is regarded as a masterpiece; a play enjoying the longest run is accepted as the best. Our motion pictures are conceived on a vast scale, and endowed with sumptuous trimmings and accessories. The same is true of our sculptures and monuments, our World's Fairs and Radio Cities. The bulk of our daily newspaper often exceeds the life output of many an eminent thinker. A person enjoying the biggest income, a college with the largest enrollment, a crooner or radio artist with the biggest public, a phonograph record or automobile sold in the largest quantity, a preacher or professor having the largest audience, a research project entailing the largest cost—in short, any material or immaterial value that is in some respect the biggest becomes for this very reason the greatest or best. That is why—to multiply instances—we brag of possessing the largest number of schools and colleges; the largest number of books published or pictures produced; the largest number of museums, churches, plays, and the like. This, again, is the reason for our pride in mass art education, musical education, and adult education. This attitude makes possible the following criteria of artistic progress in this country offered by a serious scientific work with a foreword by the President of the United States.

> One hundred and eighty thousand copies of a government pamphlet on furniture, its selection and use, were distributed in 1931. . . .
> Six hundred thousand objects are lent annually by the St. Louis Educational Museum alone. . . .
> The sale of Navajo blankets is reported as above $1,500,000 in 1930. . . .
> The town of Ottawa, Kansas, with a high-school population of 431, has an orchestra of 90. . . .

These are but variants of the famous boast: "England has only two universities, France has four; but in Ohio alone we have thirty-seven colleges."

Such a quantitative mania ordinarily operates to the detriment of quality. The greater and more varied the mass of the material, the more intractable it becomes and the harder it becomes to integrate it in a single consistent unity. Hence colossality inevitably leads to qualitative deterioration. On the other hand, the emphasis on size proves the way of least resistance. Anyone can pile mass upon mass, quantity upon quantity; but only a genius can achieve (often with the maximum economy of means) a masterpiece. Hence the inner emptiness of our biggest creations. Our cathedrals are devoid of genuine religious spirit. Our universities and colleges produce few, if any, authentic geniuses. The art of our Radio Cities and theaters is supremely vulgar and supremely mediocre. In spite of our art education, no Phidias, Beethoven, Goethe, or Shakespeare has emerged. (What *has* emerged consists chiefly of crooning and jazz, a yellow press, yellow literature, yellow movies, and yellow paintings!) After a few brief weeks our best-sellers sink into permanent oblivion. The same is true of our weekly song hits and cinema successes. At first almost everyone seems to be humming the tune or attending the "show"; but it is not long before these are irretrievably submerged beneath a flood of more novel offerings. Thus the malady of colossality not only sacrifices qualitative excellence, but eventually destroys the art that it has invaded.

The same degeneration is brought about by *the tendency of our culture to substitute means for ends, technique for genius*. The decadent periods, whether in art or science, religion or philosophy, have regularly been marked by the substitution of means for ends, of specific training in technical skills for genuine creativeness. Scientists of such an age talk mainly of the scientific technique of research (though they rarely produce anything above the level of mediocrity); critics and artists talk of the technique of scoring, of playing, of writing, of painting. Technique becomes the alpha and omega of art. Artists strive to exhibit, first of all, their mastery of it, and particularly their own technical inventions. Hence the cerebral character of music or painting, created according to the prescriptions of the approved technique. Hence the mediocrity of research. Hence the striving for technical *tours de force* as the evidence of supreme mastery. Hence the technical virtuosity of philosophy and religion. The nemesis of the deification of technique is the growing aridity of artistic, scientific, religious, and philosophic achievement. The greater the attention to technique, the greater the neglect of the central, inner end-values. We seem to forget that, after all, technique is a mere means—not the end of creative work. We must remember, also, that genius creates its own technique. In the hands of a moron, technique can produce nothing but what is moronic. In the hands of a master, by the grace of God, any technique will yield a masterpiece. Thus the very concentration upon technique, instead of upon the creative end-values, is a sign of the bankruptcy of genius. Technique is mechanical in its nature. Many can learn the mechanical operations. But they do not result automatically in a *chef-d'oeuvre*. Indeed, our technical facility has been in inverse ratio to our ability to achieve genuine and durable art masterpieces.

*The professional character of sensate art, though a boon under certain conditions, turns, at its decadent stage, into a veritable malady.* When an art, such as that of ideational or idealistic culture, is collective, the foremost artists—let us repeat—are but *primi inter pares* in the community or

How true this is of course in education!

collectivity. Thus an intimate contact obtains between society and its artists, who serve as the exponents of its culture. There is, accordingly, neither a sharp hiatus between the values of society and those of its artists nor a danger of transforming art into an expression of individual vagaries or into the pseudo-values of an isolated individual fancy. Art is an organic part of the culture of such a society, performing a highly important cultural function. It is not divorced from the other fundamental social values, be they truth and goodness, patriotic and civic virtue, or eternal beauty itself. But when art becomes professionalized, and artists are separated from the public, acquiring complete freedom from the control exercised by other values, the situation presents distinct dangers. Instead of springing from the soil of social culture, such an art is rooted solely in the erratic fancy of the individual artist. This soil is much more shallow, uncertain, and arid. If it sometimes produces a work of genius, more often than not it yields only shallow, hollow, grotesque pseudo-values. The dependence of a professional artist on the market leads, as we have seen, to the same result. An artist who pompously declares his unqualified independence becomes a minion of the commercial dealer or the boss and has to meet his demands, no matter how vulgar they may be.

Again, professionalism in art results in the unionization of music-makers, show-makers, picture-makers, fiction-makers, and art-makers generally. Such a unionization coincides with the decadent stage of sensate culture. So it was in Greece, where, in the third and second centuries B.C., there arose numerous unions, such as the Dionysiac Synods (*ca.* 300 B.C.), the Dionysiac Association of Artists of Ionia and the Hellespont (*ca.* 279 B.C.), and the Union of Itinerant Musicians. So it is in the contemporary West, which has developed similar unions striving to control, for the sake of better wages, the creative activity of every artist. Instead of dedicating themselves to a sacrosanct activity, to the disinterested service of God and their fellow men, these organizations are purely political and economic in nature, intent mainly on the economic improvement of the conditions of professional art-makers, especially of the mediocre rank and file. These politico-economic objectives drive more and more into the background the esthetic objectives. A union becomes a sort of political faction, dominated by leaders frequently devoid of artistic distinction and quite incapable of understanding the cultural and esthetic mission of art. This leads to an artificial control of the artists and their creative activities by ignorant political bosses, to a disregard of art values as such, to a suppression of everything that runs counter to the predilections of the bosses. Thus, instead of fostering creative art, these associations tend to strangle it. Is it any wonder that the period of domination by the professional Apollonian and Dionysiac unions of Greece and Rome was quite sterile? Is it surprising that in our day we observe the ignorant politicians of the art unions suppressing the activities of the most eminent artists (whether musicians, painters, or sculptors) and fostering, instead, the mediocre or inferior values and performances of pseudo-artists subservient to these bosses?

*The Revolt against Sensate Art.* All these consequences are spontaneously generated by sensate art in the process of its development. They are definite symptoms of its growing disintegration. At the present times these symptoms are so unequivocal that they constitute a veritable *memento mori* foreshadowing the extinction of contemporary sensate art. Since it is becoming ever more incoherent, imitative, quantitative, and sterile, it is small wonder that its decadence evokes a growing spirit of revolt. Such a revolt had already broken out at the close of the nineteenth century, after the decline of the Impressionistic School, in painting and sculpture and in other fields of the fine arts. Impressionism, as we have seen, represented the farthest limit of sensate art. Its motto was to reflect the surface of sensory reality as it appears to our eyes or other senses at a given moment. *What* to render was wholly unimportant. The important thing was to produce an illusion of the appearance of the person, landscape, or thing represented. Hence a given landscape, since it looks different at different times, might become the subject of a series of different paintings. In all these respects the Impressionistic School constituted the uttermost limit of a sensate art based on momentary glimpses of mere surface phenomena. No further development in this direction was possible.

After its brief heyday, impressionism declined under the assaults of hostile criticism. Its place was taken by cubists, futurists, pointillists, expressionists, Dadaists, constructivists, and other "ists," not only in painting and sculpture but also in other fields of the fine arts. Whether in painting and sculpture, in architecture, in music, in literature, or in the drama, these modernists openly revolted against the decadent sensate art. They refused to reproduce the mere visual surface of phenomena, as does sensate art.

They rebelled against impressionistic photography, seeking to express, rather, the essence of the phenomenon dealt with—the inner soul or character of a person, the dominant traits of an inanimate object, and the like. What they strive to present is substantiality, the three-dimensional materiality, beneath the visual surface. Hence their cubist planes and similar technical devices, so strange to a sensate person. Again, they rebelled against an art debased to a mere instrument of pleasure and entertainment. Hence their music, so discordant to the habitual sensate ear. Hence their literature, which appears so unpleasant and indigestible to the habitual readers of sensate fiction. Hence their eccentric and incomprehensible sculpture. In a word, the modernists take issue with almost all the basic characteristics of declining sensate art. The revolt is both fundamental and relatively successful. Modernism is destined to enjoy a fairly long lease of life. It may be seen at any museum or it may be heard at almost any concert; it is solidly entrenched in the field of architecture; it has invaded both literature and the drama. Most of the leading composers—for example, Stravinsky, Prokofieff, Hindemith, Honegger, Schönberg, Berg, and Shostakovitch—are modernists. In painting and sculpture the proportion of modernist works rose from zero in the eighteenth century to 2.8 per cent in the nineteenth and 35.5 per cent in the period from 1900 to 1920. A similar situation prevails in the other fine arts. Such a successful revolution is in itself sufficient evidence of the disintegration of our sensate art. Together with other symptoms, it establishes beyond any doubt the profound gravity of the crisis.

Does this mean that modernism is a new organic form

of Western art destined to dominate the succeeding decades or centuries? Such a diagnosis is hardly sound. More accurate is the conclusion that modern art is one of transition from a disintegrating sensate to an ideational or idealistic form. As such, it is revolutionary *vis à vis* the dominant sensate form. But it has not yet arrived at any definite goal. Whereas its negative program is as clear as any merely negative program of revolution can be, its positive program has not yet emerged. If the style of modernist art is definitely divorced from that of sensate art, its content still remains thoroughly sensate. It does not attempt to depict anything supersensory or idealistic. The world it deals with is fundamentally materialistic. It seeks to portray not God but matter, in all its three-dimensional substantiality. Its revolt is not in the name of God or some other supersensory value, but in that of the material world, against the thin surface materiality of sensate art. In this respect modern art is hypersenate. It is somewhat similar to communism or fascism in the political world. Communism and fascism are materialistic in the highest degree. They elevate the economic factors or those of "race and blood" to the level of a god. In this sense they are the legacy of the bankers and money-makers, the captains of finance and industry, only still more economically minded than these. On the other hand, they are in revolt against the sensate capitalist system, not because it is materialistic or economically minded, but because it is not sufficiently materialistic, confining luxury and comfort, wealth, and sensory power to the few instead of bestowing it upon the many.

The communists and fascists in politics are the analogues

of the modernists in the fine arts. Both groups are in rebellion against the dominant sensate politico-economic and art systems; but both are essentially sensate. Accordingly, neither group can constitute the politico-economic or art system of the future. They are mainly destroyers and rebels—not constructive builders. They flourish only under the conditions peculiar to a period of transition. Being charged with destructive force, the modernists are too chaotic and distorted to serve as the bearers of a permanent art culture. But as a symptom of revolt against the prevailing forms, the movement is significant. Whether we like it or not, sensate art seems to have performed its mission. After the decline of the ideational culture of the Middle Ages, it infused new vitality into the art of the West; produced for four centuries notable values and evolved unique standards; and finally exhausted its creative forces and, together with the whole system of sensate culture, began to show increasing signs of fatigue, sterility, perversion, and decadence. This decadence is now in full swing. Nothing can stop it. It is destined to be succeeded by a different type of art, either ideational or idealistic, as these types gave way to it six or seven centuries ago. While we should be grateful to it for its enormous enrichment of the treasure house of human culture, we must not seek to revive what is already dead. "*Le roi est mort! Vive le roi!*" After the travail and chaos of the transition period, a new art—probably ideational—will perpetuate in a new guise the perennial creative *élan* of human culture. (*Dynamics*, Vol. I, chaps. 8-13)

# CHAPTER III

# THE CRISIS IN THE SYSTEM OF TRUTH: SCIENCE, PHILOSOPHY, AND RELIGION

## I. THREE SYSTEMS OF TRUTH: IDEATIONAL, IDEALISTIC, AND SENSATE *Truth (empiricism)*

The wisdom of this world is foolishness with God.—SAINT PAUL

Deum et animam scire cupio. Nihilne plus? Nihil omnino.—SAINT AUGUSTINE

Sensory cognition is occupied with external, sensible qualities, but intellectual knowledge penetrates to the very essence of the things. . . . In the things which we hold about God there is truth in two ways. For certain things that are true about God wholly surpass the capability of human reason; for instance, that God is three and one; while there are certain things to which even natural reason can attain, for instance, that God is. . . . Accordingly some divine truths are attainable by human reason, while others altogether surpass the power of human reason.—SAINT THOMAS AQUINAS

Science is the most economic adaptation of man to environment, his thoughts to facts, and facts to one another.—E. MACH

In logic, there are no morals. Everyone is at liberty to build up his own logic, *i.e.*, his own form of language, as he wishes. All that is required of him is that, if he wishes to discuss it, he must state his methods clearly, and give syntaxical rules instead of philosophical argument.—R. CARNAP

Science is not concerned with reality. . . . It is not for us as scientists to worry about "reality."—A young contemporary scholar

Pilate said unto him, Art thou a king then? Jesus answered, . . . To this end was I born, and for this cause came I into the world, that I should bear witness unto the truth. Every one that is of the truth heareth my voice. Pilate said unto him, "*What is truth?*"

Pilate's question is perennial, still awaiting an adequate answer valid for all cultures and all minds. This answer apparently presupposes an omniscient, superhuman mind. For the limited human mind, only a relative answer seems possible. While these relative solutions have been many, they all fall into three classes, each giving its own conception of truth, its source and its criteria. These three main systems of truth correspond to our three main supersystems of culture. They are the ideational, sensate, and idealistic systems of truth and knowledge. Ideational truth is *the truth revealed by the grace of God*, through his mouthpieces (the prophets, mystics, and founders of religion), disclosed in a supersensory way through mystic experience, direct revelation, divine intuition, and inspiration. Such a truth may be called *the truth of faith*. It is regarded as infallible, yielding adequate knowledge about the true-reality values. Sensate truth is *the truth of the senses*, obtained through our organs of sense perception. If the testimony of our senses shows that "snow is white and cold," the proposition is true; if our senses testify that snow is not white and not cold, the proposition becomes false.

Idealistic truth is *a synthesis of both, made by our reason*. In regard to sensory phenomena, it recognizes the rôle of the sense organs as the source and criterion of the validity or invalidity of a proposition. In regard to supersensory phenomena, it claims that any knowledge of these is impossible through sensory experience and is obtained only through the direct revelation of God. Finally, our reason, through logic and dialectic, can derive many valid propositions—for instance, in all syllogistic and mathematical reasoning. Most mathematical and syllogistic propositions are arrived at not through sensory experience, nor through direct divine revelation, but through the logic of human reason. Human reason also "processes" the sensations and perceptions of our sense organs and transforms these into valid experience and knowledge. Human reason likewise combines into one organic whole the truth of the senses, the truth of faith, and the truth of reason. These are the essentials of the idealistic system of truth and knowledge.

Such, in brief, are the three principal systems of truth, which embrace practically all the answers to the eternal question, "What is truth?" given by the great thinkers of mankind. There remain only the purely negative, skeptical answers. According to one of the formulas of the negativistic solution, we cannot know anything; even if we did, we could not adequately express it; if we did express it, we could not convey it to others. Such a despairing skepticism flares up once in a while in the history of human thought; but it is always limited to a comparatively small circle of thinkers, and functions as an intermittent current. Mankind cannot live and act under the conditions of such a skepticism.

This preliminary outline of the three systems of truth shows that each is derived from the major premise of one of our three supersystems of culture. Each dominates its respective culture and society. If we have a preponderantly ideational culture, its dominant truth is always a variety of the revealed truth of faith; in a sensate system of culture the truth of the senses will prevail; in an idealistic culture the idealistic truth of reason will govern men's minds. With a change of the dominant cultural supersystem, the dominant truth undergoes a corresponding change. Later on we shall perceive the factual accuracy of the foregoing statements.

It is necessary to realize clearly the profound difference, in particular, between the ideational truth of faith and the sensate truth of the senses. *If either is regarded as "the truth, the whole truth, and nothing but the truth," the two become mutually irreconcilable.* What appears true from the standpoint of ideational truth is ignorance and superstition from the standpoint of sensate truth, and vice versa. Many a revealed truth of religion is utterly false from the point of view of an exclusive truth of the senses, and vice versa. This explains the sharp clash of these systems of truth that marks especially the periods of decline of the one and the rise of the other. An excellent example is furnished by the clash between the emerging revealed truth of Christianity with the sensory truth dominant in the Greco-Roman society of the first centuries of our era. To the pagan Greco-Roman thinkers, swayed by the truth of the senses, Christian revealed truth appeared but mere superstition and ignorance. The foremost intellectuals of the time, like Tacitus, called it "dangerous superstition," "infamous and abominable." Pliny characterized it as "nothing but a debased superstition carried to an extreme." To Marcus Aurelius it was only an unreasoned and intemperate spirit of opposition; to Suetonius it was "a novel and maleficent superstition." Celsus regarded the Christians as "illogical folk. . . . They will not reason or listen to reason about their faith, but stick to their *'Ask no question but believe,'* or *'Thy faith shall save thee,'* or *'The wisdom of the world is a bad thing and the foolishness a good.'* " To Celsus, as to other partisans of sensory truth, the Christians, with their truth of faith, were mere charlatans, ignoramuses, prestidigitators, and the like. Even Christ and the Apostles were ignorant and "notorious vagabonds"; the Virgin Mary, a girl with an illegitimate child; and so on. From the point of view of sensory truth, the Christian truth of faith, revelation, and God—indeed the whole Christian religion and movement—could not appear other than an absurdity and superstition.

On the other hand, from the standpoint of the revealed truth of Christianity, the truth of the senses and the sensory knowledge derived from it could not appear anything but foolishness. As Saint Paul formulates the principle, "The wisdom of this world is foolishness with God." Other early Christians and all the Church Fathers designate sensory knowledge as "doubtful, uncertain, and probable rather than true" (Minucius Felix); as a mere "vanity" (Basil the Great); as "deceit and tricks," "babbling," "lies," "errors," and the like (Saint Augustine); as something that is misleading; and, finally, as something opposed to the truth (Tertullian, Origen, *et alii*). Tertullian's famous statement sums this up very cogently.

> Cruxifixus est Dei Filius; non pudet, quia pudendum est. Et mortuus est Dei Filius; prorsus credibile est, quia ineptum est. Et sepultus resurrexit; certum est, quia impossibile est. (The Son of God is crucified; that is not shameful because it is shameful [that is, from the sensate standpoint]. And the

Son of God died; that is credible because it is absurd. And
He rose from the dead; that is quite certain because it is
impossible.)

In this statement the clash is formulated in the most
masterly manner. What is impossible or untrue from the
sensate standpoint may be possible and quite true from the
standpoint of the Christian truth of faith; and vice versa.

The clash of these two systems was as sharp as possible
and lasted for centuries, until Christian faith emerged victorious around the sixth century. This system was not
much concerned with empirical knowledge, which was
deemed a second-hand truth, being admitted as a "handmaid" in so far as it did not contradict the supersensory,
superlogical, and superrational revealed truth of Christianity. Its simple objective was excellently formulated by
Saint Augustine. It reduced itself exclusively to the knowledge of God and of the soul. *Deum et animam scire cupio.
Nihilne plus? Nihil omnino*—such is the categoric formula
of this system of thought.

If we now turn to the Renaissance, when the submerged
truth of the senses reemerged and began rapidly to drive
out the revealed truth of Christianity, we note that the clash
was as sharp as at the period of the rise of Christian truth,
with revealed truth now on the defensive and sensory truth
taking the offensive.

It must be clear that the whole mentality of human
society—what is regarded as true or false, knowledge or
ignorance; the nature of education and the curricula of the
schools—all this differs according to the dominant system
of truth accepted by a given culture or society. Let us
glance a little more closely at the characteristics, implica-

tions, and consequences of the sensate system and, more briefly, the other systems of truth.

*The Sensate System of Truth and Knowledge*. Since, according to the major premise of sensate culture, the true-reality value is sensory, cognition is obviously derived only through the sense organs. Sensate truth is mainly the truth of the senses. John Locke's dictum, *Nihil esse in intellectu quod non fuerit prius in sensu* (Nothing is in the mind that was not already in the sense), is its exact formula. In this system of truth the sense organs become the principal source of cognition of sensory reality; their testimony decides what is true and what is false; they become the supreme arbiters of the validity of any experience and proposition. Another name for this truth of the senses is empiricism. From the basic character of sensory truth are derived its other characteristics. *A to H*

*A.* Any system of sensate truth and reality implies *a denial of, or an utterly indifferent attitude toward, any supersensory reality or value*. By definition, supersensory reality either is nonexistent or, if it exists, is unknowable to us and therefore equivalent to the nonexistent. Being unknowable, it is irrelevant and devoid of interest (Kantian criticism, agnosticism, positivism, etc.). Hence it follows that the sensory cultures regard investigations of the nature of God and supersensory phenomena as superstitious or fruitless speculation. Theology and religion, as a body of revealed truth, are at best tolerated, just as many hobbies are tolerated; or are given mere lip service; or are transformed into a kind of scientific theology, and sensory religion reduced to the level of empirical disciplines devoid of revealed truth.

*B.* If the sensate system disfavors any preoccupation with the supersensory aspects of reality, *it most strongly favors the study of the sensory world, with its physical, chemical, and biological properties and relationships.* All the cognitive aspirations are concentrated on the study of these sensory phenomena, in their materiality and observable relationships, and on the technological inventions that aim to serve our sensory needs. Knowledge becomes equivalent to the empirical knowledge represented by the natural sciences. Hence in a sensate society natural science replaces religion, theology, and even speculative philosophy. This generalization is well supported by the data of scientific discoveries and technological inventions. The figures on page 88 summarize this movement during the centuries studied.

During the ideational centuries of Greco-Roman culture (from the eighth to the sixth centuries B.C.) the number of discoveries and inventions is low. With the second half of the sixth century B.C. the number greatly increases, remaining on a high level up to the fourth century A.D.—a period dominated (as we have seen) by a sensate art and (as we shall see) by the truth of the senses. Beginning with the fifth century A.D., it sharply declines, remaining very low until the thirteenth century—a period dominated by an ideational art and (as we shall see) by ideational truth. Starting with the thirteenth century, it begins to rise more and more rapidly, until in the eighteenth and nineteenth centuries it reaches an unprecedented high level, the nineteenth century alone yielding more discoveries and inventions than all the preceding centuries together. Diagrams Nos. 2 and 3 give a pictorical summary of these and subsequent figures.

cf pg. 41

### Number of Scientific Discoveries and Technological Inventions

Centuries

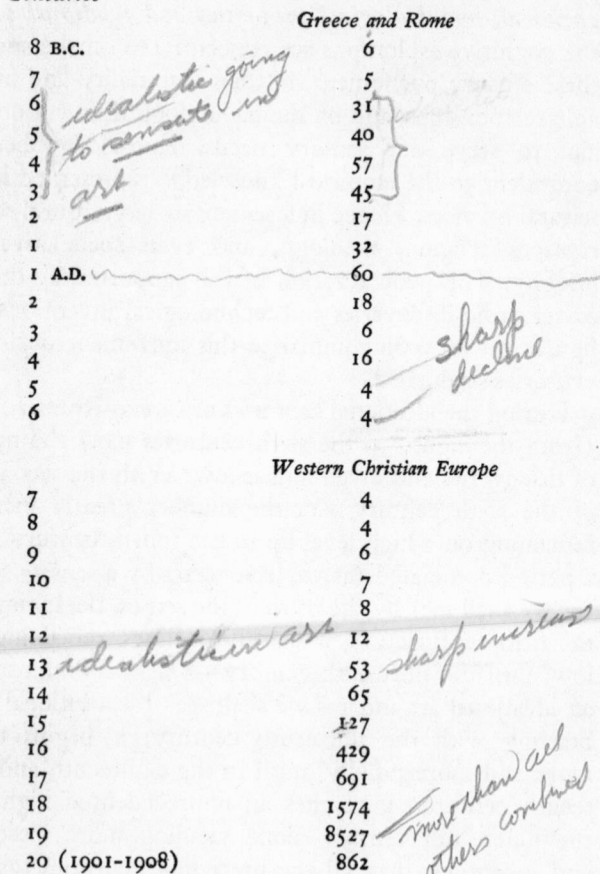

| | Greece and Rome |
|---|---|
| 8 B.C. | 6 |
| 7 | 5 |
| 6 | 31 |
| 5 | 40 |
| 4 | 57 |
| 3 | 45 |
| 2 | 17 |
| 1 | 32 |
| 1 A.D. | 60 |
| 2 | 18 |
| 3 | 6 |
| 4 | 16 |
| 5 | 4 |
| 6 | 4 |

*idealistic going to sensate in art*

*sharp decline*

| | Western Christian Europe |
|---|---|
| 7 | 4 |
| 8 | 4 |
| 9 | 6 |
| 10 | 7 |
| 11 | 8 |
| 12 | 12 |
| 13 | 53 |
| 14 | 65 |
| 15 | 127 |
| 16 | 429 |
| 17 | 691 |
| 18 | 1574 |
| 19 | 8527 |
| 20 (1901–1908) | 862 |

*idealistic in art*

*sharp increase*

*more than all others combined*

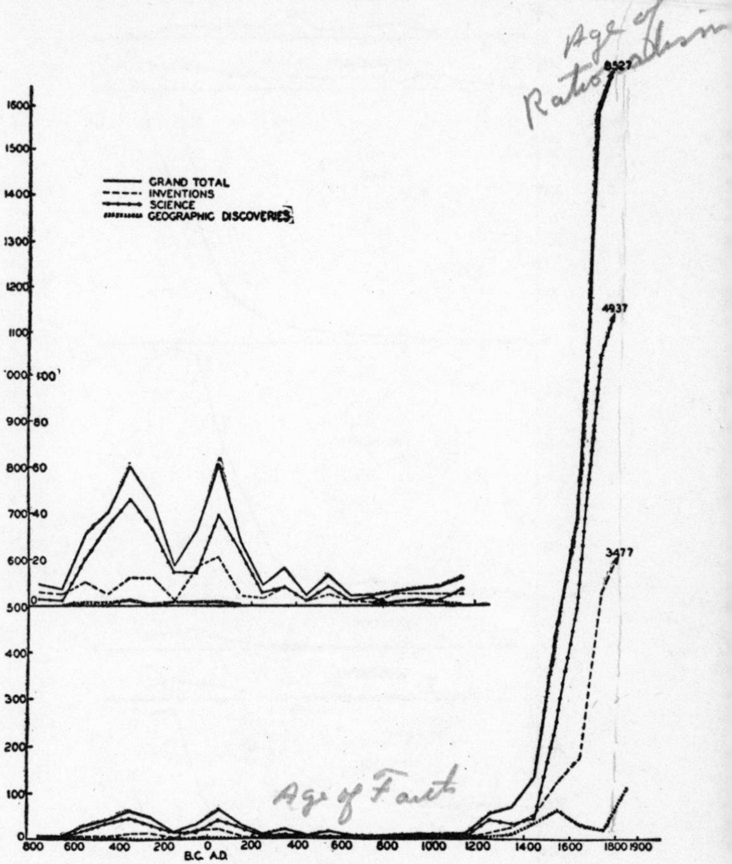

**DIAGRAM No. 2**

*Number of scientific discoveries and inventions from 800 B.C. to
A.D. 1900, by centuries*

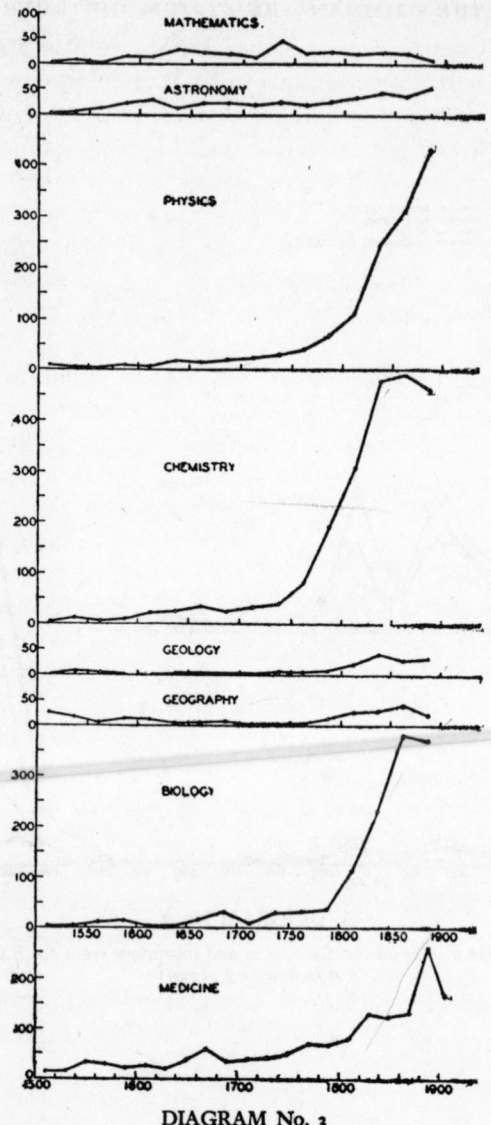

**DIAGRAM No. 3**

*Number of scientific discoveries and inventions from 1500 to 1900 by 25 year periods*

*C.* Sensate truth, or empiricism, as we have seen, rejects any revealed supersensory truth. It discredits also, to a certain extent, reason and logic as the sources of truth until their deductions are corroborated by the testimony of the sense organs. If deductive logic contradicts the testimony of the senses, its deductions are ruled out as false. Therefore in sensate cultures and societies *the empirical systems of philosophy gain in strength, while the systems of philosophy based upon ideational or idealistic truths decline*. This is well attested by the relevant historical facts. For instance, the relative percentages of empiricism among all the other philosophical systems of truth have been as follows in the specified centuries: zero per cent from 600 to 1000 A.D.; 7.7 in the eleventh century; 14.3 in the twelfth; 12.8 in the thirteenth; 17.2 in the fourteenth; 7.2 in the fifteenth; 15.8 in the sixteenth; 29.6 in the seventeenth; 37.5 in the eighteenth; 42.6 in the nineteenth; and 53 in 1900-1920. If we add to empiricism the other related systems, such as criticism and skepticism, the empirical system reaches a total of 47.5 per cent in the eighteenth century, 55.7 in the nineteenth, and 72 in 1900-1920. Thus throughout the greater part of the Middle Ages, empiricism remains close to the zero line. [Diagram No. 4 gives a pictorial reproduction of the movement of empiricism from 500 B.C. to 1900.] We have seen that these centuries were the *Blütezeit* of the ideational fine arts; they represented likewise the nadir of scientific discoveries and inventions. As we pass to the centuries marked by the reemergence of sensate art and culture we observe that, with minor fluctuations, empiricism, as the truth of the senses, begins to parallel the rising tide of scientific dis-

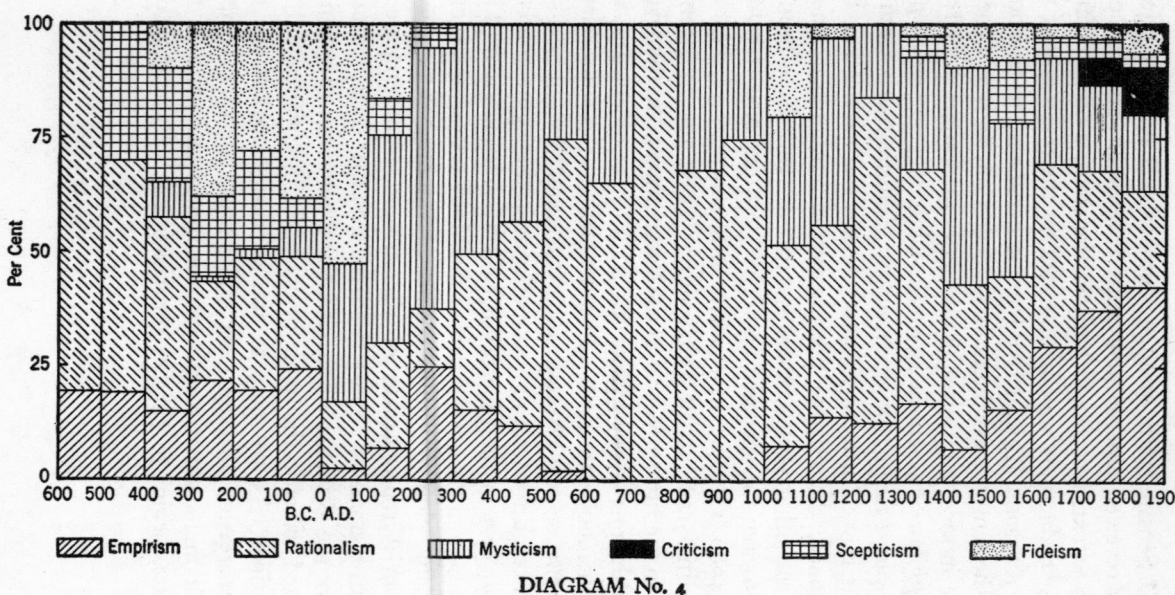

Per Cent

| | | |
|---|---|---|
| 600 500 400 300 200 100 0 100 200 300 400 500 600 700 800 900 1000 1100 1200 1300 1400 1500 1600 1700 1800 1900 | | |

B.C. A.D.

Empirism     Rationalism     Mysticism     Criticism     Scepticism     Fideism

DIAGRAM No. 4

coveries and inventions. In the last two centuries both reached an unprecedentedly high level. On the other hand, the systems of philosophy based upon ideational and idealistic truths move in the opposite direction, constituting from 80 to 100 per cent of all the systems of truth in the period from 600 to 1000 A.D., declining thereafter, with minor fluctuations, to approximately 30 and 12 per cent, respectively, in the nineteenth and twentieth centuries.

In a word, the sensate form of art, the empirical systems of philosophy, sensory truth, scientific discoveries, and technological inventions move in conjunction, rising or declining with the rise or decline of the sensate supersystem of culture. Similarly, ideational and idealistic art, and non-empirical philosophies based upon ideational and idealistic truths, likewise move together. Their movement is essentially opposite to that of sensate art, science, technology, and empirical philosophy.

*D.* A fully developed sensate system of truth and cognition is inevitably *materialistic*, viewing everything, openly or covertly, in its materialistic aspects. Whereas the mentality committed to the truth of faith spiritualizes everything, regarding even matter as a mere appearance of supersensory reality, the mentality dominated by the truth of the senses materializes everything, even spiritual phenomena themselves, viewing the latter as a mere appearance or as a by-product of material phenomena. Hence the general tendency of the sensate mentality to regard the world—even man, his culture, and consciousness itself—materialistically, mechanistically, behavioristically. Man becomes, in sensate scientific definitions, a "complex of electrons and protons," an animal organism, a reflex mechanism, a variety of stimulus-response relationships, or a psychoanalytical "bag" filled with physiological libido. "Consciousness" is declared to be an inaccurate and subjective term for physiological reflexes and overt actions of a certain kind. All the conceptions and theories predicated upon a spiritual, supersensory, immaterial reality are dismissed as a sort of superstition or ignorance or as a result of the tyranny of misused words. Such a trend manifests itself in hundreds of ways. Our statistical studies show that the periods marked by the growing domination of sensory truth have always been paralleled by an intensification of the materialistic mentality and by a corresponding decline of idealistic and ideational philosophy. Thus, during the medieval centuries the percentage of the materialistic philosophy among all the other philosophies from 500 to 1300 was zero; and that of the idealistic philosophy and *Weltanschauung*, 100. In the nineteenth and twentieth centuries materialism increased, respectively, to 12.7 and 23.3 per cent; whereas idealism decreased, respectively, to 55.9 and 40.3 per cent, the remainder being represented by composite philosophies blending materialism and idealism. Diagram No. 5 shows this movement pictorially. Scientific theories based upon the truth of the senses tend, as we have seen, to become progressively materialistic, mechanistic, and quantitative, even in their interpretation of man, culture, and mental phenomena. The social and psychological sciences begin to imitate the natural sciences, attempting to treat man in the same way as physics and chemistry treat inorganic phenomena. In the field of the social sciences all mental and cultural phenomena come to be treated behavioristically, physiologically, "reflexologi-

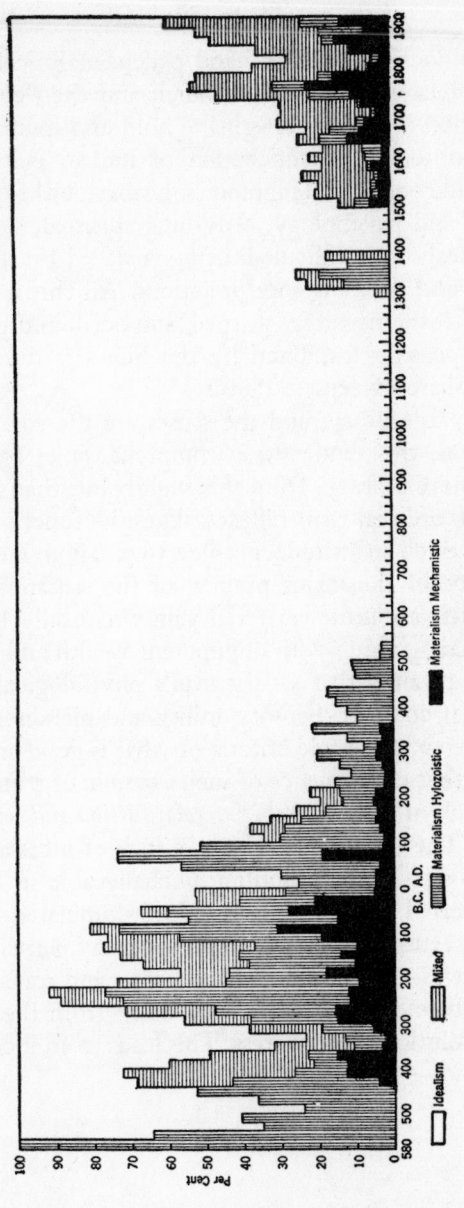

DIAGRAM No. 5

Idealism    Mixed    Materialism Hylozoistic    Materialism Mechanistic

cally," "endocrinologically," and psychoanalytically. Society becomes economically minded, and the "economic interpretation of history" begins to hold undisputed sway. A quasi-pornographic conception of human culture acquires a wide vogue, in biographies, history, anthropology, sociology, and psychology. Anything spiritual, supersensory, or idealistic is ridiculed, being replaced by the most degrading and debasing interpretations. All this is closely analogous to the negative, warped, subsocial, and psychopathic propensities exhibited by the fine arts during the decadent phase of sensate culture.

If reality is sensory, and the senses are the sole source of cognition, this tendency is comprehensible; for what could be more sensory, from this standpoint, than matter, and what more real than reflexes, digestive functions, sex, and so on? Such an attitude, needless to say, is an inevitable consequence of the major premise of the sensate system.

*E.* In such a culture, material values naturally become paramount, beginning with omnipotent wealth and ending with all the values that satisfy man's physiological needs and material comfort. Sensory utility and pleasure, as we shall see, become the sole criteria of what is good and bad.

*F.* A further consequence of such a system of truth is the development of a *temporalistic, relativistic, and nihilistic mentality.* The sensory world is in a state of incessant flux and becoming. There is nothing unchangeable in it—not even an eternal Supreme Being. Mind dominated by the truth of the senses simply cannot perceive any permanency, but apprehends all values in terms of shift and transformation. Sensate mentality views everything from the standpoint of evolution and progress. This leads to an increasing neglect of the eternal values, which come to be replaced by temporary, or short-time, considerations. Sensate society lives in, and appreciates mainly, the present. Since the past is irretrievable and no longer exists, while the future is not yet here and is uncertain, only the present moment is real and desirable.

Hence the sensate *Carpe diem*, as tomorrow is uncertain; snatch the present kiss; get rich quick; seize the power, popularity, fame, and opportunity of the moment, because only present values can be grasped. As the tempo of change accelerates, this "present" grows ever shorter and more transitory. To the same source is attributable the stupendous rôle of *time* in the life and activities of such a society. *Tempus fugit, tempora mutantur et nos mutamur in illis*, and *tempus edax rerum* become the mottoes of the sensate mentality.

From the same system of truth and values follows the doctrine of *relativism*. Since everything is temporal and subject to incessant change, and since sensory perception differs in the case of different organisms, individuals, and groups, nothing absolute exists. Everything becomes relative—truth and error, moral and aesthetic considerations, and what not. A thing may be good today and bad tomorrow; in a given set of conditions a proposition may appear to be true and under other conditions false. Sensory observation shows that scientific, philosophical, religious, moral, aesthetic, and other values, norms, and beliefs vary according to the individual, the group, and the period. Hence the dictum, "Everything is relative in this world," as the motto of sensate truth. Hence its negative attitude toward any absolute whatsoever. But relativism, once accepted, inevitably becomes more and more uncompromising, until finally all relative truths and values are completely "relativized" and reduced, so to speak, to atoms. Sooner or later, relativism thus gives place to skepticism, cynicism, and nihilism. The very boundary line between the true and the false, between right and wrong, disappears, and society finds itself in a state of veritable mental, moral, and cultural anarchy. No society can long exist under these conditions. Either it perishes or it substitutes another system of truth—one sounder and more adequate to its needs. (See the figures and the diagram on movement of relativism in Chapter IV.)

G. All this means that sensory truth, when made exclusive, inevitably develops into a kind of *illusionism* in which it undermines itself. Instead of valid cognition of the true reality and values, it increasingly gives us relative and conditional hints respecting the ever-fleeting shadows of ever-changing sensory impressions, which differ with different individuals, groups, and conditions. Instead of revealing truth as the *adaequatio intellectus et rei*, it yields mere impressions and artificial constructs relating to something essentially unknowable. Decadent sensory science even declares that it is not concerned with any true reality. It offers merely certain propositions based upon sensory observations which appear to be convenient and therefore speciously true. Such a formulation of the task of sensory science is equivalent to burying the truth, reality, and science itself. The whole situation becomes distinctly bizarre, no one knowing precisely what a sensory proposition is, what it is concerned with, or what it claims. Since it is not concerned with any reality, and does not represent the statement of the cognizing mind about this reality, then just what is it? In this way sensory truth eventually digs its own grave.

*H.* The same system of truth gives rise to the *nominalistic and singularistic mentalities characteristic of sensate society.* Sensory impressions are always singularistic. For example, we cannot perceive the *genus* horse or the *genus* homo—that is, essences, categories, and universals. We perceive only an individual horse, or other object, in their sensory appearances. Hence the vogue of nominalism, with its axiom *Universalia sunt nomina:* all universals, categories, concepts, and essences are but mere words, unscientifically used, and corresponding to no objective reality. They are merely the result of the tyranny of words over unscientific minds. Hence the reluctance to recognize the reality of universals and essences. Men prefer, and delight to deal with, concrete phenomena. Such a mentality regards society as simply a sum of interacting individuals. It cannot see the forest for the trees. This attitude, in turn, leads to increased superficiality, whereby, as in the case of sensate painting, only the sensory surface appearances of phenomena are perceived. The theories of science grow progressively thinner and shallower, ultimately resolving themselves into imaginary, make-believe propositions or purely utilitarian and conventional fictions, at once empty and irresponsible.

*I.* Let us consider next the *utilitarian, hedonistic, pragmatic, operational, and instrumental character of the science and philosophy, pseudo-religion, and ethics of sensate culture.* Since sensory cognition does not seek anything absolute (including valid truth, independent of sensory peculiarities), and since it views any "truth" as a mere means of adaptation to the sensory universe, designed to make life pleasanter or less painful, the propositions and theories that prove to be useful, enjoyable, and convenient become authentic, whereas those that prove to be useless, inconvenient, or noneconomical are regarded as false. *Savoir pour prévoir, prévoir pour pouvoir* is the main motto of such a science.

I. Science and philosophy, as we have seen, come to be imbued with utilitarian aims. Only those disciplines which, like physics and chemistry, biology and medicine, geology and geography, technology, politics and economics, are eminently practical and serviceable and are intensively cultivated. Hence the aforesaid progress of the natural and technological sciences. Other disciplines, either metaphysics and "nonpragmatic" philosophy, or transcendental religion and absolute ethics, are relatively ignored. In so far as they are cherished, they assume the same utilitarian, sensory, and pragmatic, or instrumental, character. Psychology, as a science of the human soul, turns out to be a physiology of the nervous system and its reflexes. Religion, as a revelation of God, degenerates into a second-hand "social gospel"—a sort of political creed. Philosophy, as the cognition of essences and true reality, with presuppositions of knowledge, becomes a vague ideology devoted to either the justification or the castigation of this or that system of sensory values and appearances; or a mere generalization based upon the conclusions of utilitarian natural science; or a finical, formal, empty semantic inquiry into the "logical syntax of language," with its imitative pseudomathematics and pseudo-symbolic logic, and its Baconian belief in the possibility of a purely mechanical technique of constructing "sensorily valid propositions"; or a demonstration of the nonexistence of anything save sensory reality; or, ultimately, a system of negative criticism, agnosticism, and skepticism (we cannot know any true reality; even if we did, we could not express it; if we did somehow express it, we could not convey this knowledge to others). In short, philosophy turns out to be a second-class sensory utilitarian science composed of empiricism, positivism, neopositivism, pragmatism, criticism, agnosticism, skepticism, instrumentalism, and operationalism—all marked by the same utilitarian and economical traits.

And so with other disciplines. *Savoir pour pouvoir* becomes one of the supreme criteria. Anything that does not permit a utilitarian control tends to be neglected; anything that does is elevated to the dignity of a scientific or valid proposition.

II. Of like character is the educational system, which is first and foremost a training school devoted to "useful knowledge" and the crafts. Its chief business is to prepare successful businessmen, craftsmen, engineers and technicians, politicians, lawyers, doctors, teachers, preachers, and so on. Mastery is sought in such arts as amassing a fortune, farming, home cooking, barbering, the invention of machines, research work, teaching, and preaching. Elementary, high-school, and college education—all are oriented principally in the same direction, paying scant attention, if any, to the forgotten purpose of real knowledge and wisdom: the nature of true reality and true values. Since this is deemed devoid of any immediate, short-time sensory utility, it is given merely lip service, playing little part in the actual curriculum of the schools of sensate society.

Such, in brief, are some of the characteristics of the system of sensory truth and of the society in which it flourishes.

*The Ideational and Idealistic System of Truth and Knowledge.* The *ideational system of truth* is the very opposite of the sensate system. It is preoccupied primarily with supersensory reality and values. It is based on revelation, divine inspiration, and mystic experience. As such, it is considered to be authentic and absolute. Its main concern is with God and his kingdom as the true reality. Therefore revealed religion and theology become the queen of genuine wisdom and science, empirical knowledge serving as a mere handmaid. The mentality dominated by the truth of faith is dedicated to the eternal verities, in contradistinction to the temporal truth of the senses. It is idealistic in that reality is viewed as spiritual, or nonmaterial. It is absolutistic, nonutilitarian, nonpragmatic.

Finally, the *idealistic system of truth* occupies an intermediary position between the sensate and ideational systems, blending in its crucible the three distinct elements of sensory, religious, and rationalistic truth. The systems of Plato and Aristotle, of Albertus Magnus and Saint Thomas Aquinas, are the supreme examples, attempting to embrace in one organic whole divine as well as sensory and dialectic truth. (*Dynamics*, Vol. II, chaps. 1, 2, 3, *et passim*)

## 2. THE RHYTHM OF DOMINATION OF SYSTEMS OF TRUTH IN HISTORY, AND ITS REASON

The foregoing characterization of the sensate system of truth, science, and culture is a sketchy portrait of the system that has dominated Western society for the past four centuries. Our principal body of truth is scientific. Our science is primarily a nexus of empirical, sensory knowledge derived from observation of, and experimentation with, sensory facts. Some elements of the logical truth of reason—certain basic concepts, including mathematico-logical conclusions—it undoubtedly contains. But even such concepts and deductions are valid only in so far as they are corroborated by sensory experience. The essential character of this logico-sensory fabric of thought is revealed by the fact that the terms "scientific" and "true," "unscientific" and "false," are used as synonymous.

The question arises: In what does the contemporary crisis consist? What are its symptoms? What are the reasons for this crisis, and how did it come about? For many, the very possibility of such·a crisis appears improbable. They still think that the truth of the senses incorporated in science is the only system of genuine truth; that, as such, it cannot experience any crisis (except, perhaps, a replacement of one kind of scientific theory by another); that it is destined to progress, because at the present stage of human science and culture no retrogressive movement from science to ignorance, from truth to error, from tested sensory knowledge to untested magical and speculative beliefs, is possible. Such reasoning is still prevalent and sounds thoroughly convincing. Nevertheless, like many current beliefs, it is fallacious.

Its first fallacy is the illusion that there can be only *one* valid system of truth—that of the senses. We have seen that, as a matter of fact, there have been at least three fundamental systems: ideational, idealistic, and sensate. Its second fallacy is the belief that in the course of time there has been a steady linear trend in the direction of sensory truth at the expense of faith and of dialectical and speculative reasoning. Such a conception, as we have seen, is contradicted by incontrovertible facts. In the course of Greco-Roman and Western history each of these systems of truth has repeatedly prevailed. The sensate truth of the Creto-Mycenaean culture gave way to ideational truth in the Greece of the eighth to the sixth century B.C., and this to the idealistic truth of the fifth century B.C. This was displaced, in turn, by the sensate truth of the period from the third century B.C. to the fourth century A.D., which was followed by the ideational truth of Christianity during the period from the sixth century to the end of the twelfth. In the thirteenth century idealistic truth once more became paramount, to be succeeded by a third phase of sensate truth, which has maintained its sway from the sixteenth century up to the present time. Accordingly, instead of the alleged progressive linear trend of sensate truth throughout the course of history, we witness a series of oscillations from one dominant system to another.

The reason for such oscillations is readily comprehensible. *No single system comprises the whole of truth; nor is it, on the other hand, entirely false.* If one of these systems constituted the whole truth and nothing but the truth, whereas the others represented unalloyed error, the fluctuations which we have just noted could not occur. Not even an individual person could long exist if all his beliefs were mistaken. If he ascribed the properties of a cow to a dog, took an enemy for a friend, and a friend for an enemy, ate what is uneatable, failed to distinguish poison from food, knew nothing about the weather, and so on, he would soon perish. Still less would it be possible under these conditions for a *society* to survive for decades and centuries, as has been true of a multitude of societies governed by the truth either of faith or of reason. The ideational truth of faith dominated medieval Europe for well-nigh six hundred years; yet Western society did not perish. The historical record thus proves that neither faith nor reason is wholly false. Each is partly valid, yielding cognition of some important aspect of the complex of true reality.

It can be demonstrated, indeed, that *each source of knowledge—the senses, reason, and intuition—affords a genuine cognition of the manifold reality*. Intuition in its ordinary form as a momentary and direct grasp of a certain reality—the grasp distinct from sensory perception or logical reasoning, yields a knowledge of this aspect of reality like, for instance, the certain validity of anyone of us that "I exist." In its extraordinary form, as a charismatic and mystic experience accessible, through the grace of God, to only a few prophets, great thinkers, great artists, and great religious leaders, it opens to us certain aspects of the true reality inaccessible to our logic and senses. Each source of knowledge discloses some aspect of the manifold reality, the truth of the senses giving a knowledge of the sensory and nonrational aspects of the true reality; the truth of reason its rational aspect; and the truth of intuition its metalogical and metasensory aspect. As has already been pointed out, even contemporary natural science and technology embody not merely the truth of the senses but, in the field of mathematics and logic, for instance, a large portion of the truth of reason as well; and both of these truths are ultimately rooted in intuition or faith as the basic postulates of science.

*Importance of Intuitional Cognition*. The validity of sensory experience and, in a less degree, of logical reasoning is pretty well established nowadays. More doubtful appears intuitional truth. Intuition lies at the roots of any science, from mathematical axiom to the natural sciences. The deductive and inductive superstructure of science rests not upon logic or the testimony of the senses but upon the ultimate intuitional verities. Intuition is also the basic foundation of the beautiful, of moral norms, and of religious values. It has furnished the initial impulse to an enormous number of sensory and dialectic discoveries in all fields of human knowledge and values, including mathematics, physics, and technology. More scientific discoveries and technological inventions—especially the more important ones—are attributable to intuition than to plodding, mechanical sensory observations. The discoveries of Newton, Galileo, Robert Mayer, and Henri Poincaré, for instance, arose, respectively, from an intuitional grasp of such laws as those of gravitation, the oscillation of the pendulum, the mechanical equivalence of heat, and the *fonctions fuchsiennes* in mathematics. Just as most technological inventions are primarily the products of intuition, so also are most of the important achievements of the philosophical, humanistic, and social sciences. The same is true in the field of art in all its forms, as well as that of religion and morals —particularly where creative endeavor is vitalized by the rare intuition of a genius or that of a prophet or mystic. We must not forget that *any genuine creation is a real cognition, just as any real discovery is a creation.* When Mozart or Beethoven, Raphael or Dürer, Phidias or Shakespeare, Buddha or Saint Paul, Plato or Kant, created their artistic or religious or philosophical systems, they actualized the hidden potentiality existing in the reality; they discovered it and disclosed to us what we had not yet seen or known. In this sense any creation is a cognition and discovery—a discovery of a new combination of sound values (as in great music), or of the new values of architectual forms disclosed by an original combination of stone, marble, wood, and other elements of architecture, or of the new aspects of reality revealed by painting, literature, religion, and ethics. If all artistic, religious, philosophical, and ethical values were eliminated, and all our knowledge reduced to strictly "scientific discoveries" formulated in dry propositions, how greatly our cognition of the world and reality would be impoverished and diminished! From millionaires we should be turned into beggars!

Similarly, any scientific discovery is also a creation—not necessarily in the sense of an imposition upon nature of what is manufactured by our mind, as Kant and his followers say, but in the sense of actualizing the hidden potentiality in the reality, bringing it to the light, and thus enriching our knowledge. From this point of view, Newton *created* his law of gravitation, Robert Mayer his law of the conservation of energy, Lavoisier and Lomonosoff their law of the conservation of matter, and so on.

The following are a few typical examples of the rôle of intuition in discoveries and inventions. Let us consider some of the personal experiences of Henri Poincaré.

"For two weeks I tried to demonstrate that no function analogous to what later on I called *les fonctions fuchsiennes* could exist. Every day I sat down at my working table and attempted a great number of combinations, but arrived at no result. One evening, contrary to my habit, I took black coffee and could not fall asleep; ideas thronged my mind; I felt as though they were pushing one another (*se heurter*) until two of them became intertwined, as it were (*s'accrochassent*), and made a stable combination. In the morning I established the existence of the class of *fonctions fuchsiennes*. All that I had to do was to repeat the results, which took only a few hours."

Again he tells that the solution of another mathematical problem came to him instantaneously as he was stepping into a bus. Having arrived at Caen, he verified it and found it correct. He cites several other instances of this kind and stresses that in all of them the solution came "with the same characteristics of brevity, suddenness, and immediate certitude" (*avec les mêmes caractères de brièveté, de soudaineté et de certitude immédiate*).

Scarcely different from these intuitional experiences was Sir Isaac Newton's discovery of the law of gravitation. "On one memorable day, an apple falls with a slight thud at his feet. It was a trifling incident which has been idly noticed thousands of times; but now, like the click of some small switch which starts a great machine in operation, it proved to be the jog which awoke his mind to action. As in a vision, he saw that if the mysterious pull of the earth can act through space as far as the top of a tree . . . so it might even reach so far as the moon." The biographers of Newton generally characterize as "nothing short of miraculous" the three discoveries (the mathematical method of fluxion, the law of the composition of light, and the law of gravitation) that Newton made in two years. Having failed to distinguish himself in college, immediately after graduation he retired to a lonely village and worked unaided. "As a mathematician he . . . seemed to grasp the solution of a problem immediately."

Parallel cases are those of Archimedes, with his famous "Eureka!" suddenly coming to him as he was stepping into a bath, and causing him, in his excitement, to forget to put on his clothes; of Galileo, watching a swinging lamp in the cathedral at Pisa and by "short circuit" formulating the law of the oscillation of the pendulum; of Robert Mayer, who, from two chance occurrences during a voyage, "with a sudden leap of thought . . . derived the law of the mechanical equivalence of heat." We all know of the mystic experience of Pascal, who, after his vision of the blazing cross, exclaimed: "Not the God of philosophers and scholars! *Joie, joie, pleurs de joie! Renonciation totale et douce!*" Absolute certitude!

The same principle applies even more strikingly to technological inventions, as evidenced by the testimony of the inventors themselves. Thus one observes that when the need for a certain invention arises, "I immediately eject it from the objective side of my mind; that is to say, I cease to labor over it, and consign it to the 'subjective department' of my mind." There it spontaneously ripens until it "comes out."

Another says, "Ideas come when I least expect them, often when I am half asleep, or day-dreaming." Others state that they sometimes wake with a new idea, suddenly and quite unexpectedly—"in a flash"—either in a period of relaxation (for instance, when the inventor is in the bathtub) or when the inventor is engaged in a different kind of work.

No different is the situation in the other natural sciences.

In the field of philosophical, humanistic, and social-science disciplines the rôle of intuition has indeed been preponderant. This is objectively established by the fact that almost all the principal philosophies and humanistic and social-science theories were formulated long ago, when neither laboratories, nor statistics, nor systematic data of observation, nor any other facilities or material for empirical or even rational generalizations existed. A study of the relevant data shows that a large percentage of the achievements in this field were initiated by intuition. This does not exclude the fact that in many cases the intuitional revelation was preceded by a strenuous exercise of the sensory or discursive mind. What is significant is that the *solution came about through intuition.*

As for the fine arts, the creative process is preeminently intuitional, whether it be in the realm of poetry and literature, drama, music, or painting or sculpture. The following description, by Mozart, of his habits of work is typical.

> What, you ask, is my method in writing and elaborating my large and lumbering things? I can, in fact, say nothing more about it than this: I do not know myself and can never find out. When I am in particularly good condition—perhaps riding in a carriage, or on a walk after a good meal—or during a sleepless night, then the thoughts come to me in a rush, and best of all. Whence and how—that I do not know and cannot learn. Those which please me I retain in my head, and hum them perhaps also to myself—at least, so others have told me. . . . [Farther on he describes how the "crumbs" spontaneously join one another into a whole, grow, and finally assume a finished form in his head.] All the finding and making only goes on in me as in a very vivid dream.

Finally, like Poincaré in the case quoted above, he commits the work to writing, and since it is practically ready in his mind "it gets pretty quickly onto paper."

Finally religious and moral creations are overwhelmingly intuitional. They profess the revealed truth of faith; they are based almost exclusively upon superrational, supersensory, superempirical, absolute truth and reality—namely, God. All great religions are founded by mystics endowed with the charismatic gift of mystic experience. Such are Buddha, Zoroaster, Lao-tse, the Hebrew prophets, Mahavira, Mohammed, Saint Paul, Saint Augustine, and the more recent mystics of Christianity and other religions. When some pseudo-religion arises, based upon "science," "rationality," or "reasonable, empirically verified truths," it never gets anywhere, representing at best a third-class, vulgarized social and humanitarian philosophy or pseudo-science. All great religions explicitly declare that they are revealed through the grace of the Absolute to charismatically gifted persons—prophets, saints, mystics, oracles, and other instruments of the Absolute. And mystic experience, which reveals the truth of faith, has little, if anything, to do with ordinary cognition attained through the sense organs or rational discourse. Without mystic intuition, mankind could hardly have possessed any religion worthy of the name. Since religion in general and the world religions in particular constitute one of the foremost achievements of human culture, they testify to the significance of the rôle played by intuition— especially by mystic intuition—in the history of human thought and civilization. Religion discloses an aspect of reality inaccessible through the ordinary avenues of sensory truth and the truth of reason. The founders, prophets, apostles, and mystics of the leading religious systems, together with the great artists—who also, in their own way, are instruments of mystic intuition—are the prime instrumentalities of the truth of faith that put us in touch with the superempirical and metalogical aspects of the Infinite Manifold—the *coincidentia oppositorum* of Saint Augustine, Erigena and of Nicholas of Cusa.

The foregoing discussion affords unequivocal proof that all three systems—the sensory, the rational, and the intuitional—are sources of valid cognition; that each of them, when adequately used, gives us knowledge of one of the important aspects of true reality; and that none of them, accordingly, is wholly false. On the other hand, each taken separately, not supplemented by the others, may prove misleading. The history of human thought is a graveyard filled with wrong observations and observational conclusions, with misleading reasoning and speculation, and with false intuitional conclusions. In this respect the position of intuition is in no way worse than that of sensation or dialecticism. None of them in itself, as has been said, can embrace the whole of truth. In the three-dimensional aspect of faith, reason, and sensation, integral truth is nearer to absolute truth than that furnished by any one of these three forms. Likewise, the integral three-dimensional truth, with its sources of intuition, reason, and the senses, is a closer approach to the infinite metalogical reality of the *coincidentia oppositorum* of Saint Augustine, Erigena, and Nicholas of Cusa than the purely sensory, rational, or intuitional reality disclosed by any single system. *The empirico-sensory aspect is supplied by the senses; the rational aspect, by the reason; the superrational aspect, by faith. Each of these systems, when isolated from the rest, becomes less valid and more fallacious, even within the specific field of its own competence.* The sense organs, when not controlled by reason or intuition, can furnish only a chaotic mass of sensations, impressions, and perceptions. They are incapable of supplying any integrated knowledge—anything except disorderly bits of pseudo-observation and pseudo-impressions. At best they yield merely an agglomeration of "facts," devoid of coherence, relevance, or intelligibility. Deprived of the cooperation of reason and intuition, the sense organs are definitely limited instrumentalities, even in the apprehension of the sensory aspects of reality. As Pavlov's experiments have shown, man's auditory, olfactory, and visual perceptions are less acute than those of a dog. For thousands of years such forms of energy as electricity (and, potentially, that of the electromagnetic waves employed in radio) lay, so to speak, under our very noses; yet we could not perceive them. For thousands of years many empirical uniformities of natural phenomena were similarly accessible to our sense organs; but we were unable to grasp them. When they were finally "discovered," they were discovered only through the cooperation of other sources of cognition, namely, logic and intuition. When these elementary verities are properly understood, it is evident how meager and incoherent would be our knowledge if it were confined solely to sensory cognition.

Nor can mere dialectic speculation guarantee authentic knowledge of empirical phenomena. While it can give us an unimpeachable syllogism or mathematical deduction,

such a syllogism or deduction will be empirically valid
only when its major and minor premises are also empirically valid. And this empirical adequacy cannot be derived
from the reason.

Finally, intuition uncontrolled by reason and the senses
very easily goes astray, often leading to intuitive errors. To
sum up, each of these systems of truth tends to produce
misapprehension when it is isolated from, and unverified
by, the other great sources of cognition and truth.

If, then, each system of truth is partly true and partly
false, the oscillation from one system to another becomes
comprehensible. When one of them tends to become
monopolistic and drives out the other truths, its false part
begins to grow at the expense of its valid part, and to the
detriment of the verities of the other systems. The society
dominated by such an increasingly one-sided truth tends
to be led away from reality, from real knowledge, toward
ignorance, error, hollowness of values, aridity in creativeness, and poverty of socio-cultural life. This drift leads to
an increase of theoretical and practical difficulties for such
a society. Its adaptations to reality becomes more and more
difficult; its needs less and less fully satisfied; its life, security, order, and creative experience more and more disorganized. Sooner or later the moment comes when it
faces the following alternatives: either to continue its dangerous drift and suffer fatal atrophy or else to correct its
mistake through the adoption of a different and more adequate system of truth, reality, and cultural values. (*Dynamics*, Vol. IV, chap. 16)

Some cultures, like the Greco-Roman and the Western,
were able to make such a shift several times; others could

not do so. The first cultures continued to live, passing more or less successfully through the series of recurrent rhythmic phases which we have considered above; the others either perished and disappeared, or were doomed to a stagnant, half-mummified existence, their hollow, circumscribed, and devitalized system of truth, reality, and values becoming a mere historical "exhibit" instead of remaining a creative entity. Such cultures and societies serve merely as material for other—more vigorous and creative—cultures and societies. Those which limit the reality value to only one of its three aspects—whether empirical, rational, or supersensory—needlessly impoverish themselves. Such an exclusive *Weltanschauung* invariably falls a victim to its own narrow-mindedness. So also do the cultures characterized by such one-sided mentalities. The exclusively theologico-supersensory mentality of medieval culture, which emerged and developed as a reaction to the hollow sensate cultures of the late Greco-Roman period, after several centuries of domination likewise began to atrophy, eventually crumbling in the catastrophe that marked the close of the Middle Ages. So did the one-sided sensory-rationalistic mentality of the culture of the sixteenth to the eighteenth century (that of the Renaissance and the Enlightenment), which received its deathblow in the social conflagrations of the end of the eighteenth and the beginning of the nineteenth century.

Such is the general reason for the rhythmic sequence of the three great supersystems which we have been considering. A sufficient body of evidence exists to warrant the conclusion that, in harmony with the principles governing earlier cases of decline, the contemporary one-sided empirico-sensory mentality is failing, together with the culture based upon it. The failure is not due to this or that incidental external factor, but has been generated by the system of sensory truth in the process of its own development. The seeds of decay were inherent in the system from the very first, and with its development they began to germinate and grow until they have finally become veritable lethal poisons.

### 3. THE CRISIS OF THE CONTEMPORARY SENSATE SYSTEM OF TRUTH

The crisis is at once theoretical and practical. Both aspects manifest themselves in many ways.

*A.* The theoretical phase is revealed first, in a progressive obliteration of the boundary line between sensory truth and falsehood, reality and fiction, validity and utilitarian convention. The foregoing characterization of sensory culture indicated that its temporalistic, relativistic, nominalistic, materialistic, and other traits lead to an increasing relativization of sensory truth until it becomes indistinguishable from error. The same result is produced, as we have seen, by its utilitarian and pragmatic properties. And this is exactly what is happening before our very eyes. The Western truth of the senses faces the tragic dénouement of its own dethronement. When one examines the prevailing scientific and philosophical empiricism in all its variations—empiricism, positivism, neo-positivism, Kantian or pseudo-Kantian criticism of the *als ob*, or "as if" type, pragmatism, operationalism, empirico-criticism, instrumentalism, and so on—one cannot fail to perceive how it tends to obliterate the difference between truth and falsity, reality and fiction, validity and mere expediency. When it is declared that scientific propositions are mere "conventions," and that, of several different conventions, the one which under the circumstances is most convenient, "economical," expedient, useful, or "operational" for a given individual is most true (*cf.* Henri Poincaré, Karl Pearson, Ernst Mach, William James, *et alii*), the whole fabric of truth and knowledge itself is threatened with collapse. According to this criterion, the dogmas of Stalin or Hitler are true because they are most convenient to them. Truth reduced to a norm of mere convenience, to a mere convention, or to a mere ideology or "derivation" that glorifies and rationalizes economic and other interests neutralizes itself; for every one is equally entitled to claim that any ideology is true for the simple reason that it is useful to him. Thus, in this maze of conveniences, conventions, and utilities, thousands of contradictory truths appear, each claiming to be as valid as the others: the truth of capitalists and proletarians, of communists and fascists, of liberals and conservatives, of believers and atheists, of scientists and Christian Scientists, of the privileged and the underdogs. When scientists contend that they are not concerned with reality but formulate their schemes "as if they corresponded to reality," they convert science and truth into mere fiction, into a mere *als ob*, a mere expedient arbitrary construct. If science is not concerned with reality, then what *is* it concerned with? What, then, is the difference, apart from expediency, between the "as if" construct of the inmate of an insane asylum and that of the scientist? What a distance we have traveled from the conception of truth as *adaequatio rei et intellectus* entertained by Saint Thomas Aquinas!

This trend explains the notable growth of skeptical philosophies during the past three centuries. While their percentage among the leading philosophies of truth was zero throughout the medieval period, it rose to 13.8 per cent in the eighteenth century; 19.1 per cent in the nineteenth; and 21.9 per cent in the twentieth (from 1900 to 1920).

The same impasse is reached by pragmatism, with its cult and criterion of the useful as equivalent to the true, as well as by operationalism, instrumentalism, and similar "isms." To the same category belong the current pseudo-Kantian conceptions of the laws of nature, formulated by science as mere manufactured products of our minds imposed by us upon "nature," or upon something that we call "nature" (for nobody knows precisely what it is or whether or not it exists). The result of such a conception is that we do not know what is "mind"—still less what it imposes upon what, in what way, and why. The whole of science and truth is thus reduced to a mere question mark. Still more true is this of the neo-positivist movements, of the type of the Vienna Circle, which identify thought with language, logic with the syntax of language, and truth with tautology (the "analytic propositions" of Kant), proclaiming any nontautological proposition, including the laws of science, as uncertain and arbitrary. Representing empiricism and skepticism in their most sterile, arid, and senile form, these currents destroy the landmarks between knowledge and error, reality and fiction, and leave us but a dry and hollow world of mummified pseudo-reality, devoid of life, thought, or spirit, and reduced to a formal exegesis of symbols representing nobody knows what. As the epigoni of the erstwhile full-blooded empiricism, having lost, like any epigoni, the creative spark, they seek to compensate for this loss by meticulous research into the mysteries of symbolism, conducted according to the most exact canons of pseudo-semantics and pseudo-logic. As Lao-tse aptly observed, "Wise men are never scholars, and scholars are never wise men." While the old sage exaggerated the situation, his formula well fits these twentieth-century scholars.

Moving in this fatal direction, empiricism progressively restricts its scrutiny of reality to the bare empirical aspects, which become increasingly narrow and superficial. Empiricism thus reveals itself as a discipline intent on "knowing more and more about less and less." Losing its creative genius and replacing it by "mechanicalness," it discovers less and less because it creates less and less; for—as has already been emphasized—any real creation is discovery, and any real discovery is creation.

*B.* To the same effacement of the difference between sensory knowledge and ignorance the truth of the senses has contributed through an excessive development of its *relativism.* Since empirical truth is relative, varying with different persons, groups, and circumstances, and largely representing particular ideologies, such a position leads to a complete annulment of the fundamental difference between truth and error. Everyone seems to be entitled to regard as true whatever he pleases—whatever is dictated by his special interests, his "residues," his prepotent reflexes, his environment, his socio-cultural relations, and so on. The propositions, "Property is sacred" and "Property is theft," are equally valid; for the conditions of rich owners dictate the former, whereas those of a communist proletarian suggest the reverse. And there is no sensory judge competent

Protestant idea
"Every religion equally good"

to decide which is right and which is wrong. The same applies to the Ptolemaic and Copernican cosmologies and a host of other propositions and theories. In conjunction with the "convenience" and "economy" criteria of sensory truth, relativism leads to the "atomization" of truth and the obliteration of any line of demarcation between the true and the false.

C. Similar results are produced by the *temporalistic character of the truth of senses*. Since everything incessantly changes, what is true and what is false changes *pari passu*. What appeared true yesterday is false today, and what is true today may prove to be false tomorrow. This means once again the extinction of any clearly defined boundary between the true and the false. Many an empirical scientist, faced by this danger, seeks an "escape mechanism" in the conviction that although scientific propositions are hypothetical, and though scientific hypotheses incessantly change, there is, however, a historic trend in the direction of a progressive approximation to truth. Better and more accurate hypotheses replace the poorer ones in the course of time. Such a belief, however, is pure conjecture. It amounts to a statement that a later hypothesis is necessarily better and more adequate than an earlier one. This optimistic belief in a sort of Providential guidance of hypotheses toward ultimate perfection the same scientists would be the first to deride if the theory were advanced by others than themselves!

D. Equally detrimental to sensory truth is its *materialistic* bent, which undermines the system both theoretically and practically. Theoretically it undermines it through the crudity, invalidity, and baselessness of any consistent materialism from the standpoint of even sensory truth itself. Practically it produces the same effect by degrading man and his culture and values to the level of matter and its complexes.

Let us consider contemporary science, noting just how it defines man and what it contributes both to his well-being and to his detriment. The current scientific conceptions of man exhibit him as a sort of "electron-proton complex"; "a combination of physico-chemical elements"; "an animal closely related to the ape or monkey"; "a reflex mechanism," or "variety of stimulus-response relationship"; "a special adjustment mechanism"; a psychoanalytical libido; a predominantly subconscious or unconscious organism controlled mainly by alimentary and economic forces; or just a *homo faber*, manufacturing various tools and instruments. No doubt man is all of this. But does this exhaust his essential nature? Does it touch his most fundamental properties, which make him a unique creature? Most of the definitions masquerading as scientific rarely, if ever, even raise such questions. Some, indeed, go so far as to deprive man even of mind, or thought, of consciousness, of conscience, and of volition, reducing him to a purely behavioristic mechanism of unconditioned and conditioned reflexes. Such are the current concepts of our leading physicists, biologists, and psychologists.

Other conceptions, such as those of contemporary biographers, historians, and social scientists, follow a similar pattern. The biographies of the Stracheys, the Ludwigs, the Maurois, the Hugheses, the Ellises, the Erskines, the Millars, the Henry Adamses (in part), and a legion of contemporary psychoanalytical and "scientific" biographers, debunk and debase every personage—no matter how exalted—of whom they treat. Everybody and everything they touch—God, as well as noble men and achievements—is mockingly interpreted as something passive, commonplace, abnormal or pathological, impelled by prosaic, egotistical, and, for the most part, physiological drives. Genius becomes a species of insanity; unselfish sacrifice is explained solely in terms of an inferiority, Oedipus, Narcissus, or other complex; distinguished social endeavor is motivated by the herd instincts. Sexual libido, schizophrenia, paranoia, and the like are the dominant forces. Saintliness is pictured as a kind of idiocy, and the patriotic "Father of His Country" as an abnormal sexual profligate. Piety is identified with ignorance and superstition; moral integrity, with hypocrisy; signal achievements, with mere luck; and so forth.

Whereas the medieval chroniclers viewed the whole of human history as the realization of an inscrutable divine plan, our historians view it mainly *sub specie* of the *New Yorker* or *Esquire*, of the Freudian libido, of Marxian economic factors, of Paretian "residues," and other biological, economic, and cosmic forces. The entire pageant of human history turns out to be nothing but an incessant interplay of cosmic rays, sunspots, climatic and geographic changes, and biological forces (drives; instincts; conditioned, unconditioned, and prepotent reflexes; physio-economic complexes and "residues")—forces in whose hands man is as but clay, and which stage all the historical events and create all the cultural values. Man himself, as an embodiment of superorganic energy, of thought, of consciousness, of conscience, of rational volition, plays a negligible rôle in the unfolding of this drama. In our "scientific" histories he is relegated to the back stage as a mere plaything of blind forces—a plaything, moreover, stripped of virtually every element of attractiveness. While he is deluding himself with the belief that he controls his own destiny, he is, in fact, but the puppet of a blind biological evolution that dictates his actions and thus directs the course of his history.

We are so accustomed to this point of view that we frequently fail to realize the utter degradation which it implies. Instead of being depicted as a child of God, a bearer of the highest values attainable in this empirical world, and hence sacred, man is reduced to a mere inorganic or organic complex, not essentially different from billions of similar complexes. In so far as materialism identifies him and his cultural values with matter and mechanical motion, it cannot fail to strip him and his values of any exceptional and unique position in the world. Since they are but a complex of atoms, and since the events of human history are but a variety of the mechanical motions of atoms, neither man nor his culture can be regarded as sacred, as constituting the supreme end value, or as reflections of the Divine in the material world. In a word, materialistic sensory science and philosophy utterly degrade man and the truth itself.

With the degradation of truth, man is dragged down from his lofty pedestal as a seeker after truth as an absolute value to the level of an animal who tends, by means of various "ideologies," "rationalizations," and "derivations," to exalt his greed, his appetites, and his egoism. When he does this unwittingly, he becomes a simpleton; when he deliberately resorts to such rationalizations, appealing to "truth" and other high-sounding names, he becomes a downright hypocrite who employs "truth" as a mere smoke screen in order to justify his "residues" and complexes. In either case the result is disastrous to the dignity of man and to the cause of truth and science.

All this facilitates an explosive upsurge of man's elemental forces and leads men to treat their fellows, individually or in groups, as mere material atoms, electron-proton combinations, or biological organisms. If man is only an atom or electron or organism, why stand on ceremony in dealing with him? (We do not hesitate to scotch a snake or crush an atom!) The halo of sanctity having been stripped from man and his values, human relationships and sociocultural life degenerate into a savage struggle (witness the endless succession of contemporary wars and revolutions!) whose issue is decided by sheer physical force. In this struggle many values are destroyed—among them those of sensory science, or materialistic truth, itself.

*E.* Sensory science has still further undermined its own values through a progressively *thin and narrow empiricism divorced from other social values—religion, goodness, beauty, and the like.*

The divorce of the empirical aspect of reality from its other aspects has tragically narrowed the world of meanings and values and enormously impoverished the infinite richness and creativeness of socio-cultural life and cosmic reality, including even sensate happiness itself.

This indifference of empirical science to goodness and beauty has rendered it amoral, even cynical. It has thus become an instrumentality ready to serve any master, whether God or Mammon, and any purpose, whether socially beneficial or disastrous, constructive or destructive. On the one hand, it has created a world replete with beneficial gifts; on the other hand, it has created the most devilish means for the destruction of human life and culture. Poisonous gas, bombs and other explosives, are just as truly the children of empirical science as are refrigerators, medicine, tractors, or similar inventions.

Throughout one half of this planet, freedom of thought and research is already muzzled by those who have specialized in the control of precisely the destructive forces unleashed by empirical science. Science has been degraded to the rôle of a mere handmaid of contemporary "barbarians" who have well learned the motto of empiricism: Truth is what is convenient and useful; of several possible conventions, that which is most convenient for me is most true. Hence empirical science, carried to its logical conclusion, has once again paved the way for its ultimate downfall.

*F*. Finally, because of its enormous and complicated assortment of facts—poorly integrated, often irrelevant, and, despite their alleged precision, frequently contradictory—*empirical science has distinctly impaired our understanding of reality*. The bewilderment engendered by its complexity is heightened by a feeling of uncertainty. Indeed, sensory truth may be said to have ushered in the Age of Incertitude. Its theories are at best but hypotheses, marked by contradictions and by incessant change. The world proves increasingly a shadowy jungle, at once unknown and incomprehensible. Such incertitude cannot be tolerated indefinitely. It is inimical to man's happiness, his creativeness—even his survival. In the absence of adequate certainty, he seeks an artificial substitute, even though it be but an illusion. So he did during the decline of the Greco-Roman sensate culture, in favor of the absolute verities of Christianity; and so he is already doing at the present time.

To return to the sense of helplessness and disorientation produced by the growing complexity of the contemporary system of sensory truth. Who, save almighty God, could comprehend its infinite chaos of "facts," especially since we do not know which are relevant and which irrelevant? In the face of this difficulty we elaborate endless mechanical indices and bibliographies, digests and abstracts, indices of indices, bibliographies of bibliographies, digests of digests, and abstracts of abstracts. Human life is too short to master such an overwhelming and indiscriminate agglomeration of facts. In our frantic eagerness to know "more and more about less and less" we miss the really essential things. So empirical science eventually begins to obey the law of diminishing returns. It fails increasingly to satisfy man's need for proper orientation in the universe and for an adequate understanding of this universe. Under such conditions, is it any wonder that it is less and less highly esteemed and that it tends to be supplanted—or, at least, supplemented—by another system of truth?

This is particularly true of the social and humanistic sensory sciences. In spite of their multiplicity of so-called facts, they have contributed neither to our understanding of socio-cultural phenomena nor to our ability to foresee their future course. Empirical social theories emerge, enjoy their heyday, and after a few months or years are obsolete. Almost all the empirical theories of the nineteenth and twentieth centuries—those of business forecasting, conceptions of "progress" and socio-cultural "evolution," "laws of the three stages," theories of social and cultural trends—have been refuted by the inexorable verdict of history as pompous and pretentious exhibits of barren erudition.

G. Hence the increasing sterility of sensory science, especially in the social and related sciences. Notwithstanding their imposing array of historical, statistical, pseudo-experimental, clinical, and observational data, during the last three decades they have not produced a single valid generalized theory. At the best they have only reinstated, in a vulgarized and more primitive form, the generalizations of the preceding centuries. Since Comte and Spencer, Hegel and Marx, Le Play and Tarde, Durkheim and Max Weber, Simmel and Dilthey, Pareto and De Roberty, there has appeared hardly a name worthy of mention in sociology. In this field, and in economics, political science, anthropology, psychology, and history we seem to be living in an age of eruditional Hellenic Alexandrian scholarship—very industrious, very scientific, very factual, but devoid of ability to make any really important discovery or to create a single real value. The "less scholarly" age of Plato and Aristotle, Phidias and Praxiteles, Terpander and Sophocles, Thucydides and Herodotus, which discovered and created (intuitively) the greatest values of Greek culture, was superseded by the "scientific" age of Alexandrian scholarship. Similarly, the "less scholarly" culture of Galileo and Newton, Saint Thomas Aquinas and Kant, Dante and Shakespeare, Raphael and Rembrandt, Bach and Beethoven has apparently been supplanted by a system which repeats both the virtues and the vices of the erudite, but sterile and uninspired, Alexandrian school of thought.

The situation in the field of the natural sciences and technological inventions is seemingly much better than in that of the social and humanistic sciences. Yet even here we note certain warning signals. As we study the trend of scientific discoveries and technological inventions from 3000 B.C. up to our own day, we observe, first, that with the end of the nineteenth and the beginning of the twentieth century *the rate of increase of discoveries and inventions definitely slowed down;* second, that between the outbreak of the World War of 1914 and the year 1920 *even the absolute number of discoveries and inventions declined;* third, that *the climax (in number and importance of discoveries) in most of the exact sciences was reached, not in the twentieth century, but either in the nineteenth or (for mathematics) the eighteenth century.* The following figures illustrate this movement.

| Period | Total Number of Scientific Discoveries | Total Number of Technical Inventions | Total Number of Geographic Discoveries | Grand Total |
|---|---|---|---|---|
| 1791–1800 | 149 | 113 | 7 | 269 |
| 1801–1810 | 228 | 128 | 6 | 362 |
| 1811–1820 | 286 | 157 | 13 | 456 |
| 1821–1830 | 388 | 227 | 16 | 631 |
| 1831–1840 | 441 | 313 | 9 | 763 |
| 1841–1850 | 534 | 356 | 9 | 899 |
| 1851–1860 | 584 | 423 | 13 | 1020 |
| 1861–1870 | 553 | 424 | 15 | 992 |
| 1871–1880 | 635 | 490 | 17 | 1142 |
| 1881–1890 | 663 | 477 | 13 | 1153 |
| 1891–1900 | 625 | 482 | 2 | 1109 |
| 1901–1908 | 552 | 309 | 1 | 862 |

(See also Diagrams Nos. 2 and 3.)

*Climax not in 20th century*

The climax, as regards both number and importance, of discoveries in the various natural sciences up to 1908 was attained in the following years: in mathematics, 1726-1750; in chemistry, 1851-1875 and 1900-1940; in astronomy, 1876-1940; in geology, 1825-1850; in geography, 1851-1875; in biology, 1851-1875; in medicine, 1880-1899. Thus up to 1908 the peak period for most of the natural sciences was not the latest decade but principally the first two-thirds of the nineteenth century.

The situation for the last two decades is somewhat indefinite, owing to the lack of reliable data. However, several indications suggest that it has hardly improved. The continued decrease in the rate of discoveries and inventions is definitely established. In several fields (for instance, in medicine) the decline even in the absolute number is also clear: in the period 1900-1909 there were 123 major discoveries; in 1910-1919, 94; in 1920-1928, only 43. For the World War years (1914-1918) and immediately following, the decline in most of the belligerent countries is likewise reasonably certain. Other evidences point in the same direction. To sum up, the slowing down of the rate of increase admits of little doubt. A tendency toward irregular fluctuations or even a decrease in the absolute number of discoveries and inventions, in contradistinction to the rapid increase typical of the first part of the nineteenth century and the two preceding centuries, is also practically certain. To date, the climax for most of the natural sciences falls in the eighteenth century and the first seventy-five years of the nineteenth century.

There is every reason to believe that the present war, together with totalitarian dictatorship, enormously reinforces these symptoms of fatigue, of the decline of creative vigor, which appear to have spread from the field of the social and humanistic sciences to that of the natural sciences and technological inventions—the "holy of holies" of sensory truth.

The crisis in the theoretical system of sensory truth is sufficiently evident. Its practical failure is still more obvious.

*H.* The practical failure of the decadent empiricism of contemporary culture is demonstrated by our increasing inability to control mankind and the course of the sociocultural processes, notwithstanding the optimistic empirical slogan: *Savoir pour prévoir, prévoir pour pouvoir.* The more economists have tampered with economic conditions, the worse they have become; the more political scientists have reformed governments, the more are governments in need of reform; the more sociologists, psychologists, anthropologists, and lawyers have tampered with the family, the more the family has disintegrated; the more "scientific" solutions are offered for crime, the more numerous become the crimes; and so on. Despite all the natural and social sciences at our disposal, we are unable either to control the socio-cultural processes or to avoid the historical catastrophes. Like a log on the brink of Niagara Falls, we are impelled by unforseen and irresistible socio-cultural currents, helplessly drifting from one crisis and catastrophe to another. Neither happiness, nor safety and security, nor even material comfort has been realized. In few periods of human history have so many millions of persons been so unhappy, so insecure, so hungry and destitute, as at the present time, all the way from China to western Europe.

Wars and revolutions, crime, suicide, mental disease, and other evidences of deep-seated social maladies flourish apace, some of them on a scale hitherto unknown. We are witnessing a veritable "blackout" of human culture. Failing in *savoir pour pouvoir*, sensate science has still more shockingly failed in *savoir pour prévoir*. On the eve of war most of the sciences were forecasting peace; on the eve of economic crash and impoverishment, "bigger and better" prosperity; on the eve of revolutions, a stable order and streamlined progress. Often, indeed, the ways and means recommended in the name of science for an eradication of poverty, war, tyranny, exploitation, and other social evils have actually contributed to their increase; the means for saving democracy, to its weakening; and so on. No better evidence of the nemesis of one-sided sensory truth is needed.

Such are the how and the why of the contemporary crisis of sensory truth, and such are its symptoms. As in the case of other one-sided systems of truth, the immanent forces of empiricism have eventually wrought its own destruction. Western culture is at the crossroads. It must either cling to its outmoded unilateral conception of truth or else correct its one-sidedness by reintroducing other systems. The former choice means that it will forfeit every creative possibility and become completely impotent and fossilized. The alternative will lead to the reestablishment of an integral and more adequate system of truth and values.

As we have seen, the situation in the field of sensate truth (science, philosophy, and religion) is precisely parallel to that which prevails in the realm of the fine arts. Both have reached the decadent stage—the phase of transition. While both have contributed immeasurably to the sum total of human achievement, for the time being they have outlived their usefulness. Other forms of culture are now looming on the horizon, destined to carry on, in their own peculiar manner, the task of creative evolution. When these forms, in turn, have exhausted their inner vitality, a new sensate culture will again doubtless emerge; and thus the creative "eternal cycle" will persist, as long as human history endures.

# CHAPTER IV

# THE CRISIS IN ETHICS AND LAW

## 1. IDEATIONAL, IDEALISTIC, AND SENSATE SYSTEMS OF ETHICS

Any integrated society has ethical ideals and values as the highest manifestation of its ethical consciousness. Likewise, any society has some norms of law as to what forms of conduct are expected, required, and permitted on the part of its members and what forms are prohibited and punished. Ethical ideals and legal norms differ, however, in their character and content from society to society, often from man to man. When they are integrated they produce ideational, idealistic, and sensate systems of ethics and law. The difference between these systems can easily be seen from the following examples of the supreme ethical ideals.

*Ideational Ethical Norms.* Lay not up for yourselves treasures upon earth, where moth and rust doth corrupt. But lay up for yourselves treasures in heaven, where neither moth nor rust doth corrupt.

No man can serve two masters: for either he will hate the one, and love the other; or else he will hold to the one, and despise the other. Ye cannot serve God and mammon. Therefore I say unto you, Take no thought for your life, what ye shall eat, or what ye shall drink; nor yet for your body, what ye shall put on. But seek ye first the kingdom of God, and his righteousness; and all these things shall be added unto you. . . . Love your enemies, bless them that curse you, do good to them that hate you, and pray for them which despitefully use you, and persecute you. Be you therefore perfect, even as your Father which is in heaven is perfect. . . . Our Father which art in heaven. . . . Thy kingdom come. Thy will be done in earth, as it is in heaven.

(*Matthew*, vi, 24, 25, 33, 9, 10; v, 44, 19, 20)

Different in form but similar in content are the ethical systems of Hinduism, Buddhism, Taoism, Zoroastrianism, Judaism, and any other ideational mentality. They all see the supreme ethical value not in this sensory world but in the supersensory world of God or the Absolute. They all regard the empirical world of the senses with all its values as a pseudo-value or, at the best, as an unimportant and subordinate value.

The good is one thing, the pleasant another; these two, having different objects, chain a man. It is well with him who clings to the good; he who chooses the pleasant misses his end.

Look on this world as you would at a bubble (or mirage). . . . The foolish are immersed in it, but the wise do not touch it.

All things hasten to decay and there is no permanency. Everywhere I find old age, disease, and death. Therefore I search for the happiness of something that decays not, that never perishes, that never knows beginning, that looks with equal mind on enemy and friend, that needs not wealth, nor beauty, the happiness of one . . . with all thoughts about the world destroyed.

Wise men . . . care for nothing in this world.

There is no satisfying lusts, even by a shower of gold pieces; he who knows that lusts have a short taste and cause pain, he is wise. He delights only in destruction of all desires.

A man who is free from desires . . . sees the majesty of the nonempirical Self, by the Grace of the Creator. . . . He is the greatest of all men.

The mind approaching the Eternal has attained to the extinction of all desires.

Such are Hinduist and Buddhist expressions of the negative attitude towards all the sensory values—riches, gold, pleasure, and power.

Ideational ethics aims not at an increase of the sensory happiness and pleasures of this world but at the union with the Absolute, which is supersensory. The norms of such ethics are regarded as revealed by, or emanating from, the Absolute; therefore as absolute, unconditional, unchangeable, and eternal. They cannot be disregarded under any conditions or for any other value. If the fulfillment of such norms gives as a by-product some happiness and joy, these remain mere by-products—not the objective of such ethics. If the moral commandments lead to sensory pain and grief, that does not matter either. Sensory happiness or unhappiness, pleasure or pain, are utterly irrelevant for such an ethical ideal. As a matter of fact, all ideational ethical systems regard the sensory pleasures negatively, as either a mere illusion, as a source of grief, or as an obstacle to the achievement of the transcendental objective—God.

*Sensate Ethical Norms.* Any ethical system that regards sensory happiness, pleasure, utility, and comfort, in their refined or unrefined form, as the supreme value is a sensate system of ethics. All purely utilitarian, all hedonistic, even many eudemonistic, systems of ethics are varieties of this kind of ethical ideals. Its formulae are well known to us:

The maximum happiness for the maximum number of human beings.

The supreme end is pleasure.

Let us eat, drink, and be merry, for tomorrow we die.

Wine, women, and song.

Follow thy desire, so long as thou livest. . . . Do what thou wishest on earth, and vex not thy heart.

Time is short; let us enjoy it.

There is no heaven, no final liberation, nor any soul in another world. . . . While life remains, let man live happily, let him feed on glee, even though he runs in debt. When once the body becomes ashes, how can it ever return again?

Lesbia is beautiful. . . . Let us live, let us love, my Lesbia. The sun dies to be born again, but as for us, once the ephemeral flame of our life is quenched, we must sleep the eternal sleep. Therefore give me a thousand kisses, then a hundred, then a thousand, . . . after which we will confuse the account so as no longer to know it.

*Carpe diem*
Quanto è bella giovinezza,
Che si fugge tuttavia!
Chi vuol esser lieto, sia!
Di domani non c'è certezza.

Cueillez, cueillez votre jeunesse:
Comme à cette fleur la vieillesse
Fera ternir votre beauté.

Buy a car and be happy.

Such are the eternal Chinese and Hindu, Greek and Roman, Italian and French, English and American, past and present formulae of the more rude and more refined sensate systems of ethics. Their supreme aim is to increase the sum of sensate happiness, pleasure, utility, and comfort, because they do not believe in any supersensory value.

Their rules are therefore not absolute but relative, expedient, and changeable, according to the persons, groups, and situations involved. They are regarded as man-made rules. If they serve the purpose of happiness, they are acceptable; if they do not, they may be discarded.

*Idealistic Ethical Norms.* Idealistic ethical norms are an intermediary synthesis of ideational and sensate values. Like ideational ethics, idealist ethics perceives the highest value in God or the supersensory Absolute; but, in contradistinction to ideationalism, it views positively those sensory values that are the noblest and that do not militate against the Absolute.

Its formulae likewise have been many.

> The perfect happiness of man cannot be other than the vision of the Divine essence. (Saint Thomas Aquinas)

> The soul being immortal and able to bear all evil and all good, we shall always hold to the road which leads above. And justice with prudence we shall by all means pursue in order that we may be friends both to ourselves and to the gods, . . . and we shall both here and in that thousand years' journey . . . enjoy a happy life. (Plato-Socrates)

> [The *summum bonum,* or perfectly happy life] will be higher than mere human nature, because a man will live thus, not in so far as he is a man, but in so far as there is in him a divine principle. . . . We must . . . make ourselves like immortals and do all with a view to living in accordance with the highest principle in us. (Aristotle)

> Be mindful of death. . . . Possessions do not make for happiness. Wealth is unstable. Eat no bread, if another is suffering want, and thou dost not stretch out the hand to him with

bread. . . . Be pious, diligent. Be not a drunkard. Lead an honest life. Be respectful. Learn: knowledge is useful. . . . Be careful of women.

The pleasure is only for a little moment, and it passes like a dream; and a man at the end thereof finds death through knowing it.

(Egyptian moral norms)

These formulae range from the highest ideational-idealistic plane almost to the utilitarian-sensate level, as in the Egyptian moral maxims. But the first three formulae are a variety of idealistic ethics. They virtually merge with eudemonistic ethics.

These three systems of ethics, moreover, have fluctuated in their domination throughout the history of Greco-Roman and Western cultures. Each of them has prevailed in about the same periods during which the ideational, idealistic, and sensate systems of art and truth have been in the ascendancy. The dominant Greek ethics from the eighth to the fifth century B.C. was mainly ideational—that of Hesiod, Aeschylus, Sophocles, Herodotus, Pindar, and others. This explains the otherwise incomprehensible ethics of "the wrath of the gods" in their dramas and poetry, their religion and mores. The tragedy of Oedipus is visited upon him without any guilt on his part: he did all that one could to avoid the crimes of patricide and marrying his mother, imposed upon him by destiny. From our standpoint his punishment is quite undeserved; not so from the standpoint of Sophocles. His ideational ethics passionately demands expiation for any violation of absolute moral principles, whether intentional or not. Akin is the standpoint of Pindar, Aeschylus, and Herodotus, and of the dominant religious morals of the period. They all considered, with Pindar, that "human happiness does not stay long" and is far from being the main value.

This system of ethics began to decline in the fifth century B.C. and was replaced by the idealistic ethics of Socrates, Plato, and Aristotle, with the norms quoted previously. The period from the third century B.C. to about the fourth century A.D. was marked by sensate ethics in its nobler Stoic and Epicurean forms, as well as in the crude forms of naked hedonism and of the code of *Carpe diem*. Even on many a tombstone were inscribed such vulgar sensate maxims as *Es, bibe, lude, veni* (Eat, drink, play, come hither); and "Let us eat, drink and be merry, for tomorrow we die."

After the fourth century A.D. the ideational ethics of Christianity achieved supremacy, remaining unchallenged to the thirteenth century. We know well its maxims. In their sublimest form they are summed up in the Sermon on the Mount. Being derived from God, the moral values of Christian ethics are absolute. Their cardinal principle is the all-embracing, all-bestowing, and all-forgiving love of God for man, of man for God, and of man for man. Their pathos and ethos are derived from this boundless love, and from the charismatic grace, duty, and sacrifice implied in it. Blessed by charisma, man is a child of God, and is sanctified by this relationship; regardless of his race or sex, age or social status, he is a supreme value. Making its moral principles absolute, Christianity raises man to the highest level of sanctification, and protects him unconditionally against any use as a mere means to an end. No greater glorification or sanctihcation of man is possible than that vouchsafed by the ideational ethics of Christianity.

From this attribute of Christian ethics followed the medieval—either negative or indifferent—estimation of all the values of the sensory world as such, from wealth, pleasure, and utility to sensory happiness, when divorced from the supersensory value.

*Remember man, that thou art dust & unto dust*

"*Memento, homo, quia pulvis es et in pulverem revertis.*"
"No one who loves Christ cares for this world."

This attitude is stressed by medieval monasticism and asceticism and by the medieval outlook on this life as a mere painful preparation for the transition from the sinful City of Man to the eternal City of God.

This uncompromisingly ideational system of ethics began to give way to the less rigorous idealistic ethics of the thirteenth to the fifteenth century. In the fourteenth and fifteenth centuries sensate ethics reemerges, flourishing apace during the next century—that of the Renaissance and the Reformation. The hedonism, sensuality, and paganism of the ethics of the Renaissance are well known. The period was notoriously sensuous and utilitarian, cynical and nihilistic in the teachings as well as in the conduct of its leaders. This was especially true of the Italian and French Renaissance. Less sensual, but nevertheless sensate and utilitarian, was the ethics of most of the sects of the Reformation, with perhaps an exception in ascetic Protestantism (Calvinism, Pietism, and Methodism). Though masked by its ideational phraseology, the real character of the ethics of Protestantism was largely utilitarian and sensate. Moneymaking was declared the sign of God's grace; it was elevated to the rank of a primary duty: "We must exhort all

Christians to gain all they can and to save all they can; that is, in effect, to grow rich," preaches John Wesley. Says Benjamin Franklin: "Honesty is useful because it assures credit: so are punctuality, industry, frugality, and *that is the reason they are virtues.* . . . Remember that time is money. Remember that money is of a prolific, generating nature." A similar gospel was preached by representatives of other Protestant currents. Early and medieval Christianity had denounced wealth as the source of perdition; money-making, as *summae periculosae;* profit, as a *turpe lucrum;* money-lending, as a grave crime; the rich man, as a first candidate for perdition, for whom it was more difficult to enter the kingdom of God than for a camel to go through the eye of a needle—or, as Anatole France put it, "*La miséricorde de Dieu est infinie: elle sauvera même un riche.*" Now the Reformation and the Renaissance made an about-face. "On Sundays he [the Puritan] believes in God and Eternity; on week days, in the stock exchange. On Sundays the Bible is his ledger, and on week days the ledger is his Bible." Hence the parallel growth of Protestantism, paganism, capitalism, utilitarianism, and sensate ethics during the subsequent centuries. The last four centuries have witnessed the supremacy of sensate ethics in Western society. Though from a purely quantitative standpoint, as the figures show, it has been somewhat weaker than idealistic and ideational ethics, yet from a qualitative standpoint it has certainly been the dominant system; for many of its elements have permeated and diluted many a formal principle of the ideational and idealistic systems of these four centuries.

The following tabulation, presenting the percentages of the partisans of the Absolute (ideational and partly idealistic ethics) and of the relative sensate ethics of happiness (hedonism, utilitarianism, and eudemonism) among all the eminent ethical thinkers in each specified century, gives a still more definite idea of the shift outlined.

| Period | Sensate Ethics of Happiness (Percentage) | Absolute Ideational Ethics (Percentage) |
|---|---|---|
| A.D. 400–500 | 0 | 100 |
| 500–600 | 0 | 100 |
| 600–700 | 0 | 100 |
| 700–800 | 0 | 100 |
| 800–900 | 0 | 100 |
| 900–1000 | 0 | 100 |
| 1000–1100 | 0 | 100 |
| 1100–1200 | 0 | 100 |
| 1200–1300 | 0 | 100 |
| 1300–1400 | 0 | 100 |
| 1400–1500 | 8.7 | 91.3 |
| 1500–1600 | 43.5 | 56.5 |
| 1600–1700 | 38.4 | 61.6 |
| 1700–1800 | 36.3 | 63.7 |
| 1800–1900 | 38.0 | 62.0 |
| 1900–1920 | 43.0 | 57.0 |

We have seen that throughout the Middle Ages sensate ethics was practically absent, appearing in a clear-cut form only in the fifteenth century, attaining a rapid growth in the sixteenth century, and maintaining thereafter a high level, with minor fluctuations reaching their maxima in the period of the Renaissance and the Reformation and in the present century. Diagram No. 6 shows pictorially these shifts. Looking at the movement of the sensate ethics of happiness we see clearly the periods of its rise and decline from 500 B.C. to A.D. 1920.

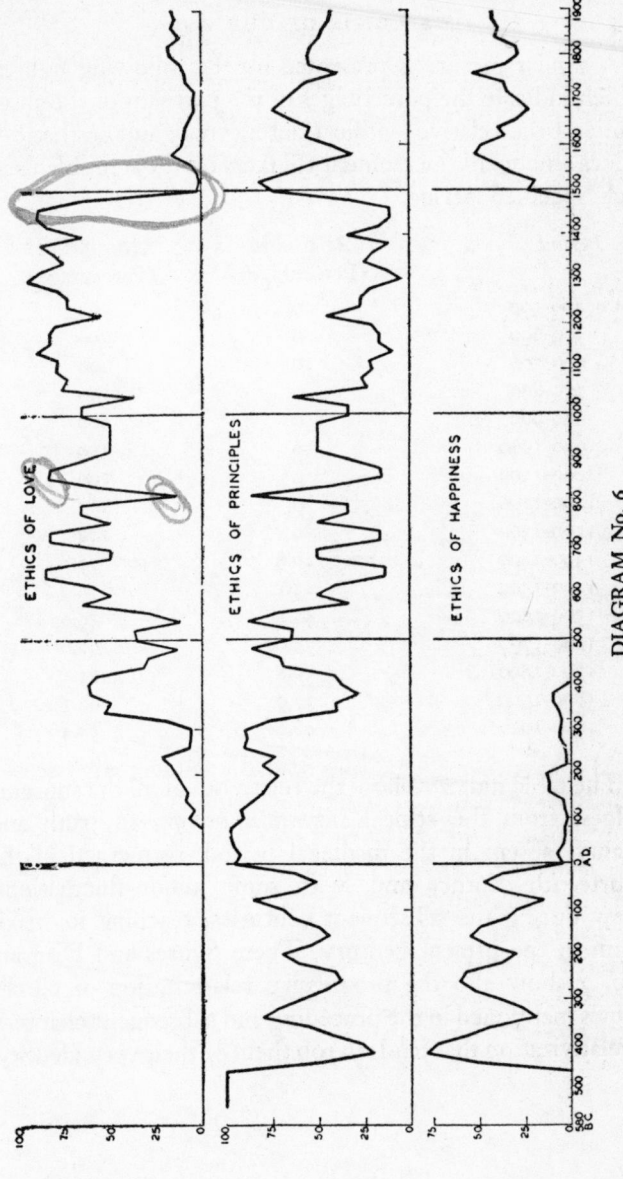

DIAGRAM No. 6

A similar picture is presented by the following figures, which indicate the percentages of the partisans of the absolute and the relative—ethical, intellectual, and aesthetic—values among all the eminent thinkers on these problems in each specified period.

| Period | Relativism (Percentage) | Absolutism (Percentage) |
|---|---|---|
| A.D. 400–500 | 0 | 100 |
| 500–600 | 0 | 100 |
| 600–700 | 0 | 100 |
| 700–800 | 0 | 100 |
| 800–900 | 0 | 100 |
| 900–1000 | 0 | 100 |
| 1000–1100 | 0 | 100 |
| 1100–1200 | 0 | 100 |
| 1200–1300 | 0 | 100 |
| 1300–1400 | 20.8 | 79.2 |
| 1400–1500 | 23.1 | 76.9 |
| 1500–1600 | 40.4 | 59.6 |
| 1600–1700 | 38.0 | 62.0 |
| 1700–1800 | 36.8 | 63.2 |
| 1800–1900 | 37.9 | 62.1 |
| 1900–1920 | 48.6 | 51.4 |

The table indicates how the relativism of all the supreme values, from the ethical *summum bonum* to truth and beauty, absent in the medieval period, reemerged in the fourteenth century and, with some minor fluctuations, grew during the subsequent centuries, reaching its maximum in the present century. These figures and Diagram No. 7 show also the progressive relativization of all the values mentioned in the preceding and subsequent chapters, a relativization that tends to rob them of their very identity,

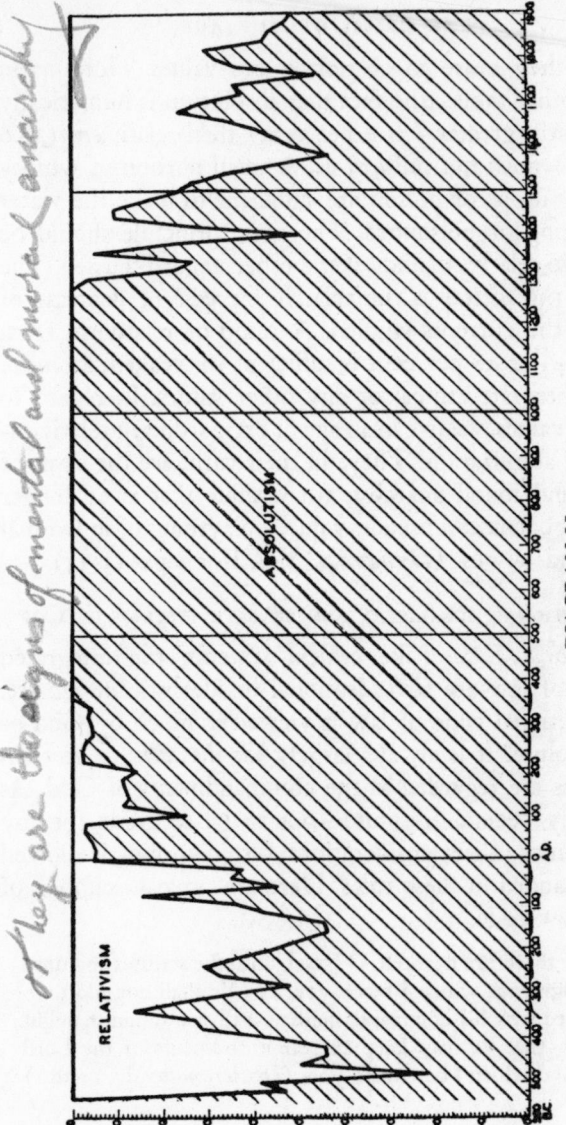

*they are the signs of mental and moral anarchy*

RELATIVISM

ABSOLUTISM

DIAGRAM No. 7

so that they cease to be norms and values. Here, as in several other tables, the fact that absolutism is numerically still slightly greater (51.4 per cent) than relativism (48.6 per cent) must not mislead us. A small portion of whisky or a few drops of poison are sufficient to make the water intoxicating or poisonous. The same principle should be applied to relativism and several other items discussed. The crux of the matter is the relative increase or decrease of each of the currents studied. A jump of relativism from zero to 40 or 48 per cent is sufficient to weaken, atomize, and disintegrate ethical or any other values. In regard to all these values, we live in an age of extraordinary relativization and atomization. They, in their turn, are the signs of mental and moral anarchy; for a value that is no longer universal becomes a pseudo-value, a plaything of individual fancy and wishes. (*Dynamics*, Vol. II, chaps. 13-15)

## 2. IDEATIONAL, IDEALISTIC, AND SENSATE SYSTEMS OF LAW

*Ideational Law.* Like ethical systems, the integrated systems of law are also ideational or idealistic or sensate. The ideational code of law is viewed as given by God or the Absolute. It is always largely *jus divinum* or *sacrum*. Its norms are regarded as the commandments of God. As such they become absolute—not to be set aside for any utilitarian or other considerations. Often nothing is allowed to be changed in these rules. Here are typical examples of such a law code.

> Now therefore hearken, O Israel, unto the statutes and unto the judgments, which I teach you. . . . Ye shall not add unto the word which I command, neither shall you diminish aught from it, that ye may keep the commandments of the Lord your God which I command you. (*Deuteronomy*, iv, 1 and 2)

And for another example:

> Now for the sake of preserving all this creation, the most Glorious [Lord] ordained separate duties for those who sprang from His mouth, arms, thighs, and feet. . . . The Lord created . . . punishment, the protector of all creatures, an incarnation of the law, framed of Brahman glory. (*The Laws of Manu*, I, 31; VII, 14)

> For verily I say unto you, Till heaven and earth pass, one jot or one tittle shall in no wise pass from the law, till all be fulfilled. Whosoever therefore shall break one of these least commandments, and shall teach men so, he shall be called the least in the kingdom of heaven: but whosoever shall do and teach them, the same shall be called great in the kingdom of heaven. (*Matthew*, v, 18, 19)

The norms of ideational law are not aimed at an increase of sensory happiness or pleasure or utility. They are to be obeyed unquestionably as the commandments of the omniscient and ever-just Absolute. We may not always understand their wisdom, and they may appear to us inscrutable, as the ways of Providence are inscrutable. Yet their wisdom and justice cannot be doubted. Being such, the ideational codes of law protect many a value that seemingly has no sensory utility or pleasure. On the other hand, they prohibit many a pleasure and utility as sinful. Their norms always contain a large portion of commandments concerning the Absolute, the forms of the proper religious beliefs, religious rituals, and religious behavior, as well as the forms of thought and conduct that sanctify or purify all the important events in man's life, such as birth (sanctified by baptism), wedding (sanctified by the sacred ceremony of marriage), and death (sanctified by the funeral rites). Almost all their norms are permeated by the central idea of facilitating man's union with the Absolute and of purifying him when he transgresses the commandments and commits a sin or a crime.

In such codes crime and sin are synonymous, just as obedience to the law is synonymous with obedience to God and salvation. Therefore in *its criminal part the ideational code of law always has among its prohibited and punished actions many an action that violates the prescribed rules in man's relationship toward God and supersensory values.* Prescriptions directed against heresy, apostasy, sacrilege, blasphemy; violation of the Sabbath, or holy day; violation of the prescribed sacred rituals; nonfulfillment of the sacred ceremonies of baptism, marriage, and funeral; infraction of the sacred rules respecting either intermarriage or contact with gentiles and disbelievers and so on—these laws comprise a large part of the punishable actions of such criminal codes. *Their system of punishment is likewise made up not of sensory punishments only but of supersensory penalties as well.* Punishment ranges from the eternal damnation of the sinful, and often of his progeny, in some inferno, or purgatory, to excommunication from the society of believers, to deprivation of the Sacraments and of the blessings of the religious rituals in burial and other events. The objective of the punishment is not so much prevention of crime, or education of the sinner-criminal, or protection of the utilitarian interests of the society, as an *expiation* of the sin committed against God: any violation of the absolute norm requires the vindication of the norm and cannot pass without expiation for the sin performed. A criminal is always *sacer esto;* therefore he must be punished, no matter whether, from a sensory standpoint, such a punishment is useful for the culprit or society, or not. The system of the *judicial evidence of such a law contains, moreover, an assortment of supersensory evidence in the form of the ordeals, "the judgment of God,"* the dicta of oracles, prophets, and pythias, and other "supernatural techniques" for finding out whether or not the accused party is guilty. This system of judicial evidence is based upon the assumption of the interference of the Absolute in judicial affairs. *Almost every law action, be it the exchange or purchase of property, or conclusion of a contract, or payment of a debt, is prescribed to the last detail through the pronouncement of certain sacred formulae, through definite sacred actions, without the possibility of changing anything, even a single letter or detail, in this sacramental procedure.* Just as no change in an important religious ritual is permitted, so no change is permitted in any judicial procedure, in the interest of the parties involved, or anyone else. For instance, in the Roman law, at its early ideational stage, when the issue before the court was the ownership of certain types of property the suitor started the procedure by holding in his hand a certain stick *(vindicta* or *festuca)* and by pronouncing a stereotyped and inflexible formula: *Hanc ego rem ex jure Quiritium meam esse ajo: sicut dixi, ecce tibi vinditam imposui.* With an equally definite formula the defendant had to answer; and so the whole judicial procedure was but a sacred ritual, as formal as any religious sacrament. The reason for this formalism of ideational law and legal procedure is that law and procedure are but a variety of religion and religious ritual prescribed by God and therefore unchangeable. Finally, *the judges in such a system of law are always—*

*directly or indirectly—priests, pontiffs, and other members of the sacerdotal order, assisted by oracles, prophets, seers, saints, and the like.* In brief, the norms of the law are absolute and rigid; the forms of its enforcement and application are also absolute and formal. No vagueness, uncertainty, relativity, ambiguity, or expediency is admitted. The legal conscience of ideational society is clear-cut, free from any doubt, and not open to any questioning or criticism. It embodies in detail the major premise of the ideational mentality.

Accordingly, ideational law is not controlled entirely by considerations of utility, profit, expediency, and sensory well-being, even in such utilitarian matters as production, exchange, and consumption of economic values—trade and commerce; money and banking; profit and interest; property and possession; rent; the relationship between the employer and employees, and other property and economic relationships. On the contrary, these all are subordinated to the ideational norms of the law, and are admitted only in so far as they do not contradict ideational values. If they do contradict these norms and values, they are rejected, prohibited, or punished, no matter how useful they may be for the society or the parties involved. This fact explains the expulsion of the merchants from the temple at Jerusalem by Jesus, with his rebuke, "My house shall be called the house of prayer; but ye have made it a den of thieves"; Christ's dictum, "Verily I say unto you, that a rich man shall hardly enter into the kingdom of God"; and the prohibition by the canon law and Christian morals upon money-lending, profit, devotion to money-making, and other economic—and profitable and useful—activities.

All these activities are restricted by, and subordinated to, ideational values. This applies also to the personal relationships of marriage and the family. The considerations of happiness in marriage receive little attention. Because marriage is a recognized sacred bond, no divorce was possible under medieval Christian law, whether the parties were happy or unhappy. In brief, ideational values transcend all other values in such a code of law.

The same is true of any other association, contract, and social relationship envisaged by ideational law. Social relationships or contracts are never left entirely to the option of the parties concerned or to a rude coercion imposed by the stronger upon the weaker. They are limited by many provisions and subordinated to the demands of the supersensory values. Such a body of law does not admit of unlimited contract and agreement or of unlimited compulsion in human relationships, however useful, pleasant, or convenient they might be to one or both of the parties concerned. On the contrary, ideational law not only restricts contractual relations and prohibits or mitigates compulsory ones among individuals and groups, but also enjoins men to be brotherly, altruistic, generous, compassionate, and solidary, or cooperative, helping one another in their relationships, loving one another, respecting one another as the children of God or the Absolute, whether or not such love, help, altruism, and mutual aid are utilitarian, pleasant, or desirable. These attributes are imposed and demanded as a duty or sacrifice required by the Absolute. This twofold, divinely authoritarian regulation of social relationships, (1) through a negative limitation of contracts and compulsions contradictory to the absolute norms of God, and (2) through the positive stimulation of duty, sacrifice, love, altruism, and good will, regardless of any considerations of profit, utility, pleasure, and happiness, is the specific characteristic of ideational law.

Finally, *such a code regards the legitimate authority of government as derived ultimately from the Absolute, or God*—not from physical force, wealth, or popular mandate. A government with authority not based on the sanction of the Absolute, and not obedient to its commands, is invalid for such a system of law and such a society. It is an arbitrary tyrant not entitled to obedience and deserving only to be overthrown. Hence in all societies ruled by ideational law the regime is always either explicitly or implicitly a *theocracy*.

Such, in brief, are the typical traits of ideational law. These traits one finds in the secular and canon law of medieval ideational Europe, of Brahmanic or Hinduistic India, or of Tibet; in the law of early ideational Rome and Greece; in that of the Incas; and in any other ideational culture.

*Sensate Law.* The characteristics of sensate law present a very different picture. It is viewed by a sensate society as man-made—frequently, indeed, as a mere instrument for the subjugation and exploitation of one group by another. Its aim is exclusively utilitarian: the safety of human life, security of property and possession, peace and order, the happiness and well-being of either society at large or of the dominating faction which enacts and enforces sensate law. Its norms are relative, changeable, and conditional; a group of rules expedient under one set of circumstances or for one group becomes useless or even harmful in different situations or for another group. Therefore they are subject to incessant change. Nothing eternal or sacred is implied in such a system of law. It does not attempt to regulate supersensory values or man's relationship toward them. It contains few, if any, provisions respecting man's relationship to God, the salvation of the soul, or other transcendental phenomena. Its criminal code virtually ignores the ideational crimes of heresy, apostasy, sacrilege, and the like. Its punishments are wholly sensory, devoid of supersensory sanctions. Their purpose is not expiation but revenge, the reeducation of the culprit, the security of society, or similar utilitarian objectives. Since it is secular, it is supplemented by no body of sacred or canon law. Its judicial evidence is invariably sensory; no "judgment of God" or ordeals are admitted. Its judges, again, are secular. Its rules and procedures are elastic, variable, free from the rigid formality of ideational law. Man's personal and property relationships are governed entirely from the standpoint of expediency, utility, and the sensory well-being, either of society at large or of the dominant group. Supersensory values and considerations do not play any important rôle in the limitation or control of these utilitarian and sensory motivations.

The social relationships regulated by sensate law are subject to the same sensory, utilitarian considerations. In this regulation the law does not invoke any divinely authoritarian sanction. All the relationships are either contractual (left to the agreement of the parties) or compulsory (imposed by the stronger party upon the weaker); and all are sanctioned by law. Such limitations of the freedom of contract or of compulsion as exist are introduced for sensory and utilitarian reasons. No nonutilitarian or anti-utilitarian limitations are imposed on property relationships, personal relationships, or any other relationships in so far as they are not required in the interest of other groups. In all these respects the whole system of legal regulation rests on a sensory plane and is determined almost exclusively by sensory motivation.

Finally, *the government that enacts and enforces such a code is a secular—not a theocratic—government*, based either upon military and physical power, upon riches and abilities, or upon the mandate of the electorate. Since no divine, supersensory sanction is demanded for the legality and authority of the law, there is no opportunity for the rise of an influential theocracy.

Such are the essential characteristics of sensate law, whether it be the Western law of the last few centuries, the law of the sensate period of Greece and Rome, or that of other sensate societies.

*Idealistic Law.* Idealistic law, in turn, occupies an intermediate position between ideational and sensate law.

### 3. SHIFTS IN THE DOMINATION OF IDEATIONAL, IDEALISTIC, AND SENSATE LAW

As in the field of ethical ideals, the fine arts, and the systems of truth, each of the main forms of law, in the history of the Greco-Roman and Western cultures, rose to a position of dominance and then declined in favor of one of the other forms of law. The early Greek and Roman law before the fifth century B.C. was mainly ideational. It was largely the *jus divinum* or *sacrum*, with the priesthood as the ruler, lawgiver, and judge, and with the legal norms prescribed by the gods. It was therefore sacred and inviolable. The transgressor became the *sacer esto*. The objective of punishment was expiation. In the words of a certain historian, "religion in early Greece was an absolute master; the State was a religious community, the king a pontiff, the magistrate a priest, and the law a sacred formula; patriotism was piety; and exile, excommunication." According to another historian, in ancient Rome (before 510 B.C.) the king was the supreme priest (*pontifex maximus, rex sacrificulus*). "He held intercourse with the gods of the community, whom he consulted and appeased (*auspicia publica*), and he nominated all the priests and the priestesses." The criminal law was sacral; many of the most flagrant crimes were of religious character. In a word, the situation exhibited all the characteristics of ideational law. Toward the end of the sixth century B.C. there appeared symptoms of its decline, and in the fifth century B.C. sensate law reemerged. Between the third century B.C. and the fifth A.D. it grew to a position of dominance, revealing all the usual characteristics. The rise of Christianity brought with it the rise of ideational law, which after the fifth century became dominant and remained so until about the end of the twelfth century. During this period the Christian law of medieval Europe—both secular and canon law—assumed all the typical traits of ideational law. Medieval criminal law, for instance, as compared with the law of the pagan barbaric tribes or of late Roman law, introduced many new, severely punishable crimes of a purely religious character—such as blasphemy, apostasy, heresy, schism, sorcery, hindering religious services, nonfulfillment of religious rites, nonobservance of Sunday, violation of

"God's peace," abuse of corpses, suicide, usury, contact with Jews, abduction, adultery, panderage, incest, fornication, and abortion. Most of these new crimes are, from the purely utilitarian and hedonistic standpoint, not necessarily harmful or painful to the parties involved. From the ideational Christian standpoint they were transgressions against the commandments of God, a violation of ideational values; therefore they were treated as criminal and severely punishable.

As we move from the codes of medieval law to those of the seventeenth and more recent centuries, most of these offenses cease to be crimes and are excluded from the list of criminal and punishable offenses. The few that remained criminal changed their nature and were punishable for purely utilitarian reasons. The terminal point in this trend toward increasingly sensate criminal law was reached in the Soviet criminal laws of 1926 and 1930, where all religious crimes were entirely abolished and, with their elimination, many a crime connected with ideational values, such as seduction, adultery, polygamy, polyandry, incest, sodomy, homosexuality, fornication, and public indecency, ceased to be regarded as crime. All such actions have become noncriminal. A similar transformation occurred in the field of constitutional and civil laws. In practically all Western countries they became almost purely sensate, and they remain predominantly sensate at the present time.

We come now to the present crisis in ethical ideals and in law. Since their dominant forms in Western countries are sensate, the crisis evidently consists in the disintegration of the sensate ethics and law of the Western countries. (*Dynamics*, Vol. II, chap. 15; Vol. III, chap. 5)

### 4. THE DISINTEGRATION OF SENSATE ETHICS AND LAW

The essence of the crisis consists in a progressive devaluation of our ethics and of the norms of our law. This devaluation has already gone so far that, strange as it may seem, they have lost a great deal of their prestige as ethical and juridical values. They have little, if any, of the sanctity with which such values and norms were formerly invested. More and more, present-day ethical values are looked upon as mere "rationalizations," "derivations," or "beautiful speech reactions" veiling the egotistic interests, pecuniary motives, and acquisitive propensities of individuals and groups. Increasingly they are regarded as a smoke screen masking prosaic interests, selfish lusts, and, in particular, greed for material values. Legal norms, likewise, are increasingly considered as a device of the group in power for exploiting other, less powerful, groups—a form of trickery employed by the dominant class for the subjugation and control of the subordinate classes. Ethical and juridical norms have both become mere rouge and powder to deck out a fairly unattractive body of Marxian economic interests, Paretian "residues," Freudian "libido," Ratzenhoger "interests," the psychologists' and sociologists' "complexes," "drives," and "prepotent reflexes." They have turned into mere appendages of policemen, prisons, the electric chair, "pressures," and other forms of physical force. They have lost their moral prestige and have been degraded and demoted to the status of a device used by clever hypocrites to fool the exploited simpletons. With the loss of moral prestige, they have progressively forfeited their controlling and binding power as effective factors of human conduct. Their "Thou shalt not" and "Thou shalt" have more and more ceased to affect human conduct as moral commandments or to guide it according to these commandments, and have grown progressively null and void. Accordingly, the question arises: "If the salt have lost its savor, wherewith shall it be salted? It is thenceforth good for nothing, but to be cast out, and to be trodden under foot of men."

Having lost their "savor" and efficacy, they opened the way for rude force as the only controlling power in human relationships. If neither religious nor ethical nor juridical values control our conduct, what then remains? Nothing but naked force and fraud. Hence the contemporary "Might is right." This is the central feature of the crisis in our ethics and law.

The crisis did not originate either suddenly or recently. It is not due to some unforeseen factor external to sensate ethics and law. On the contrary, it has been generated slowly by the sensate system itself, in the course of its development, from the pathogenic germs implicit in the system. In the earliest stages of sensate ethics and law, these poisonous germs were merely latent. Because of the sanctity and halo of ideational ethical values, the norms of early sensate ethics and law were still regarded as somewhat sacred and reasonable, still enjoyed a certain moral prestige, and hence were effective controlling forces in their own right. With a further decline of the ideational system, and with the marked growth of sensate ethics and law, these noxious germs became increasingly virulent. With their growing virulence, they came to undermine and disintegrate sensate values more and more, stripping them progressively of their sanctity and prestige, until at the present time all such norms have lost their halo.

*These poisonous germs of sensate ethics and law were inherent in the utilitarian and hedonistic—that is, relativistic and conditional—nature of the ethical and legal values of the system.* Any sensory value, as soon as it is put on a plane of relativistic and utilitarian convention, is bound to retrogress, becoming more and more relative, more and more conventional, until it reaches a stage of "atomization" in its relativism and of utter arbitrariness in its ever thinner and less universal conventionality. The final stage is bankruptcy. This is a brief summary of how and why the salt of sensate ethico-juridical values came to lose its savor. If the essence of moral and juridical values is utility and sensory happiness, then everyone has the right to pursue these values *ad libitum.* As pleasure, utility, and sensory happiness differ with different persons and groups, one is entitled to pursue them in the way one pleases and by any means one has at his disposal. As there is no limit to the expansion of sensory desires for sensory values, the available amount of these sensory values finally becomes insufficient to satisfy the desires and appetites of all the individuals and groups. The dearth of these values in turn, leads to a clash of individuals and groups. Under such circumstances the struggle is bound to become ever sharper, more intensive, and more diversified in its means and forms. The ultimate result is the emergence of rude force assisted by fraud as the supreme and sole arbiter of the conflicts. Under such conditions no logic, no philosophy, and no science can invoke any transcendental value to mitigate the struggle and to distinguish the right moral relativism from the wrong, the right means for the pursuit of happiness from the wrong, or to distinguish moral obligation from selfish arbitrariness, and right from might. The simple reason is the nonexistence of any transcendental value or norm in sensate ethics or law. Aside from subjective utility and happiness, relativism and convention, sensate ethics and law have no absolute judge, no objective and universal criterion to decide the issue. Hence we can deduce the inevitable "atomization" and self-annihilation of the sensate system of values from the very process of its development.

The sensate thinkers of the fourteenth, fifteenth, and sixteenth centuries, the period of the reemergence and growth of the sensate system, already well understood this danger and tried to reinforce sensate ethics and law by a "mythology" of religion and ideational ethics. Pierre Du Bois, Marsilio of Padua, Machiavelli, and J. Bodin, to mention but four, all warned that purely sensory control of man by policemen and other agents of physical power was insufficient. They pleaded, therefore, the advisability of adding to them the artificial controls of absolutistic religion and of ideational moral mythology. The priest, playing upon "the fear of hell," must supplement the police and the prison. Legislators must invent a God from whom nothing was concealed and who commanded the observance of the law under supersensory penalties. "The sagacious politician will always respect religion, even if he has no belief in it." So ran the argument of these initiators of sensate ethics. Unfortunately, they appear to have forgotten that if religion and ideational norms were a mere artificial mythology invented as a useful adjunct to the policeman and the gallows, such an illusion could not last long without being exposed. With this fraud exposed, sensate values themselves could not help losing their "saltiness," and hence their prestige and controlling power. Without power, they necessarily forfeited their efficacy as sensate norms and had to be replaced by sheer physical force.

Coming on the historical scene as a successor to, and as a substitute for, Christian ethics and law, the modern system of sensate ethics and law in its immanent development sowed the seeds of the degradation of man, as well as of the moral values themselves. Declaring the moral values to be mere conventions, it dragged them down to the level of utilitarian and hedonistic calculations, completely relative in time and space. If they were expedient for a given man and group, they could be accepted; if they were a hindrance, they could be rejected. In this way a limitless relativism was introduced into the world of moral values, whose arbitrariness engendered conflict and struggle. This, in turn, produced hatred; and hatred led to rude force and bloodshed. In the chaos of conflicting norms moral values have been more and more ground to dust; they have progressively lost their binding power and given way to rude arbitrary coercion. The pathos of binding Christian love has tended to be supplanted by hatred— the hatred of man for man, of class for class, of nation for nation, of state for state, of race for race. As a result, might has become right. *Bellum omnium contra omnes* has raised its ugly head. These are exactly the conditions we face.

At the present time there is hardly any ethical value common to and equally binding upon communists and capitalists; Hitlerites and Jews; Italians and Ethiopians; the

British alliance and the German alliance; Catholics and atheists; multimillionaries and the underdogs; employers and the employed; oppressors and the oppressed; and so on. Their ethical and juridical values are quite contradictory and irreconcilable. What one faction declares good, another brands as bad. And the tragedy of it is that there is no sensate arbiter, acceptable to all these factions, whose decision is equally authoritative for all. If any mediator attempts such arbitration, he becomes, in turn, only an additional faction denounced by the others. We are thus a society of endless contesting parties without a moral judge to decide the contests. The result is moral chaos and anarchy. Everyone becomes his own lawgiver and judge, deeming his own standard just as good as anybody else's. Inertia still causes appeals to "public opinion" or to "the world's conscience," but they are either voices crying in the wilderness or else smoke screens masking the egotistic aspirations of this or that "pressure group." Instead of one genuine public opinion, we have thousands of pseudo-public opinions of factions, sects, and individuals. Instead of a "world conscience," we have millions of contradictory "rationalizations" and "derivations." The whole body of ethics accordingly becomes a plaything of unscrupulous "pressure groups," each of which tries to snatch as big a share of sensate values as possible at the cost of other groups. Under these circumstances the motivating, binding, and controlling power of ethical ideals tends to vanish. Since there is no uniform moral code, there is no united pressure of homogeneous public opinion to mold one's sentiments and convictions during his early formative years. Hence there is no uniform moral conscience to wield an effective motivating power in human behavior. Is it any wonder that crimes, wars, revolutions, have increasingly afflicted Western society? "Everything is permitted, if you can get away with it" is the main moral maxim of our time. This is supplemented by an insane preoccupation with utilitarian values as the supreme criterion. "If a belief in God is useful, God exists; if not, he does not exist." "If science has survival value, science is appreciated; if it does not, it is useless." Hence our money-madness; our unabashed struggle for wealth. "Money can buy everything." We turn into money and profit any value—quintuplets, scientific invention, religious revivals, novel crime, and what not. Successful money-makers compose our aristocracy. Hence our ferocious "business is business" and all the barbarity of the struggle for sensory values. Hence our supposedly scientific "mores" and "folkways," instead of moral imperatives—our anthropological and sociological "Mores are conventional and differ from group to group." Hence the millions of other characteristics of our *urbs venalis*, with all the tragic consequences of such moral cynicism. When a society dispenses with God, with the Absolute, and rejects all the binding moral imperatives, the only binding power that remains is sheer physical force itself.

Thus sensate society, with its sensate ethics, has prepared its own surrender to the rudest coercion. "Liberating" itself from God, from all absolutes and categoric moral imperatives, it has become the victim of undisguised physical coercion and fraud. Society has reached the nadir of moral degradation and is now paying the tragic price of its own folly. Its vaunted utilitarianism, practicality, and realistic expediency have turned into the most impractical and unrealistic dis-utilitarian catastrophe. Nemesis has at last overtaken it!

Hence the contemporary tragedy of sensate man himself. Stripping man of his divine charisma and grace, sensate mentality, ethics, and law have reduced him to a mere electron-proton complex or reflex mechanism devoid of any sanctity or end-value. "Liberating" him from the "superstitions" of the categorical imperatives, they have taken from him an invisible armor that unconditionally protected him, his dignity, his sanctity, and his inviolability. Divested of this armor, he finds himself but a plaything in the hands of the most fortuitous forces. If he is useful for this or that, he may be treated decently and cared for as we care for a useful animal. If he is harmful, he can be "liquidated," as we exterminate harmful snakes. No guilt, no crime, no valid reason, is needed for such a liquidation. The very existence of a man or group as an unintentional obstacle is enough to eliminate them. Without any compunction, remorse, regret, or compassion, millions of guiltless people are uprooted, deprived of all possessions, of all rights, of all values, subjected to all kinds of privations, banished, or killed by bombs and bullets, simply because their mere existence is an unintentional obstacle to the realization of a lust for power, for wealth, for comfort, for some sensate value. Rarely, if ever, have even cattle been treated with such cynicism! Released from all the inhibitions of supersensory values, sensate man suicidally murders sensate man—his pride and self-confidence; his values and possessions; his comfort, pleasures, and happiness. In this tornado of unleashed sensate passions, the whole of sensate culture is being blown to pieces and swept away.

As has happened several times before, in the insanity of a decadent mentality, sensate man again today is destroying the sensate house he has so proudly been building for the past five centuries. Sensate ethics and law have once again entered a blind alley. This alley marks their *finis* for the present epoch. Without a shift towards ideational ethics and law, without a new absolutization and universalization of the values, they cannot escape from this blind alley. Such is the verdict of history in regard to the past crises of sensate ethics and law, and such must be its verdict regarding the present crisis. The subsequent chapters will further unfold all the disastrous consequences of the moral atomism and ethical cynicism of our overripe sensate morality.

Meanwhile, Diagram No. 8 shows the great waves of rise and fall of eight of the variables of sensate culture from the sixth century B.C. up to the present century. Though each of these sensate streams fluctuated not quite parallel with the others, so far as minor fluctuations are concerned, in their major movements they oscillated together, giving the tidal waves of rise and high level of sensate culture from the sixth century B.C. to the third century A.D.; its enormous decline and almost disappearance from the fourth century A.D. and throughout the mediaeval centuries; and its new tidal wave started in the twelfth century and risingly continued up to the present day.

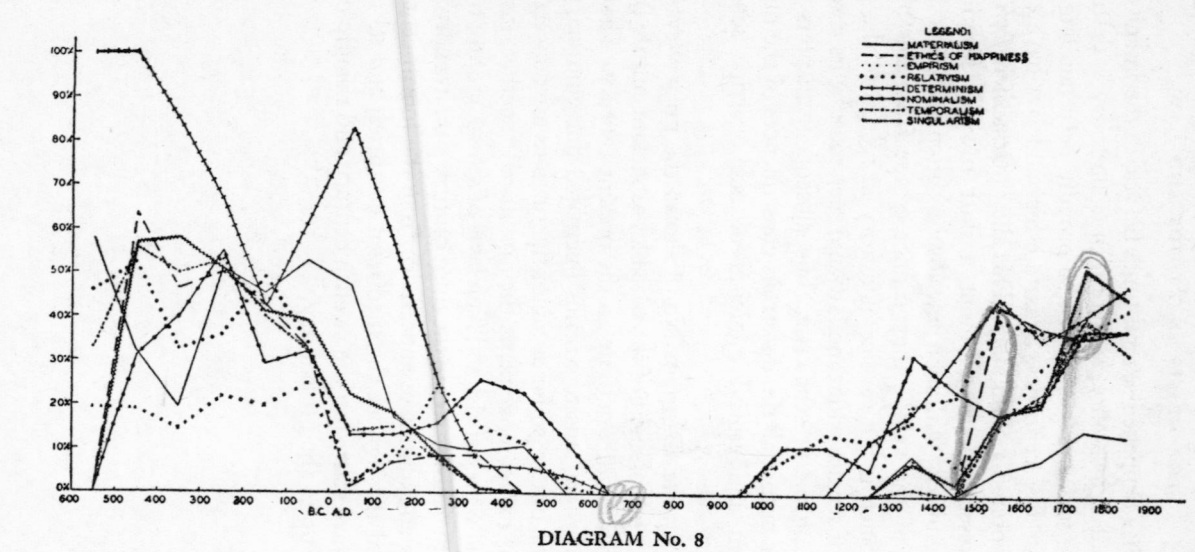

**DIAGRAM No. 8**

# CHAPTER V

# THE CRISIS OF CONTRACTUAL FAMILY, GOVERNMENT, ECONOMIC ORGANIZATION, LIBERTY, AND INTERNATIONAL RELATIONS

## I. FAMILISTIC, CONTRACTUAL, AND COMPULSORY RELATIONSHIPS

In spite of the infinite variety of the patterns of social relationships of man to man, or of group to group, they all fall into three main classes: *familistic* relationships, permeated by mutual love, devotion, and sacrifice; free *contractual* agreements of the parties for their mutual advantage, devoid either of love or of hatred, but profitable to both; and *compulsory* relationships imposed by one party upon the others, contrary to their wishes and interests.

The familistic relations are most frequently found among the members of a devoted family or among real friends. In such contacts the individual ego is merged in the sense of "*we*." Joys and sorrows are shared in common. The individuals need one another, seek one another, love one another, and gladly sacrifice themselves for one another—in brief, they represent a single solidary body. This is the supreme and noblest type of social relationship, a real *consortium omnis vitae, divini et humani juris communicatio*. In such a unity a special contract, with its prescription "no more and no less," becomes superfluous. Unlimited, all-embracing, all-forgiving, and all-bestowing mutual devotion renders unnecessary any contract, with its limitations and reservations.

In contrast to the familistic relation, the contractual relationship is *limited and specified*. It does not cover the whole life of the parties, but only one narrow sector, such as a contract between employer and employee, buyer and seller, or plumber and householder. Contracts tend to specify carefully the rights and duties of each party: "fifteen cents for a package of cigarettes" or "fifteen dollars a week for forty hours of honest work."

Within the circumscribed sphere of the voluntary contract the contracting parties are solidary. But this solidarity is somewhat egotistical: it does not spring from spontaneous devotion, but from a desire to obtain some advantage—pleasure, profit, utility, or the like—rooted in a sober calculation of advantage. In this sense it is utilitarian and self-centered. Not infrequently a contracting party tries to get from the other as much as possible for as little as possible—as good a bargain as the other will agree to. Otherwise the parties remain strangers to one another, one party being little interested in the well-being, activities, and outlook of the others. The contractual relation does not fuse them into a homogeneous "we," animated by a sense of mutual love, devotion, and sacrifice. Each person or group remains egocentric and individualistic. Such is the second fundamental form of social relationship. Though not so noble as the familistic type, it has at least the merit of constituting a voluntary agreement of free parties for their mutual benefit.

Finally, many human relations are *compulsory*, imposed by one party upon another coercively, contrary to its wishes and desires. Antagonism and hatred, not love and solidarity, are the binding cement. One of the parties is the victim and prey of the other. It is exploited, degraded, cruelly treated, deprived of many of its rights. It is not regarded as a free and sacred human entity. It becomes a mere instrument in the hands of the other party. The reaction of the coerced is one of dislike or even hatred. Examples are afforded by the cruel master and his ill-treated slave, the executioner and his victim, the ravisher and the ravished, the conqueror and the conquered. It goes without saying that this is the crudest and worst form of social relationship. (*Dynamics*, Vol. III, chap. 1)

### 2. THE RISE OF CONTRACTUALISM IN MODERN SOCIETY

These three forms of relationship have been present in virtually all large societies and groups, but not always in the same proportions. The social relationships of a good family are principally familistic; so also are those of many a religious organization in which God is known as "our Father," the church as "our Mother," and the members as "brethren" or "sisters." On the other hand, the social relations of a prison society, of coercively drafted soldiers, of slaves and serfs, or even of the citizens of a state, with its obligatory and compulsory rules, are essentially compulsory.

The relative proportions of these fibers change in course of time, even in the fabric of the same society. For instance, the texture of European medieval society from the eighth to the twelfth century was mainly familistic (the all-embracing medieval *fidelitas* in the relations of men and of groups); in lesser degree compulsory (in the relations of the free and unfree classes); and only slightly contractual. The total network of social relationships in this society changed notably between the thirteenth and the sixteenth century in the direction of contractual relation-

7 AD to 11 AD - familistic (fidelitas)
12 AD to 15 AD - contractual
15 AD to 17 AD - great increase in compulsory
18 AD to present - golden age of contractualism

ships. Between the sixteenth and the eighteenth century the relative proportion of compulsory relations greatly increased. The nineteenth and the beginning of the twentieth century constituted the golden age of contractual society. If we were to characterize modern Western society in a single word, one such word would unquestionably be *contractualism*. It denotes the most essential characteristic of the Euro-American society of these centuries. During this period Western society attempted to build a comfortable sensate society based upon covenant, contract, or agreement for the mutual advantage of the members of society, of the citizens and their government, of employers and their employees, and of the members of other special groups of free men. For some time this aim appears to have been pretty well achieved. Western society throughout the nineteenth century was a well-ordered contractual house inhabited by free men governed by free agreement. *Its dominant capitalist system of economy was a contractual system of economic relationship between the parties involved.* In contradistinction to a system of compulsory slavery or serfdom, or the system of relationships governing the members of a good family, the capitalist system rests upon a contract between free parties, the employer and the employee. In this contract both parties agree—one to perform certain services, the other to pay a certain wage. The parties are not tenderly attached to one another, as are the members of a good family, nor does one party coerce the òther, as in a compulsory system. As a consequence of this contractual capitalistic system, Western society witnessed the liquidation of serfdom, slavery, the plantation system, and other coercive systems of labor. The capitalist contractual system produced an enormous number of signal achievements, such as the increased efficiency of labor and machines, the extraordinary multiplication of technological inventions, a fundamental improvement in the material standard of living, and the substitution of a contractual agreement for the compulsory feudal system of economy.

In the *political field* the rise of contractual relationships in the nineteenth century resulted in the elimination of autocratic, coercive governments and in their replacement by democratic political regimes, with the government contractually elected, contractually limited in its power, contractually bound to respect the inalienable rights of the citizen—his liberties, his equalities, and his individualism. By means of constitutions, and such special instruments as bills and declarations of rights, these prerogatives were promulgated and guaranteed: equality of citizens before the law; religious liberties; freedom of speech, the press, and assembly; the right to form unions; free choice of occupation; and so on. The rights and duties of every individual were definitely fixed and mutually limited. The elective principle became the main principle of recruiting public officials in the state, in municipalities, in associations, and other organizations. Even the army in many countries became contractual to a notable degree. In brief, free contract of free parties became the principal fiber out of which the fabric of the political regime was made. *Contractual government is a more precise definition of so-called democratic political systems—of government of the people, by the people, and for the people.*

In other social organizations the same contractual principle became paramount. Liberty of religion meant *a transformation of religious organizations into contractual bodies:* one was free to become, or not to become, a member of any religious organization. A similar transformation occurred within the *family*. Marriage was declared a purely civil contract between free parties, in contradistinction to a compulsory marriage in which the parties were chosen, often against their wish, by parents or other authorities. The free consent of the parties was now made an indispensable condition of the marriage itself. Becoming contractual in its establishment, marriage was made also more contractual in its continuity and dissolution. While a medieval marriage, as a rule, was indissoluble, it was now, in principle, dissoluble. The number of the legal bases for its dissolution systematically increased, and ever-wider possibilities were thus opened for a divorce at the option of one or both parties. Not only in the relation of husband and wife but also in those of the parents and children, the family tended to become an increasingly contractual institution.

With individualism, the period became the century of triumphant *sensate liberty*, in contradistinction to *ideational liberty*. If liberty means the possibility for one to do whatever he pleases, he is free when he can do what he wants. If his desires are satisfied, he is free; if not, he is unfree. If the sum total of his wishes exceeds his means of satisfying them, he is unfree; *per contra*, if the sum of his wishes does not exceed or is smaller than the total sum of his means of satisfying them he is free. Hence we derive the general formula of liberty as $\dfrac{\text{Sum of means}}{\text{Sum of wishes}}$. When the numerator exceeds or is equal to the denominator, one is free; otherwise he is not. A person can therefore become free in two different ways: either by decreasing his wishes to make them equal to or smaller than the means of their satisfaction, or by expanding his wishes and increasing proportionally the means of their satisfaction. The first is the way of ideational liberty, consisting in a reduction of one's wishes, especially sensory ones. The second is the way of sensate liberty, consisting in an ever-increasing expansion of one's wishes for sensory values, accompanied by an equal or greater expansion of the means of satisfying them. The extreme case of ideational liberty is ascetic liberty. Its formulae are well known. "Freedom is not gained by satisfying, but by restraining, our desires." "Not only ambition and avarice, but even the desire of ease, of quiet, of travel or of learning, may take away our liberty." "*Non qui parum habet, sed qui plus cupid, pauper est.*" "A very little can satisfy our necessities, but nothing our desires." "Who has most? He who desires least." "Seek not that the things which happen should happen as you wish, but wish the things which happen to be as they are, and you will have an even flow of life." And so on.

Ideational liberty is inner liberty, rooted in the restraint and control of our desires, wishes, and lusts. It is the liberty of Job with his imperturbable "The Lord gave, and the Lord hath taken away; blessed be the name of the Lord." Such a liberty does not multiply sensory wishes; it does not lead to an incessant struggle for an ever-increasing expansion of the means of their satisfaction—wealth, power, fame, and what not. It is little interested in political and civil rights, in the external guarantees of such rights, such as constitutions and political declarations. Its "kingdom is not of this world." On the other hand, it is inalienable—unconquerable by anybody or anything external.

Sensate liberty is the opposite of ideational liberty. It

strives to expand endlessly both wishes and the means of
their satisfaction. The more one has the more one wants.
There is no limit to the expansion of sensory desires, and,
according to the modified Weber-Fechner law, the discrepancy between what one has and what one wants increases progressively in a vicious circle. Such a liberty leads
to an incessant struggle of men and groups for as large a
share of sensate values—wealth, love, pleasure, comfort,
sensory safety, security—as one can get. Since one can get
them mainly at the cost of somebody else, their quest ac-
centuates and intensifies the struggle of individuals and
groups. Sensate liberty is thus mainly external. It is vitally
interested in the external reconstruction of social, economic, and political conditions—in guarantees of freedom
of speech, of the press, and of thought, and of other "inalienable rights of man." For this reason it leads to political
and economic struggle: each group or person wants to gain
as many rights as possible, either by snatching them from
others or by sensibly entering into a contractual compro-
mise guaranteeing a minimum number to all the contracting parties.

With the rise of ideational culture, ideational liberty
becomes the principal form of liberty, as, for instance, in
the early and medieval Christian culture. With the advent
of Christian ideational culture, ideational liberty replaced
the sensate liberty of the last centuries of Greco-Roman
culture. Upon the reemergence of sensate culture at the
end of the twelfth century, sensate liberty also reemerged
in the form of the Magna Charta of 1215, and in the struggle of the cities for their freedom in the thirteenth and
fourteenth centuries. As it continued to grow, ideational

liberty continued to decline. Reinforced by the Declaration of the Rights of Man at the end of the eighteenth century, and by subsequent laws expanding the scope of personal liberties, sensate liberty finally became supreme in the nineteenth century. After the violent struggles of the preceding centuries of the sensate era, sensate liberty now came to assume at last the contractual form. All factions and persons had discovered that the best and most advantageous form in which it could be vouchsafed to everyone, without the risk of disastrous struggle, was a free agreement guaranteeing a minimum share of such liberty to all groups and persons. Hence the contractual liberty of the nineteenth century and its free associations, with the emphasis upon inalienable rights and their political guarantees. Hence the true enthusiasm of the slogan, "Give me liberty or give me death!" All these liberties—inalienable rights, equality, individualism, free association—were the fruits and manifestations of the sensate culture of Western society in the nineteenth century, with contractual relations as the dominant social relationships. And who can deny the value of these achievements? In many ways they were unquestionably extraordinary, ranking among the most brilliant constructive achievements in the field of social relationships—in building a free society of free men.

The success of the nineteenth century in this field warranted the general optimism of Western society respecting "bigger and better" progress; man's capacity to build, without the invocation of any supernatural power, in his own right and by his own efforts, a better, more free, more just, and more noble society; his ability to eliminate most social evils—crime, exploitation (including the remnants of slavery and serfdom), and autocracy. The road of the future destiny of mankind appeared to point to ever fairer prospects.

### 3. THE CRISIS OF CONTRACTUALISM

Carried away by this optimism, Western society failed to notice the underground forces that were keeping pace with the growth of triumphant contractualism. It forgot that not everything is contractual and arbitrary in any real contract; that to be truly contractual the pact must satisfy four indispensable conditions which must not be changed or eliminated by the contracting parties. They are necessary conditions if a contract is to be really contractual and beneficial to society as well as to the contracting parties themselves. The first of these is that all the contracting parties shall be equally free and independent. A pact entered into under conditions of duress, of open or disguised coercion, ceases to be a contract and represents a compulsory relationship. Second, the freedom of the contracting parties must not be used to the detriment of either a contracting party or—what is more important—to that of society as such. The free contract of a group of murderers to cooperate faithfully in the enterprise of "Murder, Incorporated," becomes a downright menace to society. It imposes upon it the grossest and most harmful coercion. A third indispensable condition is the old Roman stipulation *pacta sunt servanda:* the contracted duties must be faithfully fulfilled by all the parties concerned. Fourth, one party must not twist the pact to the detriment of any other. Contracts in which the stipulations are not fulfilled by all the parties, or which are misused by one party to exploit another, cease to be a genuine contract and come to represent a disguised compulsory relationship. With the growth of moral relativism, nihilism, and "atomism," all these conditions began to disappear in the contractual fabric of Western society towards the end of the nineteenth and the beginning of the twentieth century. Hence arose *the contemporary crisis in contractual relationships as the dominant form of social relations in recent Western society*. Since contractual relationships were the principal fibers of all societal and associational organizations—economic and political, familial and religious, national and international—*the crisis of contractualism meant a fundamental crisis for practically all the social organizations and institutions of Western society, from the smallest to the biggest, from the bottom to the top*. The process was similar to the decay of the chief material of which a great building is constructed. When this material rots, all parts of the structure are likewise bound to crumble and decay. That is exactly what is now happening to Western society. Let us examine more closely the symptoms of this crisis and then try to decide how it has come about.

*Symptoms.* There is no scarcity of symptoms in the institutions and organizations of our Euro-American society. As a matter of fact, they are so numerous, and the decline in question has already progressed so far, that a bare enumeration of the most important institutions and organizations in which contractualism has declined will be sufficient for our purpose.

Let us begin with our *political institutions and relationships*. In almost all the Western states, with the exception of Switzerland, the United States of America, and the

*political*

British Commonwealth, the contractual form of government has ceased to exist. Its place is taken by noncontractual totalitarian regimes of different forms—Communist, Nazi, or Fascist—with their mainly compulsory and partly familistic fabric of social relationships. The totalitarian government is self-appointed—not elected or contractual. It is purely authoritarian and autocratic in character. Being dictatorial, it is absolutistic and unlimited. It enacts any law, any decree, anything it pleases, and it imposes upon its citizens—or, rather, subjects—anything that it wants to impose, without the necessity of consent or contract. In this sense, like all despotic and noncontractual governments, it is *legibus solutus est*—that is, above the law. One may say of it what was said of the absolute monarchial power of ancient Rome: *quod principi placuit legis habet vigorem*—whatever it desires has the power of law. Such is its legal status; and still more, such is its factual position. In its actions the totalitarian and dictatorial government of today is as autocratic as any autocracy in human history— certainly more absolute than most of the absolute monarchies of the recent past. It can arbitrarily seize the property of any subject; can impose any taxes or duties; can arrest, imprison, banish, or "liquidate" anybody (as it does with thousands, even millions, of its victims); and can change by fiat any laws, constitutions, and other institutions (which it does in the most drastic manner, both in its own country and in conquered territories). Neither religious norms, nor mores, nor moral commandments, nor contractual and treaty obligations, nor the guaranteed and supposedly inalienable rights of man, nor "the will of the majority" curbs its unbridled arbitrariness. We live, indeed, in one of the most absolutistic and autocratic ages in all human history. *compulsory forms.*

In the Anglo-Saxon countries and in a few others where democratic contractual government still survives, we have only remnants of the erstwhile full-blooded contractualism. Even these survivals are rapidly disappearing. They have also been moving away from contractualism toward a compulsory and familistic relationship. The trend is in the same direction as in totalitarian countries.

Quantitatively unlimited, the modern autocracy is becoming progressively more and more unlimited also in the extent of its regimentation of, and its interference with, the social relationships of its subjects. Since the end of the nineteenth century, and especially since the beginning of the war of 1914-1918, we have witnessed the most rapid expansion of such control and regimentation. In the contractual nineteenth century, most of the relationships among the persons and groups of Western society were left to their own discretion. Beginning with the economic relations of production, distribution, and consumption, of employers and employees, and ending with the choice of occupations, amusements, and places of abode, with marriage, religion, and the like, all these matters were subject to the free decision of the persons and groups concerned. Apart from a few legal regulations, the government did not interfere with these relationships.

The present picture is quite a different one. Not individuals and private groups but the government now decides, controls, and regulates all these relationships. In the dictatorial countries the regimentation and control is well-nigh complete; the government decides practically everything and the citizen nothing, except, perhaps, the choice of alternatives: of obeying unconditionally the orders of the government or of going to prison, losing his property, and possibly forfeiting even his life. The once-proud citizen of the Declaration of the Rights of Man now dwells where the government bids him dwell; eats what he is given by the government; says only what the government tells him to say; reads only government-controlled papers and books; believes what he is ordered to believe; even marries whom he is ordered to marry. In brief, the erstwhile free citizen is practically divested of all his "inalienable rights"—of all self-direction and self-management. He has become a mere puppet of the new autocratic regime.

The area of social relationships left to individual management is reduced almost to zero; the area of governmentally controlled relationships covers virtually the whole field. In the openly nondictatorial countries, a group to which the British Commonwealth and the United States belong, the trend since the end of the nineteenth century, while slower than in the openly dictatorial countries, has been in the same direction. After 1929 it began to move with an ever-accelerating tempo towards the same objective, namely, unlimited expansion of government regimentation and control. In the United States an enormous number of economic relationships determined in the nineteenth century by citizens and private groups are now managed by the government, which controls, as well, a vast number of noneconomic relations.

As a result, in an ever-increasing number of countries the free citizen of the nineteenth century has lost almost all of his liberties guaranteed by constitutions, declarations, and similar instruments. His "inalienable rights" are already alienated. His autonomy and individualism are crushed. His lips are sealed respecting all utterances which the government regards as taboo. He is bound hand and foot— helplessly enmeshed, like a fly, in the spider web of compulsory regulations. Not only is his conduct controlled: even his mind and his thoughts are molded after the pattern prescribed by his rulers. Once an entity of the highest end-value, he is now a mere instrument of governmental experimentation.

Such is the situation in the political field. It means the well-nigh total collapse of the contractual structure of nineteenth-century political relationships. Democracy, parliamentarism, universal suffrage, or the rule of the majority, and all the other manifestations of contractualism either have completely vanished or are rapidly disappearing before our very eyes. Coercion, diluted with a certain element of familism, has taken the place of political contractualism. (*Dynamics*, Vol. III, chaps. 5, 6, 7)

The same is true of *economic relationships* in dictatorial countries. The economic regime of the nineteenth century, based on private property and a contractual capitalistic system, is in a state of hopeless decay. The decline of this regime manifested itself in two main forms: first, in a progressive undermining and splitting of the institution of private property itself, culminating in its ultimate elimination; and, second, in a progressive replacement of the contractual capitalistic economy by an obligatory, imposed economy. The latter phase has already been discussed. In the nineteenth century virtually the entire system of production, distribution, and consumption was left to individuals and private groups. Government had little to do with these matters, except for a few monopolies and the general maintenance and enforcement of the legal norms related to these fields. The overwhelming bulk of economic relationships—the choice of occupations and professions, employment, wages and prices, and the relations between employers and employees—were regulated by voluntary contracts.

All these relations have now changed. In dictatorial countries the government is the central power station. Private individuals and groups no longer decide what is to be produced, how it is to be distributed, and how and by whom it is to be consumed. The government is the principal employer and capitalist. It determines the essentials in the production, distribution, and consumption of economic commodities. It regulates money and banking, wages and prices, as well as occupations and labor (including labor unions). The rôle of private individuals and groups, with their free contracts, is as meager as it was in the old totalitarian regimes of the past—in those of ancient Egypt, Sparta, Lipara, Rome, or pre-Columbian Peru and Mexico. Of the present situation in the West exactly the same thing may be said that a historian has said about the compulsory economic regime of the ancient Roman Empire from 301 A.D. up to the so-called end of the Western Roman Empire:

> All are regimented and controlled. For this purpose an enormous army of state officials is created. It robs and steals and [thus] aggravates the situation still more. The State needs gigantic financial means to maintain the government, to feed

the mob, officials, and army, and to carry on wars. . . . The work of the population and labor unions which was before free and unregimented now becomes regimented and hereditary. [We have not reached, as yet, a hereditary grade of regimentation: so far, children are not ordered to follow the occupation of their fathers.] The *corporati* and *collegati* [the members of the governmentalized labor and occupational unions] now belong to the government, with all their possessions. The State that took upon itself the satisfaction of all needs—public and private—finally comes to the necessity of a complete regimentation of even private labor. . . . The empire is transformed into a huge factory where, under the supervision of the state officials, the population works for the government, the State, and private persons. Almost all industry is managed by the State. The State also distributes— very unequally—the produce. The members of the trade and labor unions are not free persons any more; they are the slaves of the State, that are supported, like the officials, by the State, but very poorly and inadequately. [A kind of Roman W.P.A.] Never was an administration as cruel and quarrelsome with the population and as inefficient and unproductive. The regime is based upon compulsion; everywhere is the hand of the State. Nowhere do private initiative and free labor exist.

One need not add anything to this characterization of the compulsory totalitarian economy of the declining Roman Empire. It fits exactly the present situation in the totalitarian countries, that is, in the greater part of the Western world. Of the contractual economy of the nineteenth century there remain only meager crumbs in the compulsory economy of today.

In the covertly dictatorial countries the trend has been the same—a constantly accelerating movement toward a similar situation. What a change has taken place, for instance, in the United States since the crash of 1929! For one decade we made gigantic "progress" in the reduction of contractual economy in favor of the New Deal economy of governmental regimentation. Since the outbreak of the war, contractual economy has disappeared also in Great Britain, and a compulsory war economy has taken its place.

*No less certain are the weakening, disintegration, and elimination of the institution of private property.* Private property is a part of a contractual economy, the very cornerstone of the classic capitalistic system. In some countries —for example, in the Soviet Union—it has been abolished not only factually but formally as well. In other totalitarian countries, either it has been largely eliminated, both factually and formally, or else it exists mainly on paper. No trace of its erstwhile "sacredness" and "inviolability" remains in these countries. What is left leads a precarious existence, subject to extinction at any moment by government fiat—a mere pale shadow of the robust, full-blooded private property of the nineteenth century.

In a few countries, as in the United States, while the trend has been much the same, it has not led to the same degree of "progress" that has been attained in the dictatorial countries. However, the system of private property and the classic capitalistic system have been substantially undermined as a result of the rise and extraordinary growth of American *corporation and trust economy*. At the present time, corporations and trusts possess almost one third of all the wealth of the country and almost one half of the total of American business wealth. And their proportion of the national wealth is still growing. Many do not realize that *the economy of modern corporations and trusts is already quite different from that of the capitalistic system based upon authentic private property*, and that the rise of corporation economy signifies also a decline of contractual economy. Still fewer realize that the *first mortal blow to private property and the contractual capitalistic system of the nineteenth century was dealt not by communists and socialists but by the captains of industry and finance in the second part of the century*. Communists and totalitarians only finished what these began. Let us consider this point briefly.

In creating and developing the economy of the big corporation at the close of the nineteenth century, the captains of industry and finance could not fail to undermine and split the classical form of private property and, with it, classical capitalism. Classical private property meant the right of possession, use and management, and disposal of the property. The economy of the big corporation split this indivisible right into separate functions divorced from one another: on the one hand, the owners—the thousands and millions of small shareholders and bondholders—neither manage, nor use, nor dispose of the property; on the other hand, the managers—the presidents and the boards of directors who manage, use, and dispose of the property—are not its owners. Few, if any, of them own even 1 per cent of the corporate stocks and bonds. By virtue of their positions they are, in a way, public trustees of public property. They do not bear even the risk and responsibility for the property, as private owners do. Unfortunately, the members of this new "managerial aristocracy" seem to have often forgotten their real position and, though they have frequently mismanaged the public property entrusted to them and given nothing to the owners—the shareholders—they have rarely forgotten to grant to themselves high salaries and bonuses amounting to hundreds of thousands or even millions of dollars. When the builders of the great industrial and financial empires— the Rothschilds and Morgans, the Rockefellers and Fords, the Carnegies and Cecil Rhodeses—were amassing huge fortunes, they were entitled to them: they were risking their fortunes and lives in carving empires out of the wilderness. The managerial aristocracy of present-day corporations are in the position of the decadent descendants of a full-blooded political aristocracy: they retain and even augment all the privileges of their forefathers without rendering a comparable service to society. In this sense, and by virtue of their position, they correspond exactly to the members of a mediocre state bureaucracy. Both manage what they do not own. Both reap in their own interest what they did not sow; both eliminate real private property and real capitalism in their classical form. Both are bureaucrats, administering, mainly for their own use, public property.

From this standpoint *corporate economy is a decentralized totalitarianism, while the totalitarianism of the Communist, or Fascist, or Nazi type is the economy of a centralized corporation.* The latter consists of one corporation instead of several—instead, for instance, of America's sixty families that direct most American corporations and most of the economic life of the country. The centralized corporations have one board of directors— Communist or Hitlerite or Fascist—rather than several.

This managerial aristocracy of corporations and trusts, as has been said, dealt the first decisive blow to private property and the classical capitalism based upon it. From that point it was only a short distance to the centralized economy of the totalitarian state bureaucracy, which in many European countries has finally driven out its twin, the administrative bureaucracy of the corporations, completing the work of destruction of capitalism and private property begun by the corporations and trusts. In other countries corporation bureaucracy still lingers, but steadily loses ground in favor of a centralized governmental bureaucracy. The struggle between the "Old Deal" of Wall Street and the "New Deal" of Washington, between W. Willkie and F. D. Roosevelt, is not a struggle between capitalism and totalitarianism, or private property and state property, or private business and the State in business, but between two bureaucracies both of a public nature, both undermining private property and classic capitalism. These two economic bureaucracies, in fact, have dealt a mortal blow to private property and contractual capitalism. Whereas the latter are both moribund, corporation totalitarianism and state totalitarianism are rampant, with state totalitarianism momentarily in the saddle. (*Dynamics*, Vol. III, chap. 8)

The decline of the contractual relationship in the *family* has assumed a different form from that obtaining in political and economic institutions. It manifests itself in a progressive disintegration of the contractual family, as a socially sanctioned union of husband and wife, of parents and children, and of the circle of the relatives. The disintegration shows itself in many forms: the tie binding husband and wife into one entity, normally for life, has weakened and is therefore sundered more and more frequently by divorces and separations. These have been rapidly increasing, especially in the last few decades. The bond uniting parents and children has likewise become weaker and weaker: first, because of an increasing percentage of marriages without children (in the United States 43 per cent of all married couples either are childless or have only one child); and, second, because children now separate from their parents earlier than formerly: when they are grown, they remain much less frequently with their parents and especially their grandparents. Again, the cleavage between the mores, beliefs, mentality, and social forms of conduct of parents and children has progressively widened. The "conflict between fathers and sons" has become sharper and deeper than in the old-fashioned family. As a union of relatives beyond the circle of husband and wife and parents and children, the family is virtually nonexistent nowadays, in contradistinction to the medieval family or even that of a century ago. As it has become more and more contractual, the family of the last few decades has grown ever more unstable, until it has reached the point of actual disintegration.

This disintegration manifests itself in many other ways, in the form of a shrinkage and atrophy of its size and functions. We all know that in the past few decades the number of children born to a family has been steadily decreasing, so that at the present time in most Western countries the births and survivals do not compensate for the deaths. As a result, the population is now either stationary or on the decline. Contrary to all the assurances of the multitude of birth-control partisans, one should keep in mind that a period of depopulation has fairly uniformly been associated with a period of decline in the corresponding society and culture. The Greco-Roman cases for the epoch starting with the second century B.C. in Greece and a somewhat later epoch in Rome are typical. In addition, the number of childless marriages has been steadily mounting. This fact portends many social consequences, mainly negative ones. Childless marriages are more easily broken; the partners are more susceptible to suicide, and their outlook and attitudes are more egocentric than in marriages blessed with many children. Not only is the family becoming smaller and smaller in size, but it is growing ever more unstable. This atrophy is accompanied by a striking reduction of almost all its functions.

In the past the family was the foremost educational agency for the young. Some hundred years ago it was well-nigh the sole educator for a vast proportion of the younger generation. At the present time its educational functions have shrunk enormously. Childless families obviously do not perform them at all; in families with children, the children are withdrawn from the educational influence of the home at a progressively younger and younger age, its place being taken by the nursery school, kindergarten, elementary school, high school, and college. Besides, even during the few years that a child remains in the home, the educational standards must comply to a large extent with the requirements of outside educational agencies. The actual shrinkage in the educational functions of the family is, accordingly, much greater than appears at first glance. In these respects the family has forfeited the greater part of its former prerogatives.

A similar thing has happened to the socio-moral education of children as *socii*, or members of society. In order to survive for any considerable period, the members of any society must possess a minimum of solidarity, altruism, and good will. An illiterate society can survive, but a thoroughly antisocial society cannot. Human beings are born mere biological organisms, devoid of solidary attitudes. Some agency must undertake the indispensable function of socializing them. Until recently the family was such an agency. It was the principal school of socialization for the new-born human animals, rendering them fit for social life. At present this vital mission is performed less and less by the family. Childless families, of course, do not fulfill it at all. Those with children perform it more and more inadequately: first, because the young are turned over at a very early age to such agencies as nursery schools and kindergartens; second, because an increasingly unstable family is a poor school for socialization. Instead of inculcating in its offspring a strong sense of moral and social integrity, it teaches them lessons of moral laxity and loose relationships, of antagonism and conflict between parents, of purely sensate egotism, and the like. Such a family cannot fail to produce, for the most part, unstable, loose, sensate persons. If outside agencies performed efficiently the former functions of the family, the defect might be remedied. Unfortunately, they have not successfully replaced the family in this mission. Even an illiterate mother, endowed with kindness and common sense, appears to have been a better moral educator of children than most of the highly trained educators of schools and correctional institutions. The result is a rapidly mounting juvenile delinquency, an increasing number of young people without moral integrity, strength of character, a sense of social duty, or spontaneous altruism, who swell the ranks of criminals, of irresponsible persons, of paid minions of antisocial groups, from common murderers to the praetorian guards of the dictators.

Similarly, the family has sacrificed well-nigh all its other functions. It is less and less a *religious* agency, whereas in ancient times the head of the family was a priest (the *pater familias*). With the decline of religion, its place is taken either by nothing or by Sunday schools and similar institutions. Formerly the family supplied almost the only *means of subsistence* for its members. At the present time this function, too, is enormously reduced: hundreds of other agencies, including the state and philanthropic institutions, perform it. Other *economic* functions of the family have likewise either dwindled or disappeared: our meals we eat in cafeterias and restaurants; our bread comes from a bakery; our laundry is sent out; our clothes are bought in stores; and so on. So it is also with *recreational* functions. Formerly the family circle took care of these. Now we go to the movies, theaters, night clubs, and the like, instead of "wasting our time at home." Formerly the family was the principal agency for mitigating one's psycho-social isolation and loneliness. Now families are small, and their members are soon scattered. Even when they do live together, for the greater part of the day they work and live in separate places, and in the evening they again disperse in quest of recreation. The result is that the family home turns into a mere "overnight parking place"—not even for every night, and not always for the whole of any given night.

Accordingly, the contractual family in the process of its development has unexpectedly reached the point where it has lost most of its functions and prerogatives; even those that it retains are often atrophied and poorly performed. It has shrunk in size; it has become increasingly unstable and fragile. Less and less does it furnish even pleasure and comfort—the primary objectives of the sensate contractual family. When any institution finds itself in such a situation, it is in process of decay. This is precisely the position of the contractual sensate family today.

*What is said of the decline of the contractual political, economic, and familial organizations may be said of almost all organizations, associations, and societies of Western culture.* Free contractual labor unions have progressively turned either into compulsory government unions, without any freedom of choice for its members, or into semi-compulsory political machines and "labor-racketeering gangs," manipulated by politicians and racketeers, coercively imposing their power upon a vast proportion of the laborers. A similar fate has overtaken other "free associations": they have become increasingly regimented, obligatory, and compulsory. Not even science and the arts are an exception to this rule. Free scientific and artistic associations do not exist any more in the totalitarian and half-totalitarian countries. In other countries their liberty, their free contractualism, is being curtailed from day to day in hundreds of visible or invisible ways.

Finally, *contractualism has failed shockingly in international relationships.* The self-confident free men of the nineteenth century firmly believed in an international union of free men, bound contractually through covenants of nations and peoples eliminating war and conflicts. Accordingly they began to build an international contractual house of order, freedom, and peace, striving to achieve these things through free international contracts, through the development and incorporation of international law; through international arbitration courts, such as the Hague tribunals; and finally, through the League of Nations. The objective result has been a total failure. All these covenants and treaties are now sheer scraps of paper, not binding upon any party. International law has been cast to the winds. International courts and arbitration are but a memory. The League of Nations is dead—a mere mummy. Even moral maxims and the norms of natural law are ignored. Brute force is the only arbiter; coercion in the naked form of war reigns supreme. Few periods in the entire history of nations exhibit such a complete failure of contractualism in international relations and such an unlimited rule of brute force. Failing in national relationships, contractualism became still more bankrupt in the international field. As we shall see, instead of being an era of peace and order in international relationships, the present century has turned into the bloodiest among all the thirty centuries on record. One could hardly imagine a more acute crisis in contractual relationship than that which we now face.

To sum up: Western contractual society is confronted by a mortal crisis in all its leading institutions, organizations, and associations. The contractual palace built by it in the nineteenth century has largely crumbled. A change from monarchy to republic, or vice versa; a replacement of one form of capitalistic or family contractualism by other contractual forms—these are but superficial reconstruction of the same contractual relationship. But a decline of contractual relationships in favor of quite different relations—compulsory or familistic—is a change of the most radical kind possible. It is equivalent to demolishing an old house and building a radically different one. This is the essence of the fundamental crisis of Western society.

For a person living in the time of this crisis the net result is tragic. The proud citizen of the nineteenth century finds himself deprived of virtually all his sensate values. His boasted individualism is trampled under foot: he is now an insignificant cog in a huge machine operated without regard to his wishes. His liberties and inalienable rights are gone. He has become a mere puppet. Thousands and millions of once-proud citizens, heirs of the Declaration of Rights, are shunted hither and thither, pushed and pulled about more unceremoniously than slaves by their masters. They are deported; imprisoned, tortured, or killed; or turned into cannon fodder. Even the sensate pleasure and comfort they expected to obtain through sensate contractualism are gone: since 1914, in most countries, the economic standard of living has been rapidly sinking; the lot of millions in Europe, Asia, and Africa is one of direst poverty and misery. Safety of life and security of property are extinct. The contractual society of free men—with its contractual economic order and free associations—has disappeared. Even the family is in a state of partial ruin. With the frustration of their fondest hopes and aspirations, the tragedy of their lives is complete. Few periods of human history display so deep a tragedy as that of present-day sensate man. (*Dynamics*, Vol. III, chaps. 3, 4) Such are the symptoms of the crisis of our contractual society.

#### 4. ROOTS OF THE CRISIS

The next problem is to find out how this crisis has come about. Why has this great tragedy happened? How could proud sensate man fail to foresee his degradation, and why did he not prevent it?

The answer is that no person and no special factor external to sensate society and culture produced the crisis. It developed within contractual sensate society itself, as a natural consequence of elements within that society. Under the conditions of ethical "atomism" and nihilism discussed earlier, together with an ever-expanding desire for sensory values, the contractual relationship was bound to degenerate into a pseudo-contractual relation, with all its catastrophic consequences.

The point is that not everything in a contract is arbitrary. In order for a contract to be a real contract, certain conditions must be present. There must be the condition of a more or less equal freedom of the contracting parties to enter or not to enter into the contract; and there must be a more or less equivalent advantage to be derived from it by all the contracting parties. But with ever-expanding appetites for sensory values and with each of the contracting parties seeking a utilitarian advantage, marked differences emerged between the needs of the contracting parties to enter or not to enter into the contract under given conditions. From its very beginning, the capitalist contractual regime was susceptible to periods of business depression, with an army of laborers seeking jobs and not finding them. The wish to work was there, as well as the readiness to enter into contracts of employment; but there were no jobs available and no contracting employers. Thus the value of a free contract was annulled for many who could not satisfy their needs through the purely Platonic virtue of contractual relationship. The interplay of sensate lust for sensory values not only failed to eliminate but enormously augmented the economic and other inequalities of men. In the nineteenth century the contrast between the rich and the poor, the privileged and the underdog, if anything, increased rather than decreased. Therefore the contracting parties in all fields of social life, beginning with the economic and ending with the political, were not in equal positions to enter or not to enter into a contract. As always, in order merely to live and to satisfy elementary needs, the poor and the underdog had to accept contractual conditions much more advantageous to the rich and powerful contracting parties than to themselves. In both cases, in this sensate atmosphere, the contract tended to be a pseudo-contract entered into under factual duress. In a modified way it was an old form of dependence of one party and of domination of the other. The place of the feudal nobility and the lord of the manor was taken by a rich class, and the place of the monarch's aristocracy and court by a new political aristocracy. A high-sounding phraseology, including such phrases as "equality of opportunity," "liberty," and "the rights of man," was resorted to in the effort to conceal the discrepancy between the lofty ideal of a genuine contractual relationship and its actual perversion. But no ideology can forever hide the discrepancy and convince the hungry man that he is not hungry, the exploited that he is justly treated, or the subjugated that he is free. Thus the degeneration of the contractual relationship set in even while contractualism was on the upgrade—because of the increasing host of "cheated people." The further the contractual process proceeded, the stronger grew the trends in question, increasing both the degeneration of the contracts and the number of those who failed to derive from the contract its alleged universal advantages. Placed in such a position, those who suffered composed an ever-growing army of deserters from contractual allegiance.

Similar results were produced by the progressive impairment of other conditions of a fair and genuine contract. It is only human for a sensate man or group to seek to squeeze from a contract every possible advantage. Such a tendency often led to a conflict in the interpretation of its conditions. This conflict frequently had to be decided by the courts of law. In spite of the noble principle of equality of each party before the law, the factual situation was often quite a different one; for the vastly increased complexity of the law made necessary the employment of lawyers to defend one's interests in court. A rich and privileged party could hire the best lawyers, whereas a poor one could not. Consequently the court's decision was repeatedly in favor of the rich party, in spite of the superior merits of the claims of the poor party. Thus the parties were not equally protected, and the interests of many persons were unfairly sacrificed in favor of those of the rich and strong. In similar ways bona-fide contractual relations degenerated into disguised coercion, with an increasing army of victims and deserters. Not being able to obtain from the contract what they had expected to obtain, the victims were driven to conclude that only force could correct the perennial injustice done them. In this manner the revolutionary army of opponents of the "bourgeois capitalist regime," of "the bourgeois political regime," and of other contractual institutions was bred and successfully recruited.

Furthermore, contractual relationships can be beneficial to the whole of society only if they are not grossly abused, as is the case in an overripe sensate atmosphere. The free contract of the members of a criminal society like "Murder, Incorporated" is, to be sure, a contract, but its perverse objective makes it most harmful to society. Again, a free contract of a business firm to make money by any means is a contract; but its neglect of social duties and responsibilities may be inimical to the rest of society. So also with contractual political factions, societies of pleasure-seekers, and what not.

The same thing is true of *sensate liberty*. Freedom of speech, of the press, and of thought are the greatest boons when they are not dissociated from moral and social responsibilities. When, however, they degenerate into irresponsible and unbridled propaganda, the sensationalism of the yellow press, the uncensored production of obscene plays and novels, or the means of discrediting and undermining precious values, they become a societal and cultural poison infinitely worse than the denial of freedom of thought and expression. In the atmosphere of moral nihilism, sensate liberties have been used increasingly in this pernicious way. As a result they have progressively become discredited. And rightly so. The slogan, "Give me liberty or give me death!" repeated every Fourth of July by cheap politicians sounds utterly hollow nowadays and arouses only a desire to give them a sound thrashing. This increasing misuse of the concept of liberty—so natural in an unrestrained interplay of sensory lusts and wishes—has greatly discredited both liberty and contractual relationships.

Finally, the contracted duties must be faithfully fulfilled, no matter whether they are advantageous and pleasant, or the reverse. The saying goes that a real contract requires two gentlemen, each of whom keeps his word. No genuine contract is possible between double-crossers. Every real contract involves, side by side with its advantages, some unpleasant duties. In an atmosphere of rampant sensateness, moral relativism, and "atomism," any opportunity to neglect or repudiate these duties was bound to be seized upon. If modern society were ideational or idealistic, if it believed firmly in absolute moral and juridical norms, if it were not intoxicated by the quest for pleasure, utility, and other sensory values, its deeply ingrained convictions and habits would have triumphed over any temptation to evade contracted duties or to twist the terms of a contract so as to take advantage of the other party. But we are dealing with contractual relations in a sensate society, with its skepticism concerning God and his justice; its disbelief in any absolute, sacred norms; its moral "atomism" and cynicism; and its irresistible penchant for money, wealth, profit, pleasures, and sensory happiness. Under these conditions the nonfulfillment of contracted duties was inevitable and, with the progress of moral nihilism, was bound to grow.

Such a breach of contract appeared with the rise of the contractual relationship and manifested itself in the field of marriage and the family in increasing adultery, illicit sex relations, and ever-increasing separations and divorces; in the economic field in strikes and lockouts; and in both economic and political relationships in the form of riots, revolts, and disorders. In many other spheres it revealed it-self in a similar weakening of fidelity to the plighted word. In the twentieth century this trend became explicit and overt in all manner of individual, group, national, and international relations.

In the family, breaches of fidelity became fashionable, leading to an extraordinary increase of divorce and "free" sex relations and to a mass of scandalous lawsuits, with their allegations of "breach of promise," their demands for alimony, and so on.

In the economic field, employers and employees ranged themselves in two hostile armed camps, relying on force to defend their rights. There ensued a rising curve of violence, from lockouts and strikes to open revolts and other dis-orders, with their broken heads and similar casualties. One party considered only business "profits," a goal justifying and demanding utter disregard of moral and social con-siderations. Any tactics were permissible in the interests of business—even laudable, if a clever entrepreneur could de-ceive a less clever competitor! Labor employed similar tactics: for the sake of fewer working hours and higher wages it staged strikes endangering thousands of lives. Anyone not in the union was prevented, by violent means, from doing any work, regardless of his qualifications. "The union and wages" became the sacred shibboleth of this army of labor. The result was that the rest of society suf-fered even more than the combatants themselves.

The impairment of the binding power of contracts is even more striking in the political field. The contempo-rary political parties are also engaged in a perennial war with one another, and so are the citizens. The political party has become a God for its followers. In its name everything is permitted. Its victory justifies any and all means. Hence the spoils system; bribery, calumny, overt or disguised pressure; not infrequently murder, robbery, and other forms of violent coercion—these and hundreds of other means of compulsion are incessantly exploited in order to obtain a victory at the polls, to overthrow the opposition, to seize the reins of power. Electoral campaigns are a competition in vituperation, marked by the slander of opponents. Moreover, it has become a mere matter of routine for a candidate to make an unlimited number of impossible preelection promises and to forget them, without compunction, once he is elected. We are so accustomed to these "mores" that we take them for granted.

Still more conspicuous is the breach of the covenant in the modern relationship between the government and its citizens. There exists scarcely a single government in any of the Western countries which has not broken most of its solemn promises to the citizens—which has not changed the fundamental laws (whether constitutions or statutes) or repudiated its obligations respecting the gold currency, gold certificates, and bonds, the inviolability of the courts, and countless other matters. Thoroughly honest government hardly exists nowadays. But—once again—we are so inured to this lawlessness that we take it as a matter of course: if it is not too drastic and does not impinge upon us too sharply, we actually give our rulers credit for their moderation and prudence!

This failure to fulfill contracts has reached its upper limit in the sphere of international relationships. The beginning of the war of 1914-1918 witnessed, in the invasion of Belgium, the portentous "scrapping of a mere piece of paper," the solemn international obligation to respect the neutrality of Belgium. This was symbolic of what was to become, later on, a norm. Thenceforth the binding power of contracts in international relations speedily dwindled. The years from 1914 up to the present have presented an uninterrupted succession of breaches of engagements solemnly undertaken by governments. There is hardly a single international treaty concluded since 1914 that has not been violated or deliberately scrapped by one or all of the signatories. A similar fate has attended virtually all the norms of international law. As a result we witness wars precipitated without a prior declaration of hostilities; invasions and widespread devastation without the slightest provocation on the part of the victims. Brute force reigns supreme in the Western world. Neither God, nor the moral imperative, nor juridical law, nor contracts longer possess any cogency. International relations are governed almost exclusively by rampant nihilism.

In not much better case are the national relationships between social classes, occupational groups, racial and national factions, and religious sects. Everywhere the validity of contracts is evaporating. Clever machination and unabashed or veiled coercion have replaced God, moral standards, juridical law, and pacts.

Is it any wonder, then, that contractual society is rapidly crumbling? With the collapse of the whole edifice of sensate culture and sensate contractual relationships, sensate liberty was likewise bound to collapse. The sensate man of our time finds himself standing amidst the ruins, with most of his sensate possessions and his vaunted liberties destroyed, and without even the elementary security of life and limb. *Sic transit gloria mundi.*

As has been said, we are simply reaping what was already implicit in sensate culture at the outset. Such is the nemesis of sensate society. Contractualism, in such an atmosphere, tends, by its very nature, to degenerate into lawless, normless, amoral, godless compulsion and coercion. Sensate culture releases forces which ultimately destroy the magnificent contractual edifice it proudly builds at the earlier, more sober, and more balanced stages of its development. No sunspots or other cosmic influences; no biological degeneration, disgenic selection, or racial and hereditary taints; no excessive density of population—none of these external forces is responsible for the catastrophe. Its perpetrators have been sensate culture, sensate man, and sensate society themselves!

The crisis of contractual society has gone so far, and sensate culture has reached so advanced a stage of degeneracy in all its main fields, that it is idle to expect that the decay of contractualism can be arrested and the crumbling structure patched up, or that we can return to the good old days of the golden contractualism and freedom of the nineteenth century. Genuine contractual relationships—not fictitious ones—can and will eventually be restored. They cannot be restored, however, in the atmosphere of decadent sensate society, but only in the fresh air of an entirely different cultural system, either ideational or idealistic. *A preliminary reconstruction of absolute moral values and norms, with their "dura lex sed lex," obligatory for all, universally binding, not to be brushed aside in the interest of relative, expedient pseudo-values, is necessary for such a rehabilitation.* It means the replacement of sensate mentality by an ideational or idealistic *Weltanschauung.*

This implies also the replacement or mitigation of purely sensate liberty by the infusion of a rich stream of ideational liberty. Sensate man has abdicated his sense of rationality and moral responsibility. In the frenzy of his ever-expanding appetites, he has lost all inner restraint and forfeited his own liberty. Faced by the catastrophe brought about by his misdeeds, he is once more reminded that liberty is not so much external as internal; that it cannot endure without cogent values and moral norms; and, finally, that it demands self-control and the punctilious fulfillment of one's obligations. This bitter lesson suggests two alternatives: either to remain enslaved, deprived of all essential rights and liberties; or to seek for inner ideational freedom, as, under similar conditions, Greco-Roman society did. There is hardly any doubt that the second alternative will be chosen. Greco-Roman society, at the catastrophic stage of its sensate culture, when deprived of its sensate liberties, turned inward and discovered an ideational haven in Christianity. Similarly, our society will undoubtedly prefer such inner liberty to sensate slavery. More and more inexorably it will come to perceive that sensory values are fragile and uncertain; that sensate liberty is, if anything, the most insecure and precarious form of liberty. It will, accordingly, turn increasingly in the direction of self-control, the curtailment of its desires, and inalienable inner values. When such a transformation has been effected, contractual and familistic relationships will be restored in a context of richer and fuller and less one-sided culture. Any effort to patch up the hollow pseudo-contractualism and still hollower pseudo-liberties of our sensate society are doomed to failure.

# CHAPTER VI

# CRIMINALITY, WAR, REVOLUTION, SUICIDE, MENTAL DISEASE, AND IMPOVERISH- MENT IN THE CRISIS PERIOD

## I. CRIMINALITY, WAR, REVOLUTION, SUICIDE, MENTAL DISEASE AND IMPOVERISHMENT AS THE SYMPTOMS AND CONSEQUENCES OF THE CRISIS

If a person has no strong convictions as to what is right and what is wrong, if he does not believe in any God or absolute moral values, if he no longer respects contractual obligations, and, finally, if his hunger for pleasures and sensory values is paramount, what can guide and control his conduct toward other men? Nothing but his desires and lusts. Under these conditions he loses all rational and moral control, even plain common sense. What can deter him from violating the rights, interests, and well-being of other men? Nothing but physical force. How far will he go in his insatiable quest for sensory happiness? He will go as far as brute force, opposed by that of others, permits. His whole problem of behavior is determined by the ratio between his force and that wielded by others. It reduces itself to a problem of the interplay of physical forces in a system of physical mechanics. Physical might replaces right. In a society or a set of societies composed of such persons the inevitable consequence will be a multiplication of conflicts—a brutal struggle involving domestic groups and classes, as well as nations—an explosion of bloody revolutions and still bloodier wars.

Periods of transition from one fundamental form of culture and society to another—when the old socio-cultural edifice is crumbling and no new structure has yet been erected, when socio-cultural values have become almost completely "atomized" and the clash of values of different persons and groups utterly irreconcilable—inevitably produce a struggle of the utmost intensity, marked by the widest diversity of forms. Within a society it assumes, in addition to the other conflicts, the form of an *increase of crime and brutal punishment*, and *especially of an explosion of riots, revolts, and revolutions*. Within a set of societies it manifests itself in an *explosion of international wars*. The greater and more profound the transition, the more violent the outburst of revolutions, wars, and crime and punishment, if these are not drawn in an ocean of mass brutality of wars and revolutions. Such periods are invariably times of cruelty, brutality, and bestiality unrestrained by anything except mutual force and fraud.

Another consequence of periods of transition is *an increase of mental disease and suicide*. Social life in an overripe sensate culture becomes so complex, the struggle for sensory happiness is so sharp, the quest for pleasure destroys the mental and moral balance to such an extent, that the mind and nervous system of multitudes of persons cannot stand the terrific strain to which they are subjected; hence they tend to become warped or even cracked. Deprived of generally accepted norms and values—whether scientific or philosophical, religious or moral, aesthetic, or of any other kind—and surrounded by a chaos of conflicting norms and values, these persons find themselves without any authoritative guide or any superindividual rule. In these conditions they inevitably become erratic, a prey to incidental individual expediencies, momentary fancies, and conflicting sensory impulses. Like a rudderless boat in a stormy sea, such a person is tossed hither and thither by the force of circumstances. He has no standard by which to discover how consistent his actions are and whither he is drifting; in brief, he becomes an inconsistent and unintegrated complex of fortuitous ideas, beliefs, emotions, and impulses. An increase of disintegration and derangement of personality is an inevitable result. Add to all this the painful shocks that incessantly impinge upon his mind and nervous system amid the chaotic and brutal struggles of the transition period. We well know that *the indispensable prerequisite of a sound and integrated mind is the presence of social stability and unchallenged general norms*. When these begin to collapse, an increase of nervous breakdowns ordinarily ensues, and the two trends proceed *pari passu*. Nervous breakdowns are but another aspect of the collapse of socio-cultural order.

In the light of this theory it is comprehensible why mental disease has been on the increase, particularly during the past few decades; why males show a higher rate of mental disease than females; and why almost all the psychoses (except senile psychoses and others associated with cerebral arteriosclerosis), such as dementia praecox, mental deficiency, epileptic psychoses, and psychopathic psychoses, find their victims chiefly in the younger age groups, of from ten to thirty years. It explains why the married (as in the case of suicide) show the lowest percentage of mental disease; next the widowed, and then the single; with the highest rate among the divorced, that is, among persons who have passed through the trying experience of the disintegration of family solidarity, perhaps with attendant scandal. These have witnessed the crumbling of one of the principal socio-cultural values, the sanctity and inviolability of marriage.

In several respects, though not in all, the rise and decline and social distribution of mental disease parallels the movement and distribution of suicide. In both cases we have the same main factor—disintegration of the norms and values of a given culture and society. We know well the chief causes of two main forms of suicide, the so-called "egotistic" and "anomic" types. *Whenever the system of values and standards of a given society undergoes a shock and becomes disintegrated, the curve of anomic suicide invariably goes up.* Whether the shock is due to an economic panic and a sharp change from prosperity to depression, to a sudden change from depression to prosperity, to a political upheaval, to an unpopular war, or to something else, it is followed by an increase of the rate of suicide. As the disintegration attending the transition from one fundamental form of culture to another is infinitely greater than any single economic or political or other partial disintegration or shock, the rise in the curve of suicide in such periods must be expected to be especially sharp. We know also that the chief factor of so-called egotistic suicide is an increase in the psycho-social isolation or loneliness of the individual. Whenever his intimate social ties are weakened or broken—whether with the members of his family or with his friends and associates—and he becomes a stranger to most of his fellow men, his sense of psycho-social isolation grows, and with it the danger of his becoming a victim of suicide. Complete psycho-social loneliness is an unbearable burden. This is the reason why atheists more often commit suicide than religious persons; and why, among religious persons, the members of free denominations, which bind their members less than, for instance, the Roman Catholic Church, show a higher rate of suicide than less free denominations. This explains also why single people exhibit a higher rate of suicide than the married, and childless families a higher rate than those with children; also why a particularly high rate of suicide develops among the divorced—persons whose most intimate social bonds have been sundered under conditions of scandal and perhaps ostracism.

In the light of these factors it would have been miraculous if suicide had not increased in the last few decades, and it will be equally remarkable if it does not continue to increase with the progressive disintegration of sensate cultural values and social standards.

The disintegration of social institutions and the increase of psycho-social isolation of the individual have likewise proceeded apace. We have seen how the contractual ties of all our institutions have been steadily weakening. Quantitative and qualitative decline of the family means a corresponding increase of psycho-social isolation. This is further accentuated by a decline of the contractual relations in economic, political, and labor and other occupational organizations. Modern man, in his quest for sensate liberty, has been severing most of his social bonds with his fellows. He has succeeded well! At the beginning of this century he was as free as a feather floating in the air. Like the proverbial butterfly, he flitted from one group to another: he married today only to be divorced tomorrow; he associated himself momentarily now with this, now with that, occupation; or with this or that religious, political, or business group. But all these associations, as a rule, were conditional, limited, temporary, and superficial. They rarely afforded an intimate union for life. They provided not the traditional "home, sweet home," but merely a species of temporary *pied-à-terre*. They could not satisfy the lonely heart. Like narcotics, they could give only a momentary illusion of intimate and genuine unity—no real and abiding psychosocial attachment. The individual was, indeed, free, but he found himself in a psycho-social *vacuum* where he did not know what to do with his freedom. Like a hungry millionaire in the desert, he could not buy anything with his freedom, which presently turned out to be a burden rather than an asset.

Similar isolation and ennui were engendered by the incessant expansion of his desires and lusts and by the consequent multiplication of the means of their satisfaction. In the preceding chapter it was pointed out that there is no limit to sensory desires—that the more one has, the more one wants. The painful discrepancy between what one had and what one wanted grew ever wider, and the more one strove to attain his objective, the more evanescent it became. Sooner or later this hopeless quest produced a sense of weariness, fatigue, and *vanitas vanitatum*. Life began to appear as something distasteful, empty, and futile. A few moments of pleasure turned out to be a passing illusion. Disappointment and ennui were reinforced by the conflicts, animosities, and antagonisms bred by the ruthless violation of the rights of others and by the injuries inflicted upon others in the search for sensory happiness. Thus one found himself not only a stranger to almost everyone else, but a stranger living in a psycho-social vacuum surrounded by enemies and antagonists. His psycho-social isolation was well-nigh complete. The sequel was inevitable: a mounting wave of suicide and mental derangement.

In his fatal quest for sensory values, sensate man moved from the balance of early sensatism to the unbalance of late and semisenile sensatism. Order gave way to bedlam. The noble rule of sound utilitarianism and eudaemonism was superseded by the rule of unrestrained brute force and cruelty. Instead of moral progress, men beheld an upsurge of criminality and the emergence of scientifically efficient organizations of criminal gangs. Instead of peace, they witnessed the bloodiest of wars; instead of order and stability, an inferno of anarchy and revolution; instead of a sound mind, mental disease and derangement; instead of the vaunted maximum of happiness for the maximum number of human beings, only universal weariness, ennui, misery, disillusionment, hopelessness, and suicide. Such is the tragedy of the periods of transition from one fundamental type of culture and society to another. The tragedy, as has been emphasized before, is not created by the fancy and fiat of wicked persons, be they Lenins or Stalins, Mussolinis or Hitlers—by master minds of criminality or by geniuses of perversion. On the contrary, all such leaders are the product and instrumentalities of the immanent defects of sensate culture. Only in such a social context could they arise. A stable and full-blooded culture—whether ideational, idealistic, or sensate—would produce constructive and creative leaders—not dictators wielding the instruments of brute force and dedicated to destruction.

Likewise, no cosmic or biological factors should be blamed for the tragedy, such as sunspots, intensified solar radiation, new constellations of the heavenly bodies, abnormal climatic conditions, morbid racial and hereditary factors, negative selection, or poor health. Sunspot cycles have repeatedly run their course without causing any upswing of criminality, mental disease, suicide, or revolutions, wars, and other social catastrophes. The same is true of the rotations and constellations of the heavenly bodies. The climate is much the same as it has been for decades and even centuries. If climatic and geographic conditions have somewhat changed, this has been effected mainly by man, in his own interest. The physical health of the population of the West during the past century has been rapidly improving—not declining. Our life span is longer; our physical stature is greater; we are physically sounder; we live under more healthful conditions; and we satisfy our bodily needs better than heretofore. Even disgenic selection remains in most respects an unproved hypothesis. No, these factors are not the villains of the trouble. The real culprit is sensate man himself, with his sensate culture and society.

### 2. THE BLOODIEST CRISIS OF THE BLOODIEST CENTURY

Let us now see whether history corroborates the preceding propositions. Let us begin with the trend of wars and revolutions. In this verification let us be scientific and avoid the usual pitfalls of illustrative methods. The history of mankind reveals so many wars and internal disturbances that one can always find a few which seemingly prove his point, however fallacious it may be. Instead, we shall take all the wars and revolutions of the Greco-Roman and Western cultures from about 500 B.C. to the present time. We thus avoid the bias of a one-sided selection of corroborating cases and can survey the main trends of these phenomena in a long stretch of time and in an adequate perspective.

*The Movement of War.* Following this sound method, the author investigated all the known wars in the history of Greece, Rome, and the Western countries from 500 B.C. TO A.D. 1925. This gives us some 967 important wars. Each of these was considered from the standpoint of duration, size of the armies, and casualties. Taking for the measure of war the size of the casualty list per million of the corresponding population, the war magnitude appears as follows for each specified century. For Greece: in the fifth century B.C. the indicator of war magnitude is 29; for the fourth century B.C., from 48 to 36; for the third century B.C., from 18 to 33; for the second century B.C., from 3 to 3.6. For Rome (Italy) the indicator is 12 for the fourth century B.C.; for the third century B.C., 63; for the first century B.C., 33; for the first century A.D., 5; for the third, 13. If we take the whole Roman Empire, then the respective indicators are naturally much lower: 3 for the first century B.C.; 0.7 for the first century A.D.; and 1.3 for the third century A.D. The empire as a whole, of course, enjoyed the *pax Romana.* For Europe the indicators of war movement as measured by the same yardstick—namely the number of casualties per million of the corresponding population—are as follows: for the twelfth century, from 2 to 2.9; for the thirteenth century, from 3 to 5; for the fourteenth century, from 6 to 9; for the fifteenth century, from 8 to 11; for the sixteenth century, from 14 to 16; for the seventeenth, 45; for the eighteenth, 40; for the nineteenth, 17. When we come to the twentieth century, the indicator for the first quarter alone stands at 52. Diagram No. 9 shows this movement of war magnitude pictorially.

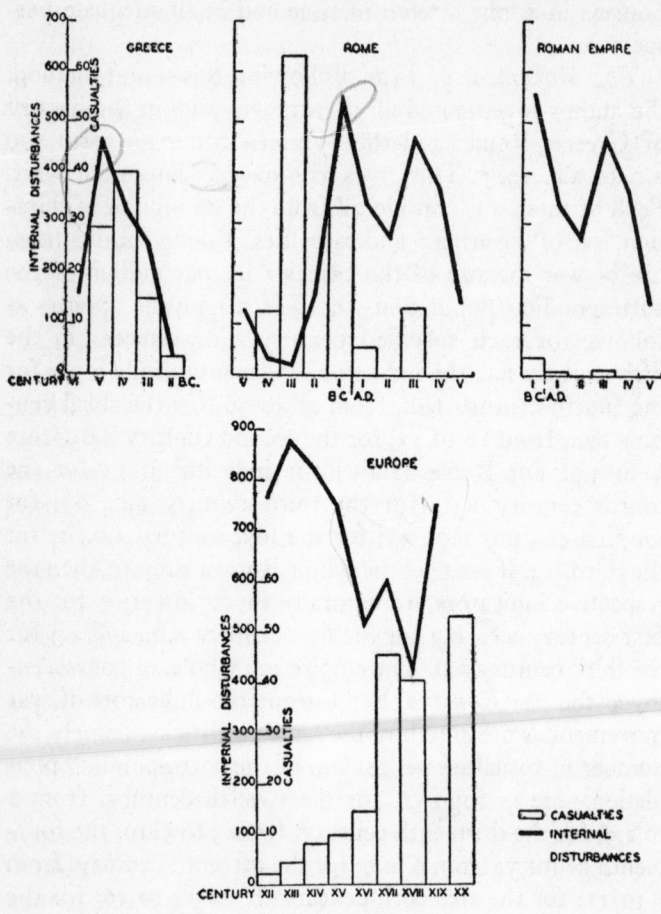

DIAGRAM No. 9

If, instead of the war casualties per million of population, we take the size of the armies, the result is similar in all essentials. The figures give a roughly accurate idea of the increase or decrease from century to century. For Greece and Rome as well as for Europe they show that war increases, with a slight lag, precisely in periods of transition from one form of society and culture to another. We know that the fifth and fourth centuries B.C. in Greece were a period of transition from the previous ideational to a sensate culture. They furnish the highest indicators of war magnitude in Greek history. When, with the end of the fourth century B.C., sensate culture became dominant and stable, war tended to decrease. In Rome the centuries from the third to the first B.C. were a somewhat similar transition period. Hence the war index for these centuries was extraordinarily high. The first and second centuries A.D. witnessed a well-established sensate culture and society. Their war indices are accordingly low. The third century saw the beginning of a decline of sensate culture and the emergence and growth of Christian ideational culture; hence the notable rise in the curve of war indices for the third century. For the period from the fourth to the sixth century, it is impossible to secure even remotely reliable data. But it is tolerably certain that these centuries were even more warlike than the third.

Still clearer is the situation in medieval Europe. We have seen that the figures for the twelfth and thirteenth centuries are very low. It is reasonable to assume that they were still lower between the year 700 and 1100, an era of settled ideational culture. This ideational system, however, had already begun to decline at the end of the twelfth century. Therefore the war index shows a slow upward trend from the twelfth to the seventeenth century, with an especially sharp rise in the latter century. Toward the close of that century sensate culture became triumphant, and many a feudal relationship was liquidated. Hence the war index for the eighteenth century falls slightly, and in the nineteenth—the golden age of contractualism and the zenith of sensate pre-Victorian and Victorian culture—sharply declines, making the nineteenth century as a peaceful era—almost as peaceful as the sixteenth. Toward the end of that period the definite signs of the disintegration of sensate culture and contractual society made their appearance—a process which assumed a catastrophic magnitude and tempo in the present century. Accordingly the war indicator registers a unique upswing; for only one quarter of the period the figures exceed those of all the preceding twenty-five centuries with the exception of the third century B.C. in Rome. But the Roman indicator (63) is for the whole century; the twentieth-century index is for only twenty-five years—from 1900 to 1925. If to the European wars of 1900 to 1925 we add all the subsequent wars up to the present time, the figures will eclipse even those for the third century B.C. If, further we add the wars that will doubtless occur from 1940 to 2000, the twentieth century will unquestionably prove to be the bloodiest and most belligerent of all the twenty-five centuries under consideration.

The extraordinary scale and depth of the contemporary social and cultural crisis are reflected by the equally extraordinary belligerency of the present century. From these summary data we perceive that the proposed theory is well corroborated by the war statistics of the twenty-five centuries studied. We see also that we live in an age unique for the unrestrained use of brute force in international relations. We observe, likewise, the tragic shortsightedness of our senescent society. Already on the edge of the precipice before 1914, it firmly believed that war was virtually obsolete. Nay, more: even after the cataclysm of 1914-1918 it continued to believe in the outlawry of war and in the possibility of an eternal peace to be established and enforced by the League of Nations. It did not realize that it was rushing headlong toward disaster. It was so blind and deaf that it still beguiled itself with the fatuous notion of an irresistible and uninterrupted historic trend toward the elimination of war from the course of human history. It did not even take the trouble to plot the course of the wars of the past statistically. Verily, whom the gods would destroy they first make mad! Such blindness is in itself a symptom of derangement and disintegration.

In the light of our theory we may safely hazard the guess that so long as the transition period lasts, and until the advent of a new ideational or idealistic society and culture, war will continue to maintain its dominant rôle in human relationships. Even if an armistice were to be signed tomorrow, it would represent merely an interlude, to be followed by an even more terrible and catastrophic Armageddon. (*Dynamics*, Vol. III, chaps. 9, 10, 11)

*The Movement of Revolutions.* Let us now turn to revolutions, revolts, and other internal disorders. Pursuing the same method, we shall review the principal disturbances that characterized the history of Greece, Rome, and western Europe from the sixth century B.C. to 1925 A.D., totaling in all some 1622. We are concerned with many aspects of the phenomenon, such as the duration of the disturbance, its social area, the population involved, and the intensity of the violence displayed. By combining these criteria we are able to assess the total magnitude of each internal disorder. By combining, in turn, all the disturbances marking each century or quarter-century, we are in a position to establish the trend as follows. In the case of Greece: for the sixth century B.C. the index is 149; for the fifth, 468; for the fourth, 320; for the third, 259; for the second (first three quarters), 36. In the case of Rome: for the fifth century B.C., 130; for the fourth, 29; for the third, 18; for the second, 158; for the first, 556; for the first century A.D., 342; for the second, 267; for the third, 475; for the fourth, 368; for the fifth (the first three quarters), 142. For Europe the figures are as follows:

| Century | Indicator of Disturbance |
|---|---|
| VI (three quarters) | 446 |
| VII | 458 |
| VIII | 733 |
| IX | 589 |
| X | 537 |
| XI | 693 |
| XII | 763 |
| XIII | 882 |
| XIV | 827 |
| XV | 748 |
| XVI | 509 |
| XVII | 605 |
| XVIII | 415 |
| XIX | 766 |
| XX (1901-1925) | 295 |

Diagrams Nos. 9 and 10 show this movement of internal disturbances pictorially.

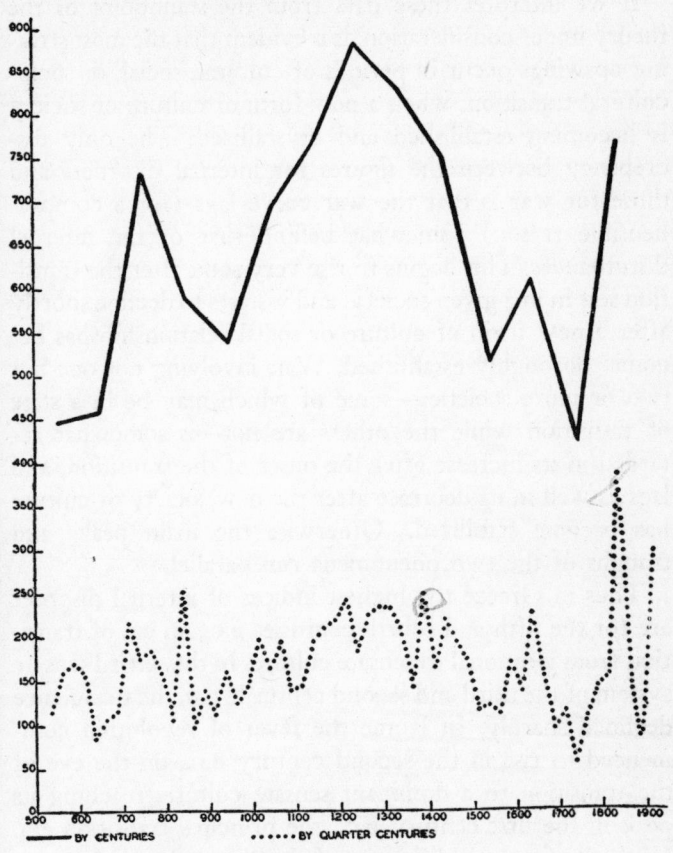

DIAGRAM No. 10

*Movement of Internal Disturbances in Europe*

If we interpret these data from the standpoint of the theory under consideration, it is evident that the most striking upswings occur in periods of cultural, social, or sociocultural transition, when a new form of culture or society is becoming established and crystallized. The only discrepancy between the figures for internal disorders and those for war is that the war curve lags (for a comprehensible reason) somewhat behind that of the internal disturbances. This begins to rise very soon after the transition sets in in a given society, and it starts to decline shortly after a new form of culture or social relationship has become thoroughly established. War, involving not one but two or more societies—some of which may be in a state of transition while the others are not—is somewhat retarded in its increase after the onset of the transition, and lags as well in its decrease after the new society or culture has become stabilized. Otherwise the main peaks and troughs of the two phenomena run parallel.

Thus in Greece the highest indices of internal disorder are for the fifth and fourth centuries B.C., an era of transition from ideational to sensate culture. In the settled sensate system of the third and second centuries B.C. the turbulence declined sharply. In Rome the fever of revolution commenced to rise in the second century B.C., on the eve of the transition to a dominant sensate culture, reaching its peak in the first century B.C., the principal transition era. With the firm establishment of the new culture, the temperature began to subside in the first century A.D., continuing to fall during the second century. The third century, in turn, was a period of transition towards a new ideational Christian culture; hence its high turbulence. By the fourth century, Christianity had been legalized as the state religion, and Christian ideational culture had become fairly well established. Hence we note a decrease of revolutionary fervor, which steadily declined throughout the fifth century, an epoch characterized by the unchallenged supremacy of ideational culture and Christian social norms.

In medieval Europe from the sixth to the twelfth century the index of internal disturbances remains low, with the exception of the eighth century, that of the Carolingian Renaissance, which temporarily injected certain sensate elements into early medieval culture and substantially remodeled social relationships along the lines of early medieval feudalism. After the tenth century the temperature begins slowly to rise, reaching a high point in the twelfth, a period of manifest decline in ideational culture and the early forms of feudalism. The thirteenth and fourteenth centuries, as has been said, were the chief centuries of transition—an epoch of idealistic culture bridging the gap between the declining ideational system and the nascent sensate system. The indices of internal anarchy, accordingly, now attain their maximum. After the fourteenth century sensate culture gained the upper hand and became more and more stable. Correspondingly, the revolutionary fever begins rapidly to subside and, with minor fluctuations, continues to do so up to the nineteenth century, or, at least, to the close of the eighteenth. The end of this stage marks a liquidation of the remnants of the late feudal regime and inaugurates an upward trend in the curve of internal disorders. With somewhat erratic fluctuations, the movement continues into the nineteenth century, becoming still more pronounced during the first quarter of the twentieth. This quarter-century exhibits an almost unprecedented outburst of internal disturbances, rivaled—if at all—by only one comparable twenty-five-year period throughout the entire two and a half millenniums embraced in this study! After 1925 there occurred a considerable number of internal disturbances and revolutions in many European countries; and many others will doubtless take place during the remaining sixty years of the century.

This analysis shows that in its principal fluctuations the movement of internal disturbances has proceeded according to our theory. A society is orderly when its system of culture and social relationships is well integrated and crystallized. It becomes disorderly when this system disintegrates and enters a period of transition. Since the present transition is one of the most crucial on record, it is necessarily accompanied by an outbreak of revolutions and anarchy well-nigh unparalleled in their number and intensity.

Here again we have proved as blind as in the case of war. Faced by the imminent menace of explosive revolutions, twentieth-century society beguiled itself with sweet illusions of orderly, streamlined progress along the smooth highway of gradual and rational change. Even in the economic field, its intellectual leaders and so-called "scientific" authorities, as late as 1927, were assuring one another quite seriously that the era of violent fluctuations from prosperity to depression was at an end; that thenceforth the fluctuations would be more and more gradual, and their amplitude narrower and narrower; and that a higher and more dependable standard of living was already in sight. Even when the explosion of the Bolshevist revolution occurred, killing and mutilating millions, many of the rich aristocracy, statesmen, politicians, professors, ministers, and journalists of Western society were entranced by what they regarded as a "wonderful social experiment." Western society behaved in this respect exactly like a degenerate aristocracy on the eve of a revolution which is to deprive it of its preeminent position, its property, and even its life. Such an aristocracy cherishes and lionizes the Rousseaus and Voltaires, socialists and communists, Karl Marxes and Lassals, in the salons of aristocratic ladies, in its academies and colleges, and in the financial quarters of the rich. Exactly the same obtuseness has been manifested in regard to all of the recent revolutions, from the socialist and communist uprisings to those of Mussolini, Hitler, and Franco.

Some understanding of the revolutionary catastrophe is finally beginning to prevail, at least in a part of our society; but even this element does not fully realize the extraordinary scale of the internal anarchy, or its real causes and consequences. Many still regard these manifestations as ordinary phenomena, due to incidental factors, including wicked men like Lenin or Stalin, Hitler or Mussolini. The preceding analysis furnishes a proper perspective and a more adequate comprehension of the profound disorderliness of our time, which is seen as the inevitable consequence of the disorganization of sensate culture and of contractual society—the terrible *dies irae, dies illa* of an acute transition period. Until a new culture and new society are thoroughly established, there is no prospect of the cessation of anarchy, of a stable order, or of a streamlined progress. No amount of experimentation with political, economic, or any other factors can eradicate the disease so long as it is carried on in the framework of a transitional period. So much for revolutions and internal disturbances. (*Dynamics*, Vol. III, chaps. 12, 13, 14)

*The Movement of Suicide.* Still less doubt prevails concerning the increase of suicide in practically all the Western countries during the nineteenth and the early part of the twentieth century. From, roughly, 1850 to 1920 its rate per one hundred thousand of the population increased in Italy from 2.8 to 8.3; in France from 7.1 to 23; in England from 7.3 to 11; in Prussia from 10.6 to 20.5; in Belgium from 6.3 to 14.2; in Ireland from 1.3 to 3.5; in Spain from 3.6 to 6.1; in Sweden from 8.1 to 12.4; in Rumania from 0.6 to 4; in Serbia from 3.8 to 5.1; in Finland from 2.9 to 5.5; in Japan from 11.0 to 20.1; and in the United States (from 1860 to 1922) from 3.1 to 11.9. During these few decades it has doubled and tripled. In itself, suicide is of small importance; even now only a small number of people die in this way. But as a symptom of the disillusionment of man in his ardent quest for sensory happiness, the phenomenon is very significant. Evidently a happy person does not commit suicide through a deliberate preference of death to life. Hence if the rate of suicide rapidly increases, it is one of the surest barometers of the failure of sensate man to attain happiness.

*Mental Disease and Criminality.* No detailed statistics are necessary here to support the claim that *mental disease* and *criminality* have been on the increase during the past few decades. As a matter of fact, almost any more or less reliable official or private publication in these fields supplies abundant statistical data showing a gradual or sudden increase of both these phenomena.

For instance, in the United States the index of criminality, as measured by total arrests, doubled in fourteen big cities from 1920 to 1930; a like increase is revealed by the arrests for major offenses from 1900 to 1930. Similar data are furnished by the statistics of the actual number of serious crimes committed, the figures for prison sentences, and other yardsticks of crime. No different is the situation in most other countries of the West.

Whether judged by the number of patients in the institutions of mental disease or by any other relevant yardstick, the figures for practically all Euro-American countries exhibit an increase of mental disease for the close of the nineteenth and for the twentieth century. For instance, per one hundred thousand of the population in England, there were 159 patients in 1859, and 360 in 1908; in the United States, 81.6 patients in 1880; 217.5 in 1910; and 220.1 in 1920. The figures for Germany and almost all other Western countries are similar. Making all the necessary allowances for possible inaccuracy of the statistics, for a possible better care of mental patients, for a longer period of detention of patients in hospitals, and the like, it is nevertheless certain that mental disease is on the upswing.

This means that Western society is progressively becoming mentally deranged and morally unbalanced. Additional novelties in the field of criminality are the calculated cold-bloodedness of crimes perpetrated for pecuniary purposes, in contradistinction to the passionate, impulsive, and spontaneous criminality of the past; the efficiency of scientifically organized criminal machines; technologically organized "racketeering" on a large scale in collusion with political leaders and "respected citizens"; and the prominence of the rôle of the lower age groups in criminal activities. In the United States, for instance, in 1930 the percentage of the age group from fifteen to twenty-four years old in the total population was 18.3, whereas the share of this age group in the total arrests for various offenses was 34.2 per cent. In England and Wales, in 1935 the number of males, per one hundred thousand of each age group, found guilty of indictable offenses was as follows: under seventeen, 998; seventeen to twenty-one, 647; twenty-one to thirty, 439; thirty and over, 163. Among females the age group from seventeen to twenty-one showed the highest conviction rate, 89, the rates for other groups being as follows: under seventeen, 64; twenty-one to thirty, 61; thirty and over, 47. We thus see that in sensate society the low age groups are generally responsible for a disproportionately large share of the crimes committed by the total population.

The increase of criminality in general, and its modern novelties in particular, point directly to the moral "atomism" and nihilism of our times. Under these conditions crime becomes a business, carried out with business-like efficiency, cold-bloodedly, calculatingly, and scientifically, for purely utilitarian purposes, without regard for moral or idealistic considerations. The kidnaper, racketeer, or murderer in most cases entertains no personal grudge or animosity against his victim. He selects this or that person or group dispassionately, solely with a view to pecuniary profit. The high rate of criminality of contemporary youth is again perfectly comprehensible. Reared in an atmosphere of unstable families, broken homes, and an "atomistic" moral atmosphere, and being young and impulsive, they seek to translate their utilitarian and hedonistic tendencies into direct action: to get rich quickly, so as to gain the wherewithal for food, drink, girls, and other instruments of pleasure and comfort.

Thus wars, revolutions, criminality, mental disease, and suicide alike bear witness to the so-called "liberation" from the bonds of ethical and legal norms, to the supremacy of unalloyed physical force, and to the upsurge of cruelty, bestiality, and inhumanity.

*The Increase in the Brutality of Punishment.* Their testimony may be supplemented by other contemporary trends—for instance, in the punishment of crime. A common belief in the nineteenth century was that, as time goes on, the penalties for crime tend to become more and more humane. Many criminologists of the nineteenth and the early twentieth century held that physical punishment was tending to disappear, just as they believed that wars and revolutions were on the wane. When such a theory is examined, however, in the light of a comparative study of the barbaric and medieval penal codes of European society and the most recent penal codes of the Soviet, Nazi, and Fascist governments, or of the actual punishment meted out to millions of contemporary human beings, it becomes utterly untenable.

The results of such a systematic study—the first of its kind—are instructive. We find that the early medieval Christian codes of secular and canon law reveal a quantitative and qualitative increase of severity as compared with the preceding barbaric codes—precisely as we should expect in the period of transition from the sensate Greco-Roman and ancient Teutonic culture to the Christian ideational system. In Rome, during the third and subsequent centuries of our era, there developed, "instead of the simple and comparatively mild system of penalties of the preceding period, a very complicated, very severe, and often barbaric system of penalties. ... The death penalty, which almost disappeared in the previous period, is now reestablished and often assumes particularly cruel forms (burning, crucifixion, *poena culei*, etc.). ... In addition, quite frequent are hard labor, imprisonment in the state mines (*condemnatio ad metallum*), banishment, exile, loss of freedom and all rights—a vast system of torturing and painful bodily punishment." Likewise, from the sixth to the ninth century, when the Teutonic tribes were passing from their "primitive state" to one of ideational Christian culture, we note a similar upsurge in the rigor of the early Christian law—both secular and canon—as compared with that of the barbaric codes.

A similar phenomenon is observable between the end of the twelfth and the beginning of the fourteenth century—an era of transition from the medieval ideational system to one of sensate culture. This period witnessed the rise and development of the Inquisition. (*Cf.* the edicts of the Council of Verona (1189) and of Pope Innocent III in 1203 and 1215.) Further evidence of the same tendency is furnished by the penal codes of the Soviet Union for 1926 and 1930, of the Third Reich for 1935, and of Fascist Italy for 1930, reflecting the conviction of contemporary lawgivers that the propensities of the would-be criminal can be inhibited only by inflicting drastic physical pain.

When we turn to the concrete figures of punishment actually imposed by the victorious faction of this or that country in periods of transition upon its defeated opponents, the magnitude of man's cruelty and brutality toward his fellows assumes truly extraordinary proportions. The great transitional periods from one main type of culture and society to another dominant type are, as we have seen, especially revolutionary and turbulent. In such revolutions, therefore, the upsurge of brutality and cruelty is particularly marked. A few data will illustrate the point. Take, for instance, capital punishment, which is typical. In Russia, from 1881 to 1905, the annual number of death penalties fluctuated only between 9 and 18. The Russian criminal code prescribed capital punishment for only a few political crimes, such as attempts against the life of the Czar or his family. During the revolution of 1905-1906 the figures jumped to 547 in 1906; 1139 in 1907; and 1340 in 1908, and then with the suppression of the revolution, dropped to 717 in 1909; 129 in 1910; and 73 in 1911. Similarly, in the French Revolution of 1789 the total number of executions amounted to 17,000 persons condemned by the revolutionary courts, and to 35,000-40,000 victims of the revolutionary terror. This rise—which occurred in a period of some five years—represented a hundredfold increase over the number of death penalties inflicted before the Revolution. A similar intensification of cruelty and multiplication of death penalties invariably occurs in any revolution during a period of sharp transition. Since in the twentieth century Western culture and society entered a crucial transition period, an extraordinary eruption of brutality was to be expected. The total number of direct victims of the Red Terror of the Communist revolution in the years 1918-1922, according to a conservative estimate, is at least 600,000—more than 100,000 a year. And this excludes the victims of the civil war, including the White Terror, and all the indirect victims of the Revolution itself. In one way or another, fifteen to seventeen millions of human lives were thus sacrificed to the idol of the revolution. Momentous also, though on a much smaller scale, was the carnage resulting from the revolutions of 1918 and subsequent years in Hungary, Germany, Austria, Poland, Spain, and other countries. Human life has lost its value and is being trampled underfoot without compunction or remorse. "Purges" have become a daily or weekly occurrence; killing, a daily routine.

Add to this the millions of persons deprived of all their property and other rights, arrested, imprisoned, kept in concentration camps and other places of detention, tortured, or banished. Add also the millions who had to flee in order to save their lives and who either perished in the migration or else became refugees—helpless derelicts without home or family and generally deprived of all means of subsistence. The ranks of the refugees are invariably swelled during periods of transition. So it was at the close of the Greco-Roman sensate era and the beginning of the Christian ideational era, in connection with the internal and external migrations of peoples in the early Middle Ages. Another conspicuous example is furnished by the history of the thirteenth and fourteenth centuries. Contemporary refugees may well echo the words of Dante, one of the most famous refugees of those centuries, who knew "how the salt of another's bread tastes and how hard it is to go up and down another's stairs." Consider, further, that at the present time neither the innocence of children nor the white locks of venerable old age nor the tenderness of girls and women is spared. If anything, they are the main victims of war, revolution, crime, and other forms of violence. The civilization that before 1914 boasted of its humanitarianism and sympathy, in contradistinction to the alleged cruelty and inhumanity of the Dark ages, has degenerated into something so base and brutal that it exceeds the alleged cruelty of the barbarians. Reemerging during the twelfth and thirteenth centuries in a spirit of humanitarianism, compassion, earthly wisdom, and noble aspiration, the sensate culture of the West has terminated this phase of its existence in a riot of subanimalistic brutality and violence. No more complete and tragic bankruptcy could be imagined. As long as society attempts to function in a disintegrating sensate framework there is no hope of arresting this process of dehumanization, demoralization, and brutalization, this progressive substitution of physical force for all moral, religious, and social values. (*Dynamics*, Vol. III, chaps. 7, 8; Vol. II, chap. 15)

*Economic Misery.* Finally, the bankruptcy of overripe sensate culture is climaxed by its failure to attain its most coveted objective—a high material plane of living accessible to all. For evident reasons, sensate culture during its sounder and more vigorous stages succeeds in this task better than does an ideational system. Ideational culture is not concerned with material standards and values. Ideational society does not invest all or even the greater part of its energies in this endeavor: it regards material comfort either indifferently or negatively. The aspiration of sensate society is quite different: it invests all its energy in the endeavor to multiply material values. Through science and technology, through more efficient production, commerce, and trade, and sometimes through the robbery of weaker peoples, it is much more successful in promoting the material comfort of its members than any ideational society.

Hence the sounder stages of sensate culture have always been characterized by a distinct improvement of material conditions. Such was the case in the Greek and Hellenistic world from the fifth to the second century B.C.—a period of the reemergence and growth of sensate culture. The standard of living rose notably in comparison with that of the sixth century B.C., which had been predominantly ideational. For the same reason, the first and second centuries A.D. show the highest level of material conditions in Rome. Finally, for the same reason, in medieval Europe the material standard of living rose markedly in the twelfth and thirteenth centuries and in the first half of the fourteenth; then, after a sharp set-back, it rose, with minor fluctuations, from the fifteenth to the twentieth century, reaching in the nineteenth century and in the pre-war period of the twentieth century a level unprecedented in human history. What is still more important, it diffused its benefits among all classes, instead of limiting them to a narrow circle of the privileged. Following this bent, it gave to Western society security of life and safety from externally inflicted pain. It contributed in striking fashion to an improvement of physical health through the prevention or elimination of many diseases. Through all these benefits the span of human life lengthened, and life became in many ways less painful and more happy.

This success was the reason for the unbounded optimism of Western society, especially from the eighteenth to the twentieth century. As late as 1927 its scholars and authorities continued well-nigh unanimously to voice this optimistic belief in the possibility of boundless improvement of material conditions, of a further extension of the span of human life, of ever-better health, of even greater happiness. They depicted the next stage of human history as a paradise where rivers of milk would flow between banks of ice cream through plains of unlimited abundance. Gastronomic delicacies—even champagne—would be within the reach of everyone. Everybody was to be freed from tedious labor, for all the work would be done by machines. Thus everyone would have abundant leisure for recreation, happiness, and education. Poverty and misery would be abolished. What was inaccessible to even the kings and millionaires of the past would be accessible to the poorest member of the society of the future. Along these and similar lines ran the Cloud-Cuckoo-Land credo of Western society up to 1914 or even 1929.

This paradise sounded quite scientific, plausible, and convincing. Being insensible to underground tremors, society was insensible also to the underground forces that were undermining the very well springs of its material prosperity.

Consequently it failed to realize that periods of sharp transition are, without exception, periods of catastrophic economic decline, especially when the transition is from a sensate to an ideational system. Demoralization, disintegration, wars, anarchy, revolutions, criminality, cruelty, and other destructive forces are not conducive to business prosperity. Under such circumstances security of possession disappears; the incentives for efficient work are undermined; and production, commerce, and trade progressively dwindle. What is created is rapidly destroyed by war and anarchy. What is earned is forthwith spent because of the uncertainty of the morrow. Long-range economics are replaced by an economy of immediate profits or downright pillage. Such periods, particularly when an overripe sensate system is succeeded by an ideational system, have invariably been attended by a formidable and often sudden economic catastrophe and by the lowering of the material plane of living. Such was the case at the end of the Greco-Roman sensate culture, in the fourth, fifth, and sixth centuries A.D. The catastrophic destruction of economic values, the lowering of the plane of living, the processes of de-urbanization, de-industrialization, and de-commercialization, together with the endless misery they entailed, are too familiar to call for detailed specification. A further example is afforded by the transition from the idealistic system of the thirteenth and the first part of the fourteenth century to the subsequent sensate system. The material well-being which was rapidly rising during the twelfth and thirteenth centuries, and which attained a level excelled only in the second part of the nineteenth, abruptly declined at the close of the fourteenth or during the fifteenth century (depending upon the country) under the transitional conditions of the period. Later on, with the complete triumph of sensate culture, the upward trend was resumed, leading to unique heights in the second part of the nineteenth century and in the pre-war years of the twentieth. Since our culture and society are in a state of basic transition, a reversal of the economic trend—towards impoverishment and a lowering of the standards of living—was inevitable.

The World War of 1914-1918 was the first of a series of cataclysms which sapped the well springs of our prosperity, reversing the trend of material prosperity. After the termination of the war, in the nineteen twenties, there was a temporary improvement; but this was very short-lived, and soon—especially after 1929—a rapid decline set in. Diagrams Nos. 11 and 12 show the described fluctuation of economic conditions from 700 A.D. to 1930, for France and Germany.

During the thirties the decline assumed enormous proportions, with millions unemployed, with or without the dole (or its equivalents), with constant shrinkage of wealth and income, and with other symptoms of acute depression. Artificial measures of alleviation were resorted to, mainly at the expense of future generations; but these measures proved entirely superficial and inadequate. With the outbreak of war in 1939 the decline in standards of living became everywhere catastrophic. Rearmament began to consume not only the surplus (if, indeed, there *was* any surplus) but the vital substance of national wealth and income—even in countries that remained neutral. As the war involved more and more of the Continent, privation and misery spread over ever-wider areas and gripped increasing millions of human beings. Their material standard of living sank to a level far below even the standards of the Middle Ages. Hunger, lack of clothes and adequate shelter (or even any shelter at all), and the lack of regular sleep and other elementary necessities became general throughout Europe, the greater part of Asia, many parts of Africa, as well as other areas. Security of property reached the vanishing point.

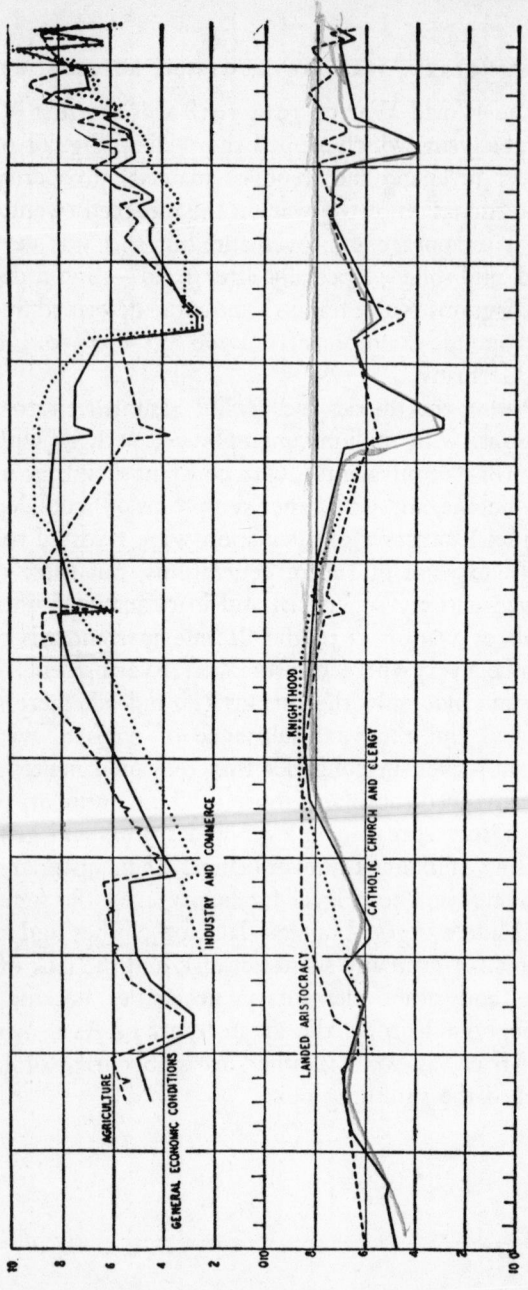

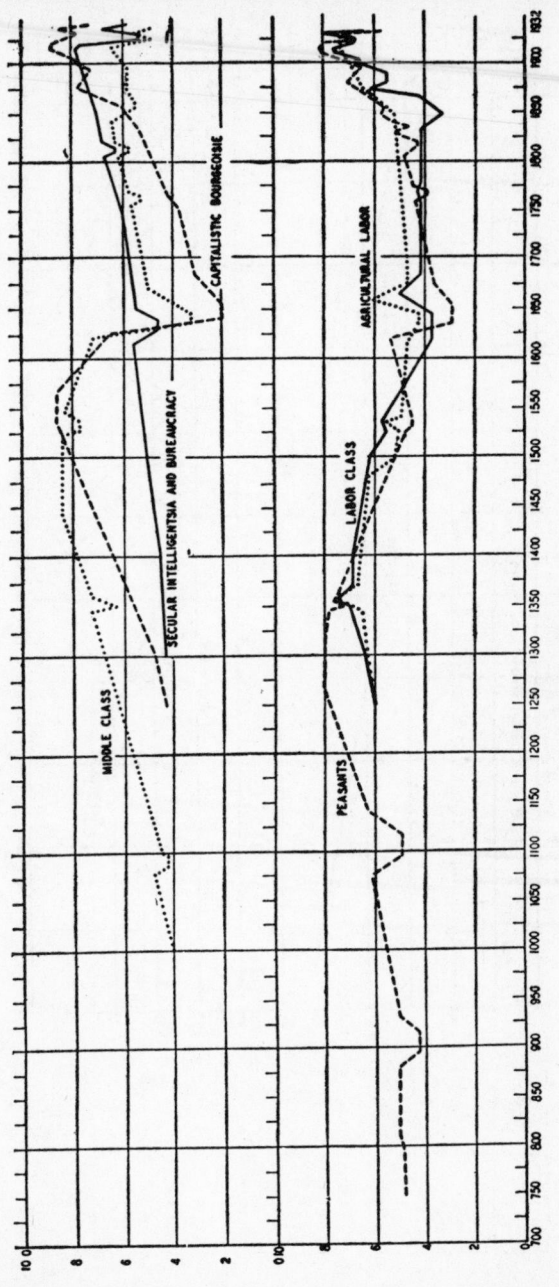

DIAGRAM No. II

*General economic situation in Germany from 700 to 1932*

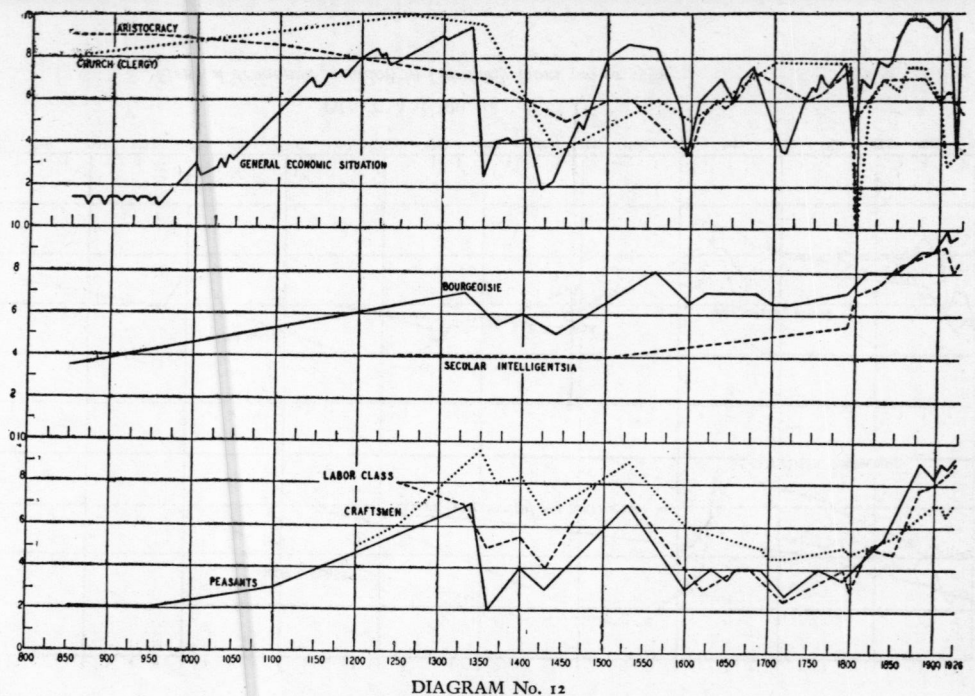

DIAGRAM No. 12

*General economic situation in France from 800 to 1926*

To these privations and miseries others, still more painful, were added. Security of life itself disappeared in all the belligerent countries. Multitudes of people were subjected to the tragedy of witnessing the sudden loss of members of their family and of friends and neighbors. Death became an omnipresent specter! This phenomenon is amply demonstrated by the swiftly mounting death rate for the years 1939, 1940, and undoubtedly for 1941, of the civilian population of European and other belligerent countries, as well as of some of the nonbelligerent countries.

Thus, within three or four decades, dying sensate culture had scrapped the material well-being and other values created during the four preceding centuries. Man sits amid the ruins of his erstwhile splendid social edifice, surrounded —both literally and figuratively—by a ghastly array of corpses. (*Dynamics*, Vol. III, chap. 8)

Additional evidences of the irony of history are furnished by the measures of so-called "social security" (insurance against old age and unemployment) introduced at a time when such security no longer exists; by pompous and high-falutin eulogies of democracy when the last remnants of democracy are vanishing (partly through the fault of those who pose as its self-appointed champions); by pretentious declarations of sensate humanism when every vestige of true humanitarianism has been discarded; and by resounding assurances that we can preserve "our way of life," be it American, German, Russian, or English, when the way of life traditional to the respective countries has become a mere historic memory! The very fervor and clamor of such measures and pronouncements are infallible indications that the values in question have already perished or else stand in the gravest danger. When the status of the family, for instance, was still secure, there was little talk about the necessity of preserving it. When, however, the family began to disintegrate, a plethora of books, lectures, courses, and societies for the conservation of this institution sprang into existence. The same is true of social security, peace, humanism, democracy, prosperity, and the like.

Investing all his energies in the control of nature, sensate man achieved a conspicuous degree of success. But in this process he lost his *self*-control. Becoming—like a child toying with a bomb—infatuated with the physical forces at his disposal, in an access of madness he directed them against himself and his own achievements. In his eagerness to serve mammon he forgot to serve God, and he now pays the tragic price of his folly!

# CHAPTER VII

# TRAGIC DUALISM, CHAOTIC SYNCRETISM, QUANTITATIVE COLOSSALISM, AND DIMINISHING CREATIVENESS OF THE CONTEMPORARY SENSATE CULTURE

## I. THE CULTURE OF MAN'S GLORIFICATION AND DEGRADATION

When any socio-cultural system enters the stage of its disintegration, the following four symptoms of the disintegration appear and grow in it: first, the inner self-contradictions of an irreconcilable dualism in such a culture; second, its formlessness—a chaotic syncretism of undigested elements taken from different cultures; third, a quantitative colossalism—mere size and quantity at the cost of quality; and fourth, a progressive exhaustion of its creativeness in the field of great and perennial values. In addition to all the signs of disintegration discussed previously, these four symptoms of disintegration have already emerged and are rampant in this contemporary sensate culture of ours. *Tragic Dualism*

Our culture in its present sensate phase is full of irreconcilable contradictions. It proclaims equality of all human beings; and it practices an enormous number of intellectual, moral, mental, economic, political, and other inequalities. It proclaims "the equality of opportunity" in theory; in practice it provides practically none. It proclaims "government of the people, for the people, and by the people"; in practice it tends to be more and more an oligarchy or a plutocracy or a dictatorship of this or that faction. It stimulates an expansion of wishes and wants, and it inhibits their satisfaction. It proclaims social security and a decent minimum of living conditions for everyone, even as it is progressively destroying security for all and showing itself incapable of eliminating unemployment or of giving decent conditions to the masses. It strives to achieve the maximum of happiness for the maximum number of human beings, but it increasingly fails in that purpose. It advertises the elimination of group hatreds, while in fact it increasingly seethes with group antagonism of every kind—racial, national, state, religious, class and others. The unprecedented explosion of internal disturbances and wars of the twentieth century is an incontrovertible evidence of that failure. Our culture condemns egotisms of all kinds and boasts of the socialization and humanization of everything and everybody; in reality, it displays unbridled greed, cruelty, and egotism of individuals as well as of groups, beginning with innumerable lobbying and pressure groups and continuing throughout economic, political, occupational, religious, state, family, and other groups. And so on, and so on.

Without attempting to enumerate all the self-contradictions of this culture of ours, let us take, instead, what appears to be its central self-contradiction. This consists in the fact that *our culture simultaneously is a culture of man's glorification and of man's degradation*. On the one hand, it boundlessly glorifies man and extols man-made culture and society. On the other, it utterly degrades the human being and all his cultural and social values. We live in an age which exalts man as the supreme end, and, at the same time, an age which vilifies man and his cultural values endlessly. The "World of Tomorrow" in the New York World's Fair is a flat symbol of one aspect of this tragic dualism; the catastrophe of the present war is a sign of the other.

Never before has man displayed such a genius for scientific discoveries and technological inventions. No previous period can rival the power of contemporary man in the modification of cosmic and biological conditions to suit his needs. At no time before has man been the molder of his own destiny to such an extent as he is now. We live, indeed, in an age of the greatest triumph of human genius.

No wonder, therefore, that we are proud of man. It is not strange that our culture has become homo-centric, humanitarian, and humanistic *par excellence*. Man is its glorious center. It makes him "the measure of all things." It exalts him as the hero and the greatest value, not by virtue of his creation by God in God's own image, but in his own right, by virtue of man's own marvelous achievements. It substitutes the religion of humanity for the religions of superhuman deities. It professes a firm belief in the possibility of limitless progress based on man's ability to control his own destiny, to eradicate all social and cultural evils, and to create an even better and finer world, free from war and bloody strife, from crime, poverty, insanity, stupidity, and vulgarity. In all these respects we live, indeed, in an era of a truly great glorification of man and his culture.

Unfortunately, this dazzling façade is not the only aspect of our cultural and social edifice. Like the mythical double-faced Janus, it has another—and more sinister—face, the face of a great degradation and de-humanization of man; of debasement, distortion, and desecration of all social and cultural values. If the dazzling façade glorifies man as a divine hero, the second face strips him of anything divine and heroic. If one face of our culture shows it as a creative flame of human genius rising higher and higher—*per aspera ad astra*—to the eternal world of absolute values, its second face sneers at such a self-delusion and drags it down to the level of a mere reflexological ant hill, to the mere "adjustment mechanism" of human ants and bees.

We do not like to parade this sinister face of our culture; it is not exhibited at any World's Fair; and yet it is as certain as any solid fact can be. Even more, in the course of time, as we have seen, it is appearing more and more frequently, and progressively tends to overshadow the sunny aspect of our cultural world. A mere glance at the main compartments of our culture will be sufficient to show this fact.

To begin with, take *contemporary science* and ask how it defines man. The current answers are, as we have seen, that man is a variety of electron-proton complex; or an animal closely related to the ape or monkey; or a reflex mechanism; or a variety of stimulus-response relationships; or a psychoanalytical bag filled either by libido or basic physiological drives; or a mechanism controlled mainly by digestive and economic needs. Such are the current physico-chemical, biological, and psycho-social conceptions of man. No doubt man *is* all these things. But do any or all of these conceptions completely explain the essential nature of man? Do they touch his most fundamental properties which make him a creature unique in the world? Most of the definitions which pretend to be especially scientific rarely, if ever, raise such questions. They pass them by.

We are so accustomed to such views that we often fail to see the utter depreciation of man and his culture implied in them. Instead of depicting man as a child of God, and a bearer of the highest values in this empirical world, and for this reason sacred, they strip him of anything divine and great and reduce him to a mere inorganic or organic complex. Thus is contemporary science permeated by the tragic dualism discussed earlier. With one hand it creates all the real values that increase man's *summum bonum;* with the other it invents cannon and bombers, poisonous gas and tanks, that kill man and destroy his culture.

Like science, *contemporary philosophy* has also contributed its share to the degradation of man and his culture: first, in the form of the growth of mechanistic materialism for the last few centuries; second, in the debasement of the truth itself either to a mere matter of convenience (Mach, Poincaré, Petzold, Richard Avenarius, K. Pearson, William James, John Dewey, and other representatives of positivism, neo-positivism, pragmatism, operationalism, instrumentalism, logical positivism, and other similar philosophical movements), or to a mere fictional and arbitrary "convention" (the philosophies of *als ob* or "as if"); or to a mere "ideology," "derivation," or "rationalization" as a by-product of economic, sensual, or other drives and residues (Marxianism, Paretianism, Freudianism); and third, in making the organs of the senses the main and often the only criterion of truth. Materialism identifies man and cultural values with matter; for this reason it cannot help stripping man and his values of any exceptional and unique position in the world. Truth reduced to a mere convenience or convention destroys itself. In the maze of contradictory conveniences and conventions, thousands of contradictory "truths" appear, each as valid as the others. For this reason the very difference between the true and the false disappears.

With the degradation of truth, man is debased from the sublime seeker after truth as an absolute value to that of the hypocrite who uses "truth" as a beautiful smoke screen for the justification of his impulses and lust, profit and greed. In so far as modern philosophy propagated these conceptions, it has its own poisonous aspect and contributes to the depreciation of man and of truth itself.

If we turn to contemporary *fine arts*, they display the same dualism, with the same contradictory consequences for man as well as for art itself. Its sunny side is well known and needs no comment. Its ominous aspect manifests itself, as we have seen, first, in debasing the socio-cultural value of art to a mere means of sensual enjoyment in the terms of "wine, women and laxatives"; and second, in its pathological exhibitionism of the negative aspects of man and of culture.

If we are to believe contemporary art in its representation, we can hardly have any respect or admiration for man and his culture. To this extent, contemporary art is an art of man's debasement and vilification. In being so, it debases itself and prepares its own downfall as a great cultural value.

Finally, a similar dualism is exhibited by contemporary *ethics and law*. These consist, on the one hand, of the system of Christian ethics created in the past and inherited by us, and on the other, of the more modern utilitarian and hedonistic rules of conduct. We have seen that these modern systems have sown the seeds of the degradation of man, as well as of moral values themselves.

Similar dualism pervades our minds, our conduct, and our social relationships. We aspire for happiness; and prepare wretchedness for ourselves. The more we try to improve our well-being, the more we lose our peace of mind, without which no happiness is possible. Instead of being serene, at peace with God, the world and his fellow men, contemporary man is a boiling pot of desires that are at war with one another, and with those of his fellows. He is torn between them, cannot control them, and is in a state of perpetual dissatisfaction and restlessness. We aspire for the maximum of material comfort; and we condone privation and misery. We eulogize love, and cultivate hatred. We proclaim man sacred, and slaughter him pitilessly. We proclaim peace, and wage war. We believe in cooperation and solidarity, and multiply competition, rivalry, antagonism, and conflicts. We stand for order, and plot revolutions. We boast of the guaranteed rights of man, of the sanctity of constitutions and covenants; and we deprive man of all rights and break all constitutions and pacts. And so on, endlessly. The tragic dualism of our culture is indisputable and is widening from day to day. Its soul is hopelessly split. It is a house divided against itself. The dark Demon in it is at relentless war with its Good Genius. And the Demon of Destruction has been progressively rising over its creative Angel. Hence the spread of the sinister blackout of our culture.

## 2. CULTURE OF CHAOTIC SYNCRETISM

An emergence of a chaotic syncretism in a given integrated culture is another general symptom of its disintegration. The classical example is given by the overripe sensate culture of Greece and Rome. In that stage it became, in the words of Tacitus, "the common sink into which everything infamous and abominable flows like a torrent from all quarters of the world." All these currents were undigested and unintegrated into one unity. The result was that the overripe sensate Greco-Roman culture turned indeed into a "common sink" or a dumping place for the most divergent elements of the most different cultures.

The reason for such a syncretism as a sign of the disintegration is evident. Any great cultural supersystem is, as we have seen, a unity integrated into one consistent whole by meaningful and causal ties. Such an integrated unity were ideational and idealistic mediaeval cultures, permeated by Christianity; such a unity has also been our sensate supersystem in the centuries of its emergence and growth. It had its sensate values strong and not ground into dust. It enriched itself by the elements of many cultures, whether Greco-Roman or Arabic, Byzantine or Egyptian, Oriental or native American. But it ingested from all these cultures only such values as did not contradict its soul, and these ingested elements it modified and digested. The irreconcilable and indigestible elements of other cultures it rejected. In this sense it was, like any great culture, highly selective and discriminatory. At the present moment it is in a very different situation. Its values have been, as we have seen, atomized and ground into dust. Further on, created by its own genius, the new means of communication and contact put it into the closest interaction with practically all the cultures of all mankind. Their elements in all their astounding variety began to flow into it increasingly. Indian tobacco-smoking, Turkish baths, coffee- and tea-drinking, polo-playing, pyjama-wearing, drug-addiction, and Oriental religious philosophy, all took root in our culture. Elements of the cultures of the Australian bushmen, of Melanesian and Esquimo tribes, as well as of all historical peoples of the present and of the past—Egyptian and Hindu, Chinese and Mayan, Greek and Roman, Turkish and Persian, infiltrated the sensate culture of the West and did so in ever-increasing currents. Like an organism, any culture at the period of its virility and strength can digest a great many foreign elements. But even for the strongest organism there is a limit to this digestion, and this limit becomes progressively narrower with the advancement of age and the decline of health. Similarly, there is a limit to the digestion of heterogeneous elements by any cultural system, and this limit narrows with the advance of the culture to its overripe phase. When the limit is passed, an increasingly richer stream of heterogeneous elements brought into such a culture will remain less and less digested. More and more they will distort the style, the soul, and the body of the host culture and finally will help its disintegration. That result is exactly what we observe now in contemporary Western culture. Its richness and variety are astounding. Everything and anything can be found in it. We can find all the existing and imaginable styles in the fine arts, from the primitive and archaic up to the ultramodern and classic. All the mores, manners, moral rules, taboos, customs, codes, ethical systems, codes of law, of all the peoples and tribes are here, living side by side. All the religious systems, indeed all manner of magical beliefs, are present in it. Our network of communication puts us in contact with them all; and all of them find somehow their devotees and apostles among us. So also with all philosophies. Again, all the scientific theories of the most different type, of the past and of the present, are in our possession and have their agents and followers. And so also with our social institutions: from the family to political regimes of all kinds, modeled along the most different patterns, they are functioning among us. Finally, in our fashions and fads of dress, courting, witticisms, up to the fashions in any field of culture, we run within a couple of decades from one possible extremity to another, from an imitative "archaic and primitive and cave-man" fashion to that of classic, romantic, Gothic and baroque, vertical and horizontal, "monastic" and "whoopee," "peaceful" and "military," and so on, in endless variety of all forms and patterns. The area of the Western culture and the area of our minds that reflect it are turned into a "World's Fair" where anything can be found, where the most heterogeneous values incessantly parade one after another. Western culture has ceased to be a selective organism. Instead, it has become a vast cultural dumping place where everything is dumped, without any restriction. It has lost its own physiognomy, its own soul, and its discriminative ability.

This all-pervading syncretism is reflected in our mentality, in our beliefs, ideas, tastes, aspirations, and convictions. The mind of contemporary man is likewise a dumping place of the most fantastic and diverse bits of the most fragmentary ideas, beliefs, tastes, and scraps of information. From Communism to Catholicism, from Beethoven or Bach to the most peppy jazz and the cat-calls of crooning; from the fashion of the latest movie or best-seller to the most opposite fashion of another movie or best-seller—all coexist somehow in it, jumbled side by side, without any consistency of ideas, or beliefs, or tastes, or styles. Today the cultural best-seller is *The Life of Christ;* tomorrow, *Trader Horn;* the next day, *Gone With the Wind;* then a psychoanalytical biography of Napoleon; then some concoction of archaism with classicism; of eroticism with sanctity; of the *Four Square Gospel* with *Why We Behave Like Human Beings;* of the gospel of Communism with that of Theosophy, crowned with all the disjointed variety of our "Information, Please," and other intellectual chewing gums.

Viewed from this standpoint, our intellectual life is but an incessant dance of jitterbugs. Its spineless and disjointed syncretism pervades all our social and mental life. Our education consists mainly in pumping into the mind-area of students the most heterogeneous bits of information about everything. Our newspapers and magazines reflect the same syncretism elevated into a dogma of "all the news" sprinkled by the sensationalism of the yellow press. Our science changes its hypotheses every decade or year. Our ethics is a jungle of discordant norms and opposite values. Our religious belief is a wild concoction of a dozen various "Social Gospels," diversified by several beliefs of Christianity diluted by those of Marxianism, Democracy, and Theosophy, enriched by a dozen vulgarized philosophical ideas, corrected by several scientific theories, peacefully squatting side by side with the most atrocious magical superstitions. So also are our philosophies and *Weltanschauung,* our fine arts and tastes. With an equal enthusiasm we accept the Gregorian Chants and "The St. Louis Blues"; the Bible and the erotic novel; behaviorism and the Neo-Thomism; the *Divine Comedy* and *Paradise Lost,* and

*Esquire* and *The Grapes of Wrath;* psycho-analysis and the *Confessions of St. Augustine;* jitterbugs and classical dance. And so on. All this lies side by side, undigested and unintegrated into any unity.

This jumble of diverse elements means that the soul of our sensate culture is broken down. It appears to have lost its self-confidence. It begins to doubt its own superiority and primogeniture. It ceases to be loyal to itself. It progressively fails to continue to be its own sculptor, to keep unimpaired the integrity and sameness of its style, that takes in only what agrees with it and rejects all that impairs it. Such a culture loses its individuality. It becomes formless, shapeless, style-less. As such, it becomes less and less distinguishable in the ocean of cultural phenomena as a striking and magnificent individuality. When it reaches this stage, its creative career is finished. From the creative actor of history, it passes into a museum of historical survivals. (*Dynamics*, Vol. IV, chap. 5)

### 3. THE CULTURE OF QUANTITATIVE COLOSSALISM

A fairly uniform symptom of disintegration in any great supersystem of culture is the substitution of quantitative colossalism for a sublime quality; of glittering externality for inner value; of a show for a substance. So it was in the past, and so it is at present.

The Greece of the most creative period of the sixth, fifth, and fourth centuries B.C., compared with the later Hellenic world and the still later Roman world, gives us a classical example. In the Greece of this creative period its temples, including the Parthenon, were of very modest size; its statues and drawings were moderate also. Its music was simple and expressed itself with few instruments, whether of the great Terpander time or later on. Its litera-- ture, its Academies and Lyceums were modest in number, size, and production. Nothing was measured by the number of copies sold or by the size of valuable objects. The size of the Greek societies was small and limited. Everything great was great by its inner value, but not by quantity or external show. Sublime quality, not a quantitative colossalism, determined whether the value was great or mediocre, positive or negative.

When we pass to the Hellenic and later Roman periods, the picture changes. Sublime quality deteriorated. Its place was taken by ever-bigger quantity, and the greater the colossalism of the quantity, the better it began to be thought. Temples, palaces, theaters, public buildings, monuments, sculptures, all became huge and enormous. The Colossus of Rhodes was 105 feet high; the Halicarnassus Mausoleum was 140 feet high. The size of sculptures and monuments like the Pergamene Frieze, the Farnese Heracles, the Arch of Titus, the Columns of Trajan, of Marcus Aurelius, and of Constantine were, comparatively, enormous. The Hellenic cities with their huge buildings and wide and long Broadways were much larger than the Greek cities of the previous period. Fortunes of the millionaires grew enormous. Gigantic choruses and orchestras, with much more complicated and numerous instruments developed. Theatrical plays involved hundreds of actors, animals, and accessories. Schools, colleges, learned and artistic societies, unions, and associations developed, each one huger than the last. Sciences and arts were now cultivated on a large scale. Mass education in arts and sciences, philosophy, and technology became established. A most widely spread school system was introduced. Mass preoccupation with politics became the rule. Mass growth—of unions, of men's and women's clubs with mass aesthetic connoisseurism; of mass amateurish philosophy; of mass theater and dramas; of mass religious revivals; of mass production of all kinds of cultural values—spread on a large scale. The size of the empire grew to pathological proportions. Quantity and show became the criteria of quality. The disease of external hugeness and of quantitative colossalism permeated the Hellenic and post-Hellenic Roman cultures.

In spite of its size, this late period could not, from a purely creative standpoint, rival at all the magnificent achievements of the earlier period. The quantitative colossalism was but a substitute for inability to create the great qualitative values. It was the line of least resistance accessible to any mediocrity. "Not being able to make them beautiful, they made them rich"—we can repeat what Pliny says about the huge theaters of his time. The more the creative quality deteriorated, the huger became the values produced. The less inner substance they had, the more showy they were. The more vulgar they were, the more successful best-sellers they became. The bigger the temples became, the more hollow was the religion. The more generally mass education spread, the less genius appeared. The larger the empires grew, the more disorganized they turned out to be and the harder the lot of the citizens became. The larger the crowd of philosophers, the fewer great philosophers emerged. Erudition replaced creative genius; technique, inspiration; mechanical skill, creative originality.

Our sensate culture of today appears to be exactly in the same position. External glitter and quantitative colossalism already reign supreme in it. "The bigger the better" is its motto: hence our enormous skyscrapers, monuments, temples, school and college buildings, railroad stations, up to the monsters of Radio City and World's Fairs. Quantitative colossalism tends to become the criterion of any great value. The best business firms are those which are hugest. The society leaders are those who are richest. The greatest empires are those which are most monstrous. The largest theaters become the best. The best show is that which attracts most people. So also the best preachers, teachers, orators, professors, ministers, and what not. The greatest scholar is he who is paid the highest salary or has the largest audience. The greatest university is that which is largest. The masterpieces of literature or art, philosophy or science, religion or politics are the best sellers bought by millions. "The biggest firm," "the largest circulation," "the biggest market of second-hand tires in the world" is our highest recommendation. Anything which is not big quantitatively, but is merely the finest in quality, tends to pass unnoticed. The very standards of fine and vulgar, good and bad, masterful and clumsy, beautiful and ugly, right and wrong, wise and smart, tend to disappear as qualitative standards and tend to be replaced by quantitative criteria. Even in science "quantitative standards" drive out thought, inspiration, intuition, and deep qualitative analysis. Pliny's "Not being able to make our values beautiful, we make them huge," is as applicable to our culture as to the sensate culture of Rome. Now, as then, the quality of the values tends to be in inverse proportion to their quantitative colossalism and external glitter. Our Radio Cities are enormous; and yet, the music and art forthcoming from these are vulgar or mediocre. Our school buildings and equipment are excellent, and the enrollment as well as the number of such institutions are enormous. And yet, in spite of all the growth of universal education, hardly any genius of the first dimension has been hatched by them. Quantitative expansion has resulted mainly in the appearance of the yellow press, a vulgar pseudo-science, and a still more vulgar "trained incapacity" in all fields of culture. Our temples are magnificent in their comfort and dimensions, but a new St. Paul would probably find them devoid of the Holy Spirit of a great living religion. More and more of us somehow feel a growing hollowness in contemporary culture. All its gigantic colossalism and dazzling glitter increasingly appear to be a rouge with which it tries to cover its inner emptiness and its decayed charms. The older it becomes and the more its beauty fades, the more rouge, more glitter, more show, and more colossalism it uses.

Shall we wonder that the results of all this quantity without quality are similar to those of the Hellenic and Roman cultures at the period of their quantitative colossalism, namely, a progressive decline of the constructive creativeness of our sensate culture and a rise of its destructive forces together with the cultural domination of mass mediocrity? This question leads us to the fourth symptom of disintegration.

## 4. DECLINE OF CREATIVENESS OF OUR OVERRIPE SENSATE CULTURE

If our culture becomes more and more torn by inner contradictions; if its soul is split and divided against itself;

if it loses more and more its identity and uniformity; if it ceases to be loyal to itself; if it begins to doubt its primogeniture; if its selective rigor and digestive power diminish; if it turns more and more into a mere dumping place; if the disease of quantitative colossalism increasingly eats away the vitals of its creative genius, what except a decline of its creativeness can be expected? To the same result it is driven by other consequences of its own nature, especially by the increasing explosion of its destructive forces that make constructive creativeness impossible, and by the feverish tempo of its accelerated change that excludes a creation of lasting values: yesterday's values are obsolete today; and today's values will be obsolete tomorrow. Who cares for, and who can create anything perennial in this inconstant Niagara of change? By virtue of this feverish change, our culture devours its own creations as soon as they emerge. Today it builds enormous buildings from steel and concrete; tomorrow it tears them down. Today it erects a temple to some new-fangled god—in science and philosophy, in religion and fine arts, and in any of its compartments. Tomorrow it will demolish the edifice in order to make a place for some newer-fashioned god that will undergo the same fate. Today it strenuously accumulates wealth; tomorrow it turns the accumulation into smoke. Today it introduces all kinds of safeguards of life, of health, of property, of everything; tomorrow it scraps them without compunction. In this sense our culture is a new Cronus incessantly devouring his own children. Hardly anything perennial can be created, and nothing can survive this perennial destruction. For these and other reasons a decline of creativeness, especially of great and perennial values, must be expected in the present phase of our sensate culture. And indeed the decline has increasingly taken place, especially since the middle of the nineteenth century.

In its whole process of reemergence and growth our sensate culture, by its very nature, was bound to be uncreative in certain fields of culture and creative in others. For instance, by its very nature it could not be greatly creative in the fields of religion, ethics, and to some extent metaphysics. It could be expected to be creative in the sensate fields like business, science, and technology. The following summary gives a more detailed picture, showing in which fields sensate culture has been creative and in which it has not. To ascertain this, all the persons mentioned in the *Encyclopedia Britannica* were classified according to the field of activity through which they became historically famous. Then the geometric average of the number of the persons and lines devoted to them was computed for all the persons in a specified activity for a given half-century. These absolute figures were turned into percentages, with all ten fields together totaling 100 per cent. Increase and decrease of the percentage for each specified field from period to period may serve as a rough measure of the comparative increase and decrease of the creativeness in these fields. The reason is that out of millions of human beings, few become historical; such historical persons must have done something that represented extraordinary, new, and, in this sense, creative activity. Here are the summary data for the last few centuries:

| Period | Religion | States- manship | Litera- ture | Social Sciences and Humanities | Science | Philosophy | Business | Miscel- laneous | Fine Arts | Music | Total 100% |
|---|---|---|---|---|---|---|---|---|---|---|---|
| 800– 849 | 46.0 | 36.7 | 2.8 | 14.5 | 8.9 | 16.6 | | | | | 100 |
| 850– 899 | 45.7 | 28.3 | | 45.0 | 1.8 | 5.4 | | | | 1.1 | 100 |
| 900– 949 | 44.3 | 29.8 | 4.3 | 8.6 | | 2.6 | | | | 4.4 | 100 |
| 950– 999 | 26.2 | 41.2 | 21.3 | 8.7 | | | | 1.4 | | | 100 |
| 1000–1049 | 33.0 | 45.1 | 4.7 | 3.1 | 10.3 | 5.8 | | | | 3.8 | 100 |
| 1050–1099 | 39.8 | 43.2 | 4.7 | 5.2 | 1.3 | 6.6 | | | | | 100 |
| 1100–1149 | 34.1 | 29.6 | 4.5 | 24.5 | | | 0.7 | | | | 100 |
| 1150–1199 | 38.1 | 31.1 | 11.0 | 9.3 | | 9.7 | | 0.8 | | | 100 |
| 1200–1249 | 28.7 | 40.9 | 8.7 | 13.1 | 3.9 | 1.9 | | 1.8 | 1.0 | | 100 |
| 1250–1299 | 28.9 | 34.3 | 8.8 | 11.9 | 2.4 | 4.0 | 3.1 | | 6.6 | | 100 |
| 1300–1349 | 18.5 | 31.0 | 18.4 | 9.0 | 1.5 | 5.8 | 2.5 | | 13.3 | | 100 |
| 1350–1399 | 30.1 | 29.8 | 21.9 | 5.0 | 2.3 | 4.5 | 4.5 | 0.8 | 5.6 | | 100 |
| 1400–1449 | 20.7 | 28.5 | 7.2 | 11.6 | 0.6 | 4.3 | 5.1 | 1.8 | 20.2 | | 100 |
| 1450–1499 | 14.8 | 25.2 | 7.7 | 13.6 | 0.8 | 0.5 | 6.4 | 1.9 | 28.3 | | 100 |
| 1500–1549 | 26.0 | 16.3 | 13.2 | 7.1 | 3.1 | 2.1 | 2.6 | 3.7 | 25.6 | 0.8 | 100 |
| 1550–1599 | 18.7 | 23.4 | 23.4 | 10.7 | 5.6 | 1.5 | 2.1 | 4.5 | 7.8 | 0.3 | 100 |
| 1600–1649 | 12.0 | 21.8 | 19.4 | 10.3 | 6.9 | 7.6 | 1.7 | 3.3 | 16.1 | 2.3 | 100 |
| 1650–1699 | 18.8 | 22.2 | 19.7 | 8.1 | 8.9 | 6.4 | 1.4 | 1.2 | 11.7 | 0.9 | 100 |
| 1700–1749 | 15.0 | 18.6 | 20.0 | 12.4 | 10.7 | 7.6 | 1.8 | 4.3 | 5.9 | 1.6 | 100 |
| 1750–1799 | 5.2 | 26.8 | 19.1 | 11.4 | 15.1 | 4.6 | 3.1 | 4.5 | 6.8 | 3.5 | 100 |
| 1800–1849 | 6.5 | 22.2 | 19.1 | 14.0 | 14.1 | 3.7 | 4.8 | 3.6 | 9.2 | 3.4 | 100 |

A glance at the figures shows that while in the Middle Ages creativeness in religion occupied about 30 to 46 per cent of the creativeness in all fields of culture, in the eighteenth and the nineteenth centuries the percentage fell to a mere 5 and 6 per cent of the whole. If the data were continued up to the present time, this per cent would probably be still lower than 5 and 6 per cent. On the other hand creativeness in science was, with the exception of one or two half-centuries, very low throughout the medieval centuries—from zero to 1 or 2 or 3 per cent of all the ten fields; in the period from 1650 to 1849 it increased to 15 and 14 per cent, and still more for the period from 1849 to the present time. While business had no single historical person throughout the medieval centuries up to 1100-1149, it had 3 and 4 per cent of all the historical persons for the period 1750-1849. A comparative decrease of the percentages for philosophy from 1750 on is also noticeable. The other fields give, as might be expected, checkered and indefinite pictures. (*Dynamics*, Vol. IV, chap. 7)

These figures give a rough idea in which fields sensate culture was fertile and in which it was not. The results are indeed corroborated by the actual study of the achievements of sensate culture in the main fields of culture. They may be summed up as follows:

The contributions of sensate culture have been mediocre in the fields of religion, ethics, and to some extent in metaphysics. It created no great new religion. It only diluted the great medieval Christianity. Its attempts to create its own religion yielded either a spiritless distortion or an atrocious mutilation of Christianity, producing the religious monstrosities of hundreds of different sects, each one more bizarre than the last. It created also many gospels of positivist and "scientific" religions, each representing an ugly hybrid of distorted science as well as of twisted religion. Finally, it gave us several varieties of atheism and of the creed of hatred, all devoid of originality and of valuable social blessings. In the balance sheet of history these religious contributions of sensate culture are either worthless or harmful.

The same is true of the *theological* contribution of our sensate culture. Any real creativeness in this field was achieved in the early and medieval centuries of Christianity. The creativeness ended with the great scholastics of the thirteenth, fourteenth, and fifteenth centuries. The enormous legion of the theologians of the subsequent centuries represented mainly the repeaters, imitators, eruditionists, political pamphleteers, and the like, with hardly any great theologian among them.

Not much better is the record of the sensate centuries of our culture in the field of *ethical and juridical creativeness*. Nothing even remotely similar to the magnificent grandeur of Christian ethics was produced by it. If anything, the ethical theories of the sensate centuries have succeeded only in the debasement, distortion, and vulgar dilution of the sublimest ethical system—Christianity. The sensate ethics of utilitarianism, hedonism, and eudaemonism, not to mention the eclectic hash of various moral teachings, were neither original creations nor even good reproductions of the ancient originals from which they were copied. The eudaemonism of Plato and Aristotle was not bettered by the eudaemonistic theories of Western ethical thinkers of the sensate centuries. The same is true of the hedonistic and utilitarian ethics of the West compared with similar ethical systems of the Chinese or the Hindus, or especially of the Greek and Roman Epicureans and utilitarianists, from Mo-Ti up to Epicurus and Lucian.

More than that, if the ethical system of Christianity had not continued to linger during these sensate centuries, the disastrous results of our sensate ethics would probably have occurred much earlier than they occurred in fact, and their destructive effect would probably have been more terrible than it has been up to the present day. Without the background of an absolute system of ethics, the purely relative ethics of utilitarianism and hedonism go to pieces much more quickly and lead to moral anarchy faster than when they have such a background.

In the field of *law* the situation has been similar. Without the *Corpus Juris Civilis* codified in the ideational period of Byzantine culture, and without the guiding principles of medieval ethics that controlled the formation of the common law, even our law codes would be something very different from what they are. At any rate, they can hardly claim any superiority over either Roman Law or medieval-secular and canon law. After all, the sensate codes of law are built upon these foundations and represent a mere variation of these: more detailed but not always better—often definitely poorer. The same is true of the theory of jurisprudence.

Likewise, by its very nature sensate culture could not create in any field of culture ideational and idealistic cultural values. What it could do and did, indeed, splendidly was to create the unique world of sensate values—first of all and most of all in the field of the natural sciences and technology. Here its discovery-creativeness has been super-brilliant and unique in the history of mankind. It is the main pride and the main contribution of the sensate centuries of our culture. Then comes the field of philosophy, where something important in the field of empiricism, criticism, and scepticism was created. But, though important, the philosophic contribution of the sensate centuries was more modest than in the field of science and technology. After all, even the greatest philosophical systems of the centuries from the fifteenth to the twentieth were but mainly footnotes to the philosophy of Plato, Aristotle, Saint Augustine, Erigena, and Saint Thomas Aquinas. Without Zeno and Heraclitus, Plato and Aristotle, Erigena and Occam, Saint Augustine and Thomas Aquinas, there hardly would be Kant and Hegel, Hume and Schopenhauer, to mention but the few important philosophers.

Great were the contributions of sensate culture in the field of the fine arts: in music and architecture, literature and painting, sculpture and drama. But even there, postmedieval architecture was mainly imitative: it did not create any new style; it gave an imitation of the old styles from the style of Phidias and Hellenic pseudo-classicism up to the imitative Romanesque and Gothic. What it attempted to create itself resulted in either baroque and rococo or the eclectic and disjointed stylelessness of the Victorian age. Only now the architecture of reinforced concrete is, perhaps, entering an original and new creative period. But even this fact is uncertain. The contributions of the sensate era were greater in painting, music, literature, drama, and sculpture. But even there its greatest contributions were but variations of what Greek and European idealistic centuries had created and passed on.

There remain, of course, the great creations of huge

business empires, political empires, and other similar empires, with their burdens and benefits for the people. Here the improvement of the material well-being of the masses was great and was mainly due to science and technology.

All in all, in the sensate fields of science, technology, and material well-being, and less in humanities, fine arts, philosophy, and law, the contributions of the sensate period of our culture were magnificent and great indeed. It need not apologize for those creations to any culture or to any period.

However, when we ask, "What is the situation in all these respects in the overripe phase of our sensate culture," the answer changes. Generally speaking, beginning with the second half of the nineteenth century, it began to show an increasing creative fatigue, in some fields more, in others less, but more or less in all fields, except perhaps in science and technology. But even there, as we have seen, we have a progressively slower rate of increase of discoveries and inventions.

If the reader surveys in his imagination each important field of our culture, and if he notes when the greatest creators in this field lived, he will see that in most of the fields the age of the *sensate* creative giants was before the second half of the nineteenth century. After that time we passed into the age of the "notable and eminent," then the "distinguished," and finally into "the age of midgets," instead of into that of the giants.

In *music* the summit was reached in the age of Bach and Beethoven. After these there have been great composers, but none of the stature of Palestrina, Mozart, Bach, and Beethoven. In the nineteenth century we had many a great composer, from Wagner, Brahms and Tschaikowsky to Debussy. In the twentieth century we have none of even the stature of the great composers of the nineteenth century. Progressive diminution of the creators of music can hardly be doubted.

In *literature* Dante, Shakespeare, and somewhat similar great giants of European literature appeared in the early centuries of the sensate period. The subsequent centuries from the seventeenth to the nineteenth yielded great writers, but none of the stature of Shakespeare or Dante. The nineteenth century still produced a large crop of great writers: Tolstoy and Dostoevski, Dickens and Byron, Goethe and Schiller, Chateaubriand and Balzac, and the like. The twentieth century has not yielded any figure equal to the giants of even the nineteenth century. All the Nobel prize winners are midgets compared with their predecessors. Instead we now have "best-sellers," sold in millions today and forgotten tomorrow.

So also in *theater and drama*. The twentieth century gave us mainly the theater of pathology and sex and obscenity and human wretchedness. Science gave us the movies, but Hollywood turned them into the most vulgar displays. Like our detective and mystery stories, the shows are all right for relaxation and momentary thrill, but nobody as yet has made of thrillers great classics, or of shows a great art.

Not different is the situation in *painting and sculpture*. After the great masters of the Renaissance and of the seventeenth and eighteenth centuries—Raphael, Leonardo, Michelangelo, Dürer, Rembrandt, and the like—nothing greater has been created in these fields. The nineteenth century yielded its own great masters, but they were in no way greater or as great as these giants. The twentieth century has not yielded any who can be put on the level with the masters of preceding centuries. We have a legion of skillful imitators of all styles from the archaic to the classic, from the romantic to the cubist. We appear to be able to use any technique of any master, but that ability is about all we have. We are in exactly the same position as were the Hellenic and late Roman imitators and technicians. In addition, something of the real skill in some of the paintings, particularly in the portraiture, seems to have been lost: most of the portraits of the twentieth century are clumsy in comparison with those of preceding centuries. Here again we regressed rather than progressed.

In the field of philosophy, even the nineteenth century did not yield as great masters as the preceding centuries of the sensate era. With Descartes and Spinoza, Berkley and Locke, Kant and Hume, Leibnitz and Hobbes, the pinnacle of philosophy of these centuries was reached. The nineteenth century gave us Hegel and Schelling, Schopenhauer and Comte, Spencer and Nietzsche, but none of these is bigger than, or even of the same caliber as, the philosophers of the centuries before. And all the philosophers of the sensate era are in no way bigger than Saint Thomas Aquinas or the other great scholastics. Finally, the twentieth century has been, so far, the age of the midget philosophers. None of them reaches even the caliber of the greatest philosophers of the nineteenth century.

Not different is the situation in the field of the *humanistic and social science disciplines*. Here the twentieth century has not yielded any figure equal to the masters of even the nineteenth century. Here we repeat and re-repeat mainly Montesquieux and Rousseaus, De Maistres and Hegels, Comtes and Spencers, Marxes and Taines, Mommsens and F. de Coulanges, Gibbonses and Ricardos, and other leaders of social science of the preceding centuries. We have accumulated an enormous mass of mainly irrelevant and fruitless facts. These facts have not yielded to us any great new theory, or important hypotheses or particularly fruitful conclusions. At the present time they are a liability rather than an asset, because we are lost in the facts and do not know which of these are reliable and which not; in addition, they hinder our vision and perspective.

*Psychology and anthropology* of the twentieth century are, again, either a mere accumulation of so-called facts or, even worse, a definite decline so far as real insight into the respective phenomena is concerned. In all the advertised conclusions of cultural anthropology there is none that was not formulated before, in the eighteenth and the nineteenth centuries, and formulated better and more adequately than in the twentieth century. Psychology of the twentieth century is but a substitution of physiology and anatomy of the nervous system for psychology as a science of the human soul, consciousness, and mental life. Most of the treatises of psychology end where real psychology has to begin: anatomy and physiology of the nervous system is not psychology but biology. The efforts to advance psychology as such have given us but a series of rapidly coming and going fads like behaviorism, gestaltism, mental tests, field-theory, and the like. They emerge, live a day, and are gone as failures.

There remain, then, only the natural sciences, the technological inventions, and, finally, the organization of the material well-being of our society. As to the natural sciences and technology, the situation here is certainly better than in any other field of our culture. They have been the backbone of it—its main achievement and source of creativeness. But even there, the greatest giants—Galileo and Kepler, Newton and Leibnitz, Mayer and Copernicus, Bacon and Boyle, D'Alambert and Harvey, Lamarque and Darwin, Lavoisier and Laplace, Pasteur, and the like—were concentrated mainly in past centuries, not in the present. The twentieth century has given us hardly any scientists who can rival the greatest masters of preceding centuries; if it has, their number is reduced to one or two, and, even so, a further test of time is necessary to assure the reality of their greatness.

As to the material well-being of our society, we have seen that the twentieth century is an insane destroyer of the well-being created by the previous centuries of the sensate era, but not its creator or promoter. Like a profligate son, it has squandered and turned into ruins what its forefathers created and accumulated.

In Chapter III it was indicated that the rate of increase of scientific discoveries and inventions in the present century has definitely slowed down and that even the absolute number of the discoveries and inventions in the present century, especially in the period from 1914 to 1919, decreased. It was also indicated that the period of the greatest discoveries in most of the natural sciences is either in the eighteenth or in the middle of the nineteenth century, but not in the present century, with the exception of perhaps two or three fields of the natural sciences.

Here, as in other fields, the mass work of mediocre scientists still keep science and invention on a fairly high level. But there is no ground to claim that the scientific and technological contributions of the present century are greater than those of preceding centuries of the sensate era. Meanwhile, in a creative field, he who does not progress slides down.

Moreover, there are one or two symptoms that make a stagnant or even a regressive trend in the natural sciences still more probable. The first of these symptoms is the increasing use of scientific and technological achievements for a purely destructive purpose. As mentioned before, bombs, bombers, poisonous gas, cannon and machine guns, incendiary devices, and other instrumentalities of destruction have been invented, after all, by the same science and technology. Science and technology of the twentieth century have increasingly been concentrating upon this kind of achievement, and now are busy mainly with discovery and invention of the most destructive means. The results are before our eyes. Being morally and socially indifferent, science and technology succeeded well in this purpose. In twenty-four hours, cities with hundreds of thousands of population are wiped out, and with them the scientific and technological laboratories and scientists themselves as the victims of their own inventions. We observe how in the course of a few months or years a whole country is laid in ruins, with thousands killed and wounded, with countless buildings, from cathedrals to universities, from museums to banks, turned into a huge mass of debris. We witness how these means of destruction in a few hours leave shambles out of what was created by the efforts of generations. These catastrophes make less and less possible a continuation of scientific and technological research itself; they destroy increasingly all the means of such research, all the conditions necessary for it, and a larger and larger portion of the existing and would-be scientists and inventors. This situation means that the children of science and technology are progressively turning into patricides, assaulting and suffocating science and technology themselves. Such an ugly turn of events does not presage well for their further development under these increasingly destructive conditions.

If science and technology remain morally and socially indifferent, serving with the same equanimity the God of Creation and the Mammon of Destruction, they will be ruined eventually: no successful continuation of scientific and technological work is possible under such conditions. If they cease to be morally and socially indifferent, they will have to stop being what they are; they will be obliged to recognize some universal—and in this sense absolute—norms and values. Such a recognition means a step far beyond sensate culture into the realm of ideational or idealistic culture. It would mean the end of the sensate era and the beginning of a new creative era different from the sensate. Such are the alternatives put before science and technology. They have to choose. The first choice leads to their stagnation and regression amidst the ruins created with the help of their own inventions and discoveries. The second choice means a step towards ideational or idealistic culture. All this signifies that the creative forces of sensate culture have begun to ebb generally, and are bound to ebb even in the field of science and invention, so long as this culture remains dominant.

The totality of the evidences and considerations given, brief though they are, hardly leaves any serious doubt that decline has begun in the creative forces of sensate culture in practically all the fields of that culture and its social life. (*Dynamics*, Vol. IV, chap. 7)

Sensate Western culture and society are given a categoric ultimatum: either persist on the road of overripe sensate culture and go to ruin, to a life uncreative, devoid of any genius, painful, and inglorious; or shift, while there is still a possibility of doing so, to another road of ideational or idealistic culture. In the same dilemma, the ideational and idealistic culture of the Middle Ages, when it became exhausted of its God-given creativeness, shifted then to the road of sensate culture, with the result that Western society continued magnificently its creative mission for five centuries. At the present time this road has brought it to a blind alley of exhaustion of the sensate creative forces. The salvation again lies in a shift to another form of culture.

The sensate phase wrote truly the most magnificent page in the whole history of mankind and culture. In this sense it discharged its greatest mission faithfully and fruitfully. Now it is tired and exhausted. It deserves a rest. It should hand on the torch of creativeness to other forms of culture. While it is resting, the ideational and idealistic cultures will carry on the great creative mission of mankind. When these in their turn are tired, then the rested sensate culture will again arise and will take the torch from the tired grasp of the fatigued cultures. And so the creative mission of mankind will go on and on to the end—if there is an end.

# CHAPTER VIII

# THE PRESENT PHASE OF AMERICAN CULTURE

## I. SIMILARITY OF EUROPEAN AND AMERICAN SOCIAL TRENDS

The preceding analysis shows that the magnificent sensate culture of our historical yesterday displays today all the signs of creative exhaustion and a mania for self-destruction.

For Europe all this already is a tragical fact. For America, which has not as yet been roughly touched by the chilling hands of the great tragedy, such a diagnosis may still sound fantastic. Here we still hear, though less and less frequently, the assurances of prosperity finally turning the corner; of the traditional "every boy" having a chance to become the President of the United States; of the marvelous progress in the next few years outdistancing that of several past centuries; of the pending plenitude of peace, happiness, satisfaction, comfort, and other sensate boons to be showered tomorrow upon everyone, from the millionaire to the W.P.A. worker. The whole course of life, the prevailing aspirations, the dominant attitudes and relationship here still run true to the pattern of a streamlined, orderly, peaceful, and prosperous sensate society. It would be strange if, in these fortunate conditions, the above diagnosis did not appear Cassandrian to many. To others it would appear such for their supposedly "scientific reasons." They contend that there is a profound difference between American and European cultures: one is young and vigorous; the other is old and withering. What happens to European culture will not necessarily happen to American culture. Their destinies have been, are, and will be different. Such is the essence of their argument.

Since considerations like the above are seriously set forth and widely accepted, it is advisable to investigate briefly whether European and American cultures are indeed fundamentally different. Have their changes been running along dissimilar lines? Are their destinies going to be unlike? If they are divergent in all these respects, then evidently the above diagnosis of the present state of the Western culture does not concern America. If they are essentially similar, then obviously American culture is also in the twilight stage of its sensate phase.

So far as the secondary characteristics of American and European cultures are concerned, there is no doubt but that they are different in many respects. But in regard to these secondary traits, no less different are the cultures of England and Italy, of France and Germany. Even different regions of the same country have many secondary differences in their culture. Even various social classes and groups of the same region, the same city, or the same town differ from one another in hundreds of cultural traits. The problem concerns not these secondary differences but the essential characteristics of both European and American cultures. When the question is put in that form, the answer is that *in spite of some three or four centuries of geographical separation, there has been for a long time and still is only one culture, the Western or Euro-American culture, identical on both continents in all its essential traits. Being essentially identical, it is of the same age on both continents, not a bit younger in America than in Europe. As such, it changes along similar lines on both continents, and passes in this change through the same main phases and exhibits similar tendencies. So it was during the seventeenth and eighteenth centuries, and has continued to be up to the present time.* Such is my thesis.

In order to demonstrate the validity of this thesis, it is enough to take the main compartments of Euro-American culture and concisely yet accurately to note the essential trends that have unfolded themselves during the last few centuries on both continents. Such a comparison shows that indeed the trends have been identical. In a short formula, both cultures and societies continued to move farther and farther from the ideational culture of the Middle Ages and the idealistic culture of the centuries from the thirteenth to the seventeenth. Both have been steadily becoming more and more sensate—empirical, utilitarian, hedonistic, materialistic, economically minded, divorced from any otherworldliness, denying its reality and value, and rooted entirely in the reality of a sensory world. In the twentieth century both cultures have reached a kind of limit in this shift toward sensate culture and are at the present time in a deep and tragic crisis of transition. Such is the summary of the road traveled by Euro-American culture during the last three hundred years and its present position on this road.

Now let us take several compartments of the culture and see whether the trends have indeed been similar on both continents.

We shall begin with the simplest compartments.

*A.* Externally, on both continents we have had a growth

of urbanization, industrialization, and mechanization, with all the numerous satellites involved.

*B.* On both continents we have had a replacement of manufacture by machinofacture; of small-scale industrial production by large-scale; of animal and man power by steam and electricity.

*C.* In the field of *social relationships* the nineteenth century witnessed on both sides of the Atlantic a decline of familistic and compulsory relationships in all fields of social life in favor of contractual relationships. Since the war period on both continents we observe a decline of contractual relationships in favor of partly compulsory and partly familistic relationships. More specifically:

I. In the *economic* field in the nineteenth century was seen the rise of the capitalistic contractual system on both continents. Coincident with the triumph of the capitalistic system, we had a liquidation of serfdom, slavery, the plantation system, and the patriarchal and coercive systems on both continents. Likewise, other concomitants of capitalism on both continents were free trade, *laissez faire*, economic liberty, economic and social individualism, and a host of other consequences of the triumphant contractualism.

One of these was a rise of the material standard of living on both continents, as well as a development of the trust and corporation economy in the decadent stage of capitalism.

On both continents, as we have seen, the rise of this trust and corporation economy has sounded the death knell to classical capitalism and private property. In Europe as well as in America the corporation economy largely replaced the private property economy; the managerial aristocracy of corporations replaced the private capitalist and proprietor. On both continents the managers do not own the property they manage, and the owners do not manage what they own.

From this standpoint, on both continents the corporation economy turned into a decentralized totalitarianism, while the totalitarianism of either the Communist, Fascist, or Nazi type represents a centralized corporation economy: with one corporation instead of several; with one—Communist, Fascist, or Nazi—board of directors, instead of several; as, for instance, "America's sixty families" which manage most of our corporations.

In many European countries, the totalitarian bureaucracy has finally driven out the corporation bureaucracy. The former finished the destruction of capitalism and of private property begun by the latter, by the corporations and trusts. In a few European countries the corporation bureaucracy still lingers, but increasingly loses ground in favor of governmental bureaucracy. In the United States, the "corporation bureaucracy" still exists, but by the relentless whip of conditions is being more and more driven out by the rising, potentially totalitarian bureaucracy of the "New Deal" and the coming "Liquidation Deal." The expansion of government control and regulation had begun already at the end of the nineteenth century, in the United States as well as in Europe. In the pre-war twentieth century it slowly progressed on both continents; in the war of 1914-18 and after, it made an enormous jump upwards, leading—in Europe—to a liquidation of capitalism and private property in Russia, Germany, Italy, and potentially in other countries; likewise, it made enormous progress in the United States during this period, and especially after 1929. With slight setbacks, the invasion of "private business" and "corporation business" by the governmental bureaucracy is progressively increasing and is going to increase. (*Dynamics*, Vol. III, pp. 196 ff.; also chap. 8) With a slight local variation, this last stage of economic organization has been the same on both sides of the Atlantic, with America lagging somewhat behind Europe but passing over the same course.

II. In the *political* field the growth of contractualism has led to the well-known phenomenon of replacement of the partly patriarchal, partly coercive autocratic regime by the democratic political systems, with the government contractually elected, contractually limited in its power, and contractually obliged to respect the inalienable rights of man and citizen, his liberties, his equalities, and his individualism. As a detail of this process, religious liberty of the individual was established, and with it, all the elements of theocracy were swept away from the governmental systems, in the Northern America as well as in the greater part of Europe. The trends in the nineteenth century were again common to both continents.

III. In the field of *social relationships* the rising contractualism signified a growth of individualism generally. Again, this phenomenon took place on both continents in spite of fairly frequent assertions that American individualism is the product of the frontier and the pioneering spirit.

IV. The post-war period is marked on both continents by a profound crisis of contractualism. This decline of contractualism has shown itself on both continents, first, in the crisis of capitalism; and second, in a decline of the individualistic *Weltanschauung* generally, and in economic life particularly. The wide diffusion of the philosophies of collectivism, communism, socialism, the corporate State, and racial collectivity is but another aspect of this crisis of individualism. This decline of contractualism has become apparent in an expansion of governmental control and regimentation on both continents. In different forms and in different degrees this expansion has occurred in Europe as well as in the United States. Hundreds of economic, social, and other relationships that in the contractual nineteenth century were left to the decision of the individual, or private groups, are now compulsorily regulated by the government. To a lesser degree than in Europe this expansion has also taken place in this country, especially in the field of economic relationships. The free *entrepreneur* of the nineteenth century has been more and more replaced by the corporation bureaucracy, and this, in its turn, by the governmental bureaucracy. The government has been more and more entering business directly; it has been more and more regimenting business indirectly; and it has been imposing an ever-increasing number of obligatory regulations upon the employer and employees, and upon every other agent of the economic process. Viewed in this light, the fact of expansion of governmental regulation, as well as the fact of the crisis of contractualism on both continents, is unquestionable. The degree and the concrete forms of these processes differ from country to country, even in Europe, but the process itself has again been Euro-American.

I have mentioned only economic and political relationships, but I could equally well have mentioned the change in the *family*, in the *unions and associations of various kinds*. It suffices to say that their "evolution" during the period considered has been similar on both continents, even in such details as the increase of divorce and instability of the family, increase of childless marriages, and so on.

D. This leads us to the field of *vital processes and the movements of the population*. Here again the main processes have run identically: on both continents we have had an extraordinary natural increase of the population in the nineteenth century, due mainly to the falling death rate; an increase of suicide; and, beginning with the end of the nineteenth century, a falling birth rate which has made the present population of Euro-America virtually stationary or even decreasing in some countries.

E. Finally, on both continents we have had an increase of *social mobility*—vertical and horizontal—during this period. Hereditary aristocracy has been practically abolished. In its place we have had a rise to power of the rich capitalistic bougeoisie, and of the middle class, with its intelligentsia and professional groups—lawyers, engineers, professors, writers, and the like. More recently, in both societies we have had an increasing effort of the laboring classes to obtain a larger share of the power and societal income and to drive out the rich and the middle class from the dominant influential position in the political, economic, and social life of the country. On both continents, the United States somewhat lagging, class cleavages and class struggle increased during the nineteenth century. In totalitarian Europe of the present time these are temporarily suppressed by governmental regimentation of everybody. In nontotalitarian Europe and in America the chasm between, and struggle of, the social classes continue to progress. In the United States the class struggle began to grow especially after 1929, with all the satellites of class antagonism and the emergence of class organizations like the C.I.O. and others.

Not to mention many other trends in the social life, the foregoing shows indeed that aside from the secondary differences from country to country, the main social processes have been similar in Europe and in the United States.

## 2. SIMILARITY OF EUROPEAN AND AMERICAN CULTURAL TRENDS

Turn now to the changes in culture—meaning by that, science, art, philosophy, religion, law, ethics, mores, modes of conduct, and the whole mentality that lies behind these cultural systems. Here again the trends have been even more similar than in the foregoing social processes. Their general nature has followed the same trend, the Euro-American culture becoming less and less ideational and more and more sensate.

*A.* On both continents we have witnessed the rise of *science*, manifested in an enormous increase of scientific discoveries and technological inventions during the period considered. The only difference is that the comparative share of the United States in all the natural science discoveries and technological inventions has been systematically growing from 1.1 per cent of the total in 1726-1750, to 25.3 per cent in 1900-8, and probably to a still larger per cent at the present time, while respectively the rôle of Europe has been decreasing. (*Dynamics*, Vol. II, chap. 3)

On both continents the universities, research institutions, and schools generally have been rapidly increasing, again faster in the United States than in Europe. But these are secondary differences. The main point is that Europe and America have both been progressing in science and technology; both have elevated science to the level of religion, and have seen in it the main hope for the future.

*B.* Parallel with this growth of science, a profound but similar transformation has taken place in the *field of the system of truth and philosophy*. The truth of faith—the divinely revealed truth of religion—has been rapidly declining, and the empirical truth of senses, based on the testimony of our sense organs, has been rising. Science is mainly an embodiment of the truth of senses, while a superrational religion, like medieval Christianity, is mainly a system of truth of faith. The growth of science involved this process of change from one system of truth to another, and it ran parallel on both sides of the Atlantic. In its more detailed forms this fundamental trend manifested itself in several narrower and more specific processes.

I. On both continents there was a decline of religious rationalism, mysticism, and fideism in favor of empiricism in its many varieties: empiricism, empirico-criticism, positivism, neo-positivism, logical positivism, realism, neo-realism, pragmatism, instrumentalism, "operationalism," and the like. This decline of religious rationalism and mysticism also partly favored the growth of criticism, agnosticism, and scepticism.

II. On both continents there was a decline of idealism in favor of materialism in its open or milder form, and in favor of monism or pantheism.

For Europe the trends are rather certain and are demonstrated in detail in my *Dynamics*. Have they also taken place in the United States? The history of American thought and philosophy answers the question positively.

American philosophy of the seventeenth and part of the eighteenth centuries was an embodiment mainly of truth of faith, whether in its Calvinistic branches (John Cotton, the two Mathers, the Boston Platform of 1680, and so on) or in its mystical and idealistic currents, embodied in such persons as Mistress Anne Hutchinson, Roger Williams, Jonathan Edwards, John Woolman, William Penn, Conrad Beissel, Thomas Hooker, John Eliot, and others.

In the eighteenth century this truth of faith begins to decline. Calvinism begins to lose its grasp, and so do other varieties of the truth of faith. Their place begins to be taken more and more by Armenianism and Methodism, and then by Deism, by the beginning of free thought, and by materialism (Joseph Priestly and others). Deism in its destructive form has not much of the truth of faith and a great deal of the truth of senses. Free thought and materialism are openly inimical to faith and try to embody the truth of senses only. Benjamin Franklin, Thomas Jefferson, Thomas Paine, Joseph Priestly, and others mark this period. In the nineteenth century this trend towards empiricism, materialism, and truth of senses becomes the main current and brings us to the present time, when the systems embodying truth of faith are almost absent in the philosophical systems, and empiricism, pragmatism, instrumentalism, logical positivism, neo-realism, "operationalism," and the like dominate the scene.

This does not mean that here or in Europe the idealistic and even religiously rationalistic and mystical systems of philosophy entirely disappeared. They certainly have continued to exist on both continents, but as ever smaller currents. The main current of philosophical thought has been as indicated above, and it has been going on in both societies.

If we pay attention to more detailed phases and currents of philosophical thought during this period, the result is still more instructive: any important current of philosophical thought of one of the societies has almost invariably been echoed by the other. In Europe we have had a rise of Kantian and Neo-Kantian criticism: we have had it here, also. In Europe, Hegelianism had its great day. America responded to it with the St. Louis School of Philosophy (William T. Harris and others). In Europe, there was a period of Comtian and Spencerian positivism and then Darwinian-Spencerian evolutionary philosophy. We had it here also; and John Fiske, J. Mark Baldwin, and Lester Ward are its apostles. Beginning with the end of the eighteenth century, Europe entered the religion of perfectionism and progress, with Turgot, Condorcet, St. Simon, Comte, Spencer, Lessing, Herder, and the English Deists as its prophets. America reciprocated with the emergence of Unitarianism, perfectionism, and so-called transcendentalism, not to mention the legion of other devotees of progress. Europe developed the "return to nature," romanticism, and romantic individualism of various types (Rousseau, Carlyle, Stirner, and later Nietzsche and Tolstoi, to mention but a few names). America echoed it with so-called transcendentalism, with Emerson and Thoreau as the main leaders, and with the back-to-nature movement, with Poe, Walt Whitman, and H. Melville as representatives of its various aspects.

The end of the nineteenth and the beginning of the

twentieth centuries has been in Europe the age of domination of empiricism and critical positivism in their various forms (E. Mach, R. Avenarius, A. Rey, H. Poincaré, P. Duhem, K. Pearson, Vaihinger, Riehl, Cohen, Rickert, Windebrandt, and others). America paralleled it with American empiricism, criticism, pragmatism, instrumentalism, "operationalism," neo-realism, and similar philosophies (Charles S. Pierce, William James, Santayana, John Dewey, Perry, Whitehead, P. Lewis, Lovejoy, and others).

In brief, the character of the philosophical currents and the main trends of philosophical thought has been quite similar in both societies.

C. If we pass now to *art*, in all its fields the trends have again been similar in both societies.

I. In *architecture* the main styles of America, namely the Colonial (the Medieval-Colonial; the Renaissance or Georgian Colonial; the Pennsylvania Dutch; the German, the French, and the Spanish Colonial), then the early republican and the romantic revival (Gothic and Romanesque)—around 1830—were but a reproduction of the respective styles of Europe, and ran practically parallel in Europe and the United States. Then on both continents came the era of the eclectic architecture, followed at the end of the nineteenth century by an emergence, under American leadership, of the steel and reinforced architecture as a great new step in the development of this art. From America it has spread over Europe. Finally, so-called modernist architecture appeared also on both continents. In a word, the dynamics of architecture have been quite similar on both continents.

II. This similarity of trend is still more true of *painting and sculpture.* American painting emerged at a period when the European painting had become definitely visual (sensate), striving to depict the objects as they look to our eyes (instead of an ideational or symbolic painting where the picture is only a visible symbol of the invisible world, as it was in the Middle Ages). Correspondingly, its characteristics and phases of development have been, even including details, practically the same as that of European painting and sculpture. It could not be otherwise, since most of the artists of the colonial periods, all the "limners," were foreign-born, and since a great part of the artists of the nineteenth century were also born in Europe (Ingham, Thomas Sully, Thomas Cole, A. Bierstadt, Thomas Hill, Keithe, Leutze, John G. Brown, John S. Sargent, and others). Others, like James Whistler, spent their childhood and most of their life in Europe; and still others—almost all the rest—got their entire training or part of it in Europe. With some modification for many of them, one can repeat what is said of John S. Sargent: "An American born in Italy, educated in France, who looks like a German, speaks like an Englishman, and paints like a Spaniard." Under these conditions, to expect that American painting can be different from that of Europe is unreasonable.

Shall we wonder therefore that in most of the histories of American painting (and sculpture) the authors classify their artists under such headings as "The English Influence," "The Düsseldorf Influence," "The Munich School," "Figure-painters of French Training," "The Barbizon School," "The Romantics," "The Impressionists," "The Expressionists," "The Neo-Classicists," "The Realists," "The Modernists," ("Post Impressionists,"

"Cubists," "Contructivists," and so on)? The very classification indicates the similarity of American painting with this or that school in Europe. Indeed, any important current in Europe has found its creative eddy in this country, and the succession of various dominant schools in American painting has run parallel with that in Europe. One may compare Reynolds, Gainsborough, Hogarth, and especially David and West in Europe with Copley, Gilbert Stuart, Trumbull, and Thomas Sully in America; Poussin, Claude, and later Turner, Constable, and others in Europe with a large group of the landscape painters in America (beginning with the "Hudson River School" and ending with the American painters of "Spectacular Scenery": Church, Bierstadt, Moran, Hill and others). Further comparison may be found in the so-called Barbizon School in Europe (Rousseau, Corot, Daubigny, Dupré, Millet, and others) and George Inness and his followers in America; the Romantic reaction to Neo-Classicism of David in Europe (Delacroix, Gericault, and others in France: the Düsseldorf School in Germany) and the similar Romantic wave in America. The subsequent Neo-Neo-Classic reaction to Romanticism in Europe was followed by a similar current in America (W. Chase, Duvenec, Eakins, F. D. Millet, G. Melchers, and others). The rise of Impressionism in Europe was paralleled similarly in America (partly Sargent, Whistler, John Alexander, Ben Foster, Charles Davis, J. Weir, and especially Theodore Robinson, J. Twachtman, Childe Hassam, W. Metcalf, and others). Finally, the rise of Modernism (expressionism, constructivism, cubism, pointillism, Dadaism, and so on) in Europe has been paralleled in America (Bellows, Robert Henri,

G. Luks, Kent, Arthur Davies, Zorach, Demuth and others).

This does not mean that America simply imitated Europe, but it does mean that since Euro-American culture is one and indivisible, it pulsates similarly on both sides of the ocean.

American and European paintings have been of the same species; not only in style but even in their content they have been similar and have undergone identical changes, including details, during the last century. My study of European art shows that the eighteenth and the first half of the nineteenth century were marked by an ascendance of portraits in the total number of paintings of all kinds. The same period was mainly a portrait-painting era in America. The nineteenth and twentieth centuries showed a strong and persistent increase of landscapes and *genre* in the total number of paintings in Europe. The same is true for America. Further, in portraiture, my study shows that in contradistinction to the centuries from the ninth to the seventeenth, when primarily, royalty, aristocracy, and clergy were depicted, the eighteenth, nineteenth and twentieth centuries witnessed in Europe an enormous decline of portraiture of royalty, the aristocracy, and clergy and an enormous increase in the number portrayed of the bourgeoisie, the professionals and intellectuals, and, finally, of the lower classes. If we take the history of American portraiture from this standpoint, we can see that it conforms with that of Europe for the last two centuries: American portraits are mainly of the bourgeoisie, of intellectuals, and of the professional classes, with some sprinkling of the lower classes. While Sargent painted mainly the well-to-do classes, the later painters depict mainly laboring types and the like.

The similarity also holds for the proportion of male and female portraits in Europe and America.

Further, in the *genre* pictures, for the last two centuries, European artists have increasingly painted, first, every-day and common scenes; and then the macabre, negative, exotic, and pathological types and events (street urchin, criminal, prostitute, and so on). In the earlier medieval centuries, art depicted mainly the supersensory kingdom of God and of the saints; or, in the centuries from the thirteenth to the fifteenth, partly ennobling and elevating events and types. A glance at the history of American painting and sculpture is sufficient to show that during the last century it depicted, like contemporary European art, mainly the daily events, the common types of persons, such as "Sand Card," "Blacksmith," "Stag at Sharkey's," "Cozy Corner," "Bathers," "Mountaineer," "Surgical Clinic," "Miners," "Sunday Morning at Mines," "The Skaters," "Lighthouse Keeper," and then increasingly the exotic and pathological types and events, such as "Street Urchin," "Prostitute," and Indians, Hawaiians, Negroes, Mexicans, and so on. Like European art, American art in its topical content has become increasingly a "muck-raking" painting.

Like the contemporary European painting and sculpture, the contemporary American art in this field exhibits similar chaos and styles, similar modernistic efforts, similar "muck-raking" and prosaic mentality in the choice of its topics. In brief, one is hardly distinguishable from the other.

III. So far as there has been a grand American *music*, it again has spoken in the idiom of the European music of the respective period (MacDowell and a few others). Contemporary American music—Gershwin, Copeland, Harris, Hill, Picton, Taylor, Carpenter, and others—is but a variety of the modern European music. On the other hand, jazz, originated in America, has successfully spread over Europe. In their character the music of both continents is almost exclusively secular. Their "heroes"—when, as in opera, there are heroes—are neither godlike, nor great and noble types of human beings, but either a common man or a pathological man, or romantic and exotic personalities: comedians (Petrushka), clowns (Pagliacci), smugglers (Carmen), pregnant women (Gurreliede), brigands (Robert le Diable), crazy persons (The Emperor Jones), and the like. Similar is the situation in drama, which has also become an exhibition of human pathology, as in the plays of O'Neill and many others.

IV. Finally, American *literature*, in form as well as in content, has passed through the same phases of transformation as European literature.

The literature of the seventeenth century was an *alter ego* of English literature, for the simple reason that its representatives (James Smith, William Bradford, John Winthrop, Roger Williams, Anne Bradstreet, Michael Wigglesworth, John Cotton, the two Mathers, Samuel Sewall, and others) were practically all immigrants. Religious works reflected similar currents of Europe; "Histories" and "Travels" and diaries reflected respective Elizabethan or later "Histories" and "Travels" (e.g. R. Hakluyt's *Principal Navigations*, and a large similar literature in other countries, Samuel Pepys' *Diary*, and so on). Likewise, many a literary figure of the eighteenth century, like Thomas Paine, or de Crévecoeur, was also an immigrant, while others, like Benjamin Franklin, spent a great portion of their time abroad. All were influenced by European writers and thinkers like Calvin, John Locke, Wollaston, Shaftsbury, Sir Isaac Newton, Godwin, and others. Therefore, whether it is the historical and narrative literature (W. Bird, de Crévecoeur), or religious (Jonathan Edwards, Woolman, and the Mathers), or political writings (Franklin, Paine, Dickinson, Hamilton), or poetry and satire (Freneau), each form and current was but a modified variety of a similar one in Europe. Poetry and the emerging novel did not present an exception to this rule. Anne Bradstreet's *The Tenth Muse* is a piece of Elizabethan literature; Wigglesworth's *Day of Doom* was only one of a number of similar religious works in verse issued in Europe of the seventeenth century.

Charles Brockden Brown, Washington Irving, James Fenimore Cooper, and their followers were American manifestations of the wave of romanticism represented in Europe in various forms by Rousseau, Goethe, Chateaubriand, and others, and especially of the English literary romanticism embodied in Samuel Richardson, Smollett, Fielding, Mrs. Radcliffe, Horace Walpole, Byron, Mary Wollstonecraft, William Godwin, Wordsworth, and Sir Walter Scott. Edgar Allan Poe finds his counterpart in Europe in Hoffman, in part in Coleridge, and the Gothic novels. To the same romantic stream belongs Herman Melville in the first part of his writings (*Typee*, *Omoo*, and in part in *Mardi*), while Melville, the philosopher of *Moby Dick*, reflects the perennial pessimistic philosophy of immanent evil and man's struggle against it, which about that time and a little earlier and later was articulated in Europe by many: Gogol, Lermontov, Byron, Schelling (second period of his writings), de Maistre, Schopenhauer, Leopardi, Baader, Renan, Goerro, de Bonald, Tolstoi, Balzac, Herzen, Dostoevski, Vigny, F. Alvorado, Richard Wagner, E. v. Hartmann, Nietzsche, Baudelaire, Renouvier, Ibsen, Taine, Nordau, Lombroso, Turgenev, Maupassant, and others. The same can be said of the pessimistic, second period of Mark Twain—Twain of the *Mysterious Stranger*, *What is Man?*, and *Personal Recollections of Joan of Arc*—and of the pessimistic philosophy of Nathaniel Hawthorne and Henry Adams.

When we pass to Emerson, Thoreau, and the Transcendentalists, their idealism, individualism, vague mysticism, optimism, and romanticism appear as but rivulets, with some individual variation, of similar currents of thought in Europe, articulated by a large group of European thinkers and writers. Optimism was the keynote of an enormous amount of believers in endless progress and a prevalence of good over evil: Comte and Spencer; John Stuart Mill and Herbart; Victor Hugo and V. Cousin; Feuerbach and Karl Marx; Hegel and Hegelians; Fichte and Lotze; Fourier and Lammenais; Schleiermacher and Jacobi; Kant and Schiller; Newman and M. de Biran; V. Solovieff and many others. Individualism was represented by Carlyle, Stirner, Proudhon, Duerhing, Bakunin, Tolstoi, Fourier, Kropotkin, E. Reclus, John Stuart Mill, Herbert Spencer, Buckle, de Tocqueville, Michelet, and others. Idealism was to be found in the works of Kant, Hegel, Fichte, Schelling, Renan, Green, Richard Wagner, E. v. Hartmann, Goethe, Carlyle, Baader, Lotze, Zeller, V. Cousin, M. de Biran,

Rosmini, Gioberty, Victor Hugo, Rosenkranz, Newmann, de Maistre, de Bonald, Secretan, and others. Mysticism and intuition were represented by Shelley, Schleiermacher, Mizkiewicz, Wronsky, Schopenhauer, Ruskin, Dostoevski, Gioberti, Hartmann, Wagner, V. Soloviev, Baader, Mathew Arnold, and others. The Concord School was just one of the brilliant varieties of this great pulsation of Euro-American culture.

*The Scarlet Letter, The Marble Faun,* and other symbolic and moral tales of Nathaniel Hawthorne appeared only a little earlier than the main works of Dostoevski and Tolstoi. One cannot fail to see that in the problems treated, in the psychological analysis, in the sense of doom and psycho-social determinism, even in the literary style of Hawthorne and Tolstoi, their works are strikingly congenial. *The Scarlet Letter* and *Anna Karenina, The Marble Faun* and *Crime and Punishment* deal with the same social, moral, and psychological problem, are pervaded with the same tragedy of doom and psycho-social fatalism—in brief, have the same atmosphere and stamina in their essential traits. They are all the same "reflex" or "pulsation" of the indivisible Euro-American culture manifested in its widely divergent regions and through persons who were hardly aware of the existence of one another. Besides Tolstoi and Dostoevski, several other European writers of the period produced works of Hawthorne's type.

As to the later leaders of American literature, Howells and Henry James's "Europeanism" and their apprenticeship and association with many a European writer like Tolstoi, Turgenev, Balzac, Flaubert, Fourier, George Eliot, Dickens, Daudet, and others, is well known and is testified to by themselves. Mark Twain as a humorist stands in a current of a large number of humorous, comic, burlesque, and satirical writers of Europe, which does not prevent him, as well as the others, from being original and individual, as individual writers. Mark Twain the pessimist, as mentioned, reflects similar currents of the European thought of his time. Then comes naturalism in Europe as well as in America. The parallelism of its development, with all its specific characteristics, on both sides of the Atlantic needs no proof. The literature of the twentieth century in America, with its diversity and chaos, as well as with its specific traits, is very similar in mentality, in form, and in style to the European literature of that century. Again, all this does not mean that America only imitated Europe, but that the indivisible Euro-American culture has pulsated similarly on both continents.

If we note some of the inner trends of the literature on both continents, they are found to be developing also along the same lines.

As we move from the Middle Ages in Europe toward more recent centuries, especially the nineteenth and twentieth, the literature becomes more and more secular and less and less religious in its topics. So does the American literature. In both, the ascetico-religious aspirations and ideals appear less and less often. Both become more and more centered around love and romance, and in the last few decades, mainly around sexual love. Both, in addition, begin to concentrate more and more on economic problems, so rare in the medieval literature. In both, the main types of heroes depicted become more and more the common man, farmer, peasant, laborer, businessman, stenographer, clerk, and sub-social types. Rogues, criminals, prostitutes, the sexually abnormal, failures, derelicts, hypocrites, murderers, and the like are now the center of the literature, instead of the noble heroes, as in the literature of the thirteenth, fourteenth, and fifteenth centuries, and instead of God, saints, and angels, as in the early medieval literature. In this larger sense, both literatures have tended to become more and more a museum of social, moral, mental, and other pathology. And this trend continues. What American historians of literature call "muck-raking" literature was in fact but a variety of this larger stream of "physio-dirty" interpretation of man and culture, that has been growing in the whole mentality of our culture and is rampant at the present time, in science, in philosophy, in art, in ethics, and everywhere.

If we note also the style of both literatures, whether it is realistic, naturalistic, romantic, symbolic, or what not, there again we find no difference. All these styles have been present on both continents, and the wave of ascendance of each on one continent was followed almost synchronously by a similar upswing on the other. The same is true in regard to such forms of literature as the novel, epic, poetry, and the like. In brief, here again similarity amounts almost to identity, so far as essential traits are concerned.

In a similar manner it would be possible to take other compartments of both cultures, such as ethics, religion, law, and the like, and to show that in these fields the phases of development have been again quite similar on both continents.

### 3. CONCLUSIONS AND DIAGNOSIS

What is the moral of this? What conclusions follow from the thesis? There are several. Let us mention a few.

1. Any contention that American and European cultures are different is wrong. There are still not two different cultures, but one, Euro-American, of the same age, that lives, changes, and pulsates similarly on both continents, so far as its essential traits are concerned. Respectively, all those who eulogize American culture as superior to European, as well as those who hold European culture superior, are wrong in so far as such contentions presuppose a difference in European and American cultures. They can talk of superiority or inferiority of some secondary characteristics, but not of the cultures themselves, since they are one and the same culture.

2. Since the culture of both continents remained the same and did not crystallize into two fundamentally different cultures for almost four centuries, when the communication and contact of America and Europe was less intensive, it is scarcely probable, in our era of intensive communication and contact, that in the future the Euro-American culture will definitely split into two different cultures with different destinies.

It is more likely that its destiny will be the same on both continents. If, after all, the destiny of the merged Greco-Roman culture happened to be the same, in spite of the fact that at the beginning they were different cultures, it is hardly probable that the destiny of the Euro-American or Western culture will be different on two continents. If it is destined to give in the future a new splendor, it will be splendor on both continents. If it is going to disintegrate, it probably will do so on both continents. This does not exclude either secondary deviations, or even a continuation of the sensate culture for a longer time on one—probably the American—continent. Many signs suggest a possibility that America may play, in a modified form, in regard to Europe, the rôle of Rome in regard to Greece. In connection with this, many evidences point to a shift of the center of world history from Europe to the Pacific Ocean, with America, China, India, Japan, and Russia as the main players of the world-history drama during the next centuries.

3. The case of the Euro-American culture testifies that any great and integrated culture is a living unity. It unfolds itself and runs its destined course, in accordance with its potential nature. It may use, as its bearers, different racial, geographic, national, economic, or occupational groups; and these groups may be separated by long distances from one another. And yet, in spite of these differences, in all these groups the culture unfolds itself in its fundamental properties along similar lines and undergoes the same essential changes in the course of its existence. Racial, national, geographic, and other differences of the groups that are the bearers of the culture rarely change the essential nature and destiny of the culture itself. They only call forth and lead to many variations in the *secondary* characteristics of the culture. These secondary traits are differently articulated by the different groups; they acquire usually different local colors. Likewise, the essential change in the culture may not occur synchronously in all the different groups that are its bearers: in some it may take place earlier than in others. Even the purity and brilliancy of the fundamental traits of the culture may be manifested more clearly in one group than in others. But, so far as the essential nature and main phases of the unfolding of the culture are concerned, they run the same course among all the different groups

which bear it. The Euro-American case is only one among many that show this organic logic of the life of culture.

4. Finally, since European and American cultures are one and indivisible Euro-American culture, they are at the same stage of development, namely, at the twilight of the declining sensate phase. Their future course is going to be essentially the same, notwithstanding secondary differences. This means that all that has been and will be said of the present phase of the Western culture and society is equally applicable to the Euro-American culture on both sides of the Atlantic. Such is the answer to the question put at the beginning of this chapter.

# CHAPTER IX

# THE DISINTEGRATION OF SENSATE CULTURE; THE ROOTS OF THE CRISIS AND THE WAY OUT

## I. THE MEANING OF THE DISINTEGRATION OF SENSATE CULTURE AND SOCIETY

At the present time, a legion of voices talk of the decline and disintegration of Western culture and society. Unfortunately, most of these voices rarely stop to define exactly what they mean. Since our diagnosis also affirms the disintegration of the sensate phase of our culture, it is advisable to outline concisely exactly what such a disintegration means and what it does not mean.

*A.* It *does not mean a physical disappearance of the Western population,* the human agents of this supersystem. Some part of it will perish in the transition, but only a part. It *means a progressively increasing defection of this population from sensate culture, with its values, and a shift of its allegiance to other forms of culture, ideational or idealistic.* Like the declining ideational phase at the end of the Middle Ages, the present sensate phase will more and more be losing its human agents, without a great physical depopulation of Western Society.

*B.* It *does not mean the total destruction of all the vehicles and instrumentalities of our contemporary culture, from its material wealth and its gadgets to its immaterial values.* A part of this material culture is bound to perish in the wars, revolutions, and anarchy of the transition. But this part will be a portion only of the total sum of the material vehicles and instrumentalities of sensate culture. The greater part of these, from buildings, roads, means of transportation and communication, to all the machines and gadgets, will survive. But surviving, they *will increasingly cease to be a mouthpiece of sensate meanings and values, and more and more will become the instrumentalities of ideational or idealistic systems of meanings and systems of values*. The tie that unites meanings and values to their material vehicles is loose. The same material vehicle, be it radio, dynamite, or airplane, can be used for the most different purposes: the radio for broadcasting religious services or obscenity, scientific theory or crooning; dynamite for building of a hospital or for bombs; the airplane for flying on an errand of mercy or for sinking a liner. So it is with all the other vehicles. Their physico-chemical or biological nature does not determine whether they will serve sensate or ideational masters. The disintegration of sensate culture means that these vehicles will progressively cease to be the servants of sensate values and will increasingly become the agencies of ideational or idealistic or integral systems of values.

C. The disintegration of the sensate supersystem of our culture *does not mean either deterioration or disintegration of our total culture*. As it has been shown earlier (in Chapter I) the *total* Western culture has never been integrated. What has not been integrated obviously cannot disintegrate. *The deterioration and disintegration of the sensate supersystem concerns and is limited to this supersystem alone, with all its subordinated systems*, leaving untouched, or only slightly touched, all the cultural systems and traits that are not parts of this sensate supersystem.

*D.* Besides the defection of human agents and of the vehicles, the decline of the sensate phase manifests itself in a *progressive deterioration and disintegration of sensate systems of meanings and values.* The deterioration means that, in contradistinction to the great achievements in all fields of culture during the growing stage of the sensate phase, its declining stage will be marked by an increasing poverty of created values. In science it means the replacement of Galileos, Newtons, Leibnitzes by a multitude of mediocre scientists, busy with a study of "the more and more about less and less," inventing destructive rather than constructive means and gadgets. Potential Galileos and Newtons, Copernicuses and Darwins, will be entering sensate science less and less; more and more they will be creating the values of ideational and idealistic types. In the period of the rise of sensate culture the best brains go into the fields of science and technology; in the periods of the rising of ideational or idealistic cultures, they become new Saint Pauls, Saint Augustines, Saint Thomas Aquinases, and other leaders of religion and new systems of truth. Such a shift of the men of genius has taken place fairly uniformly in the periods of transition from one culture to another. Deprived more and more of the men of genius, sensate science and technology are bound to slow their progress and to wither somewhat in their creative achievements. The deterioration of sensate culture in philosophy means a similar shift. The place of Descarteses, Lockes, Kants, Humes, or Comtes will be taken by the *epigoni*, of sensate philosophy, who will write learned books on the systems of great philosophers or pretentious treatises on "scientific philosophy" devoid of science as well as of philosophy. On the other hand, the potential Kants and Humes will eventually shift more and more to theology and ideational or idealistic systems of philosophy and will be enriching these instead of sensate empiricism and other sensate philosophies. In social science, the deterioration of sensate culture means a progressive replacement of the generations of Ibn-Khaldun, Vico, Locke, Montesquieu, Adam Smith, Herbert Spencer, A. Comte, and Karl Marx by a host of scholars united in big research corporations led by "social science managers and social science committees." Industriously they will cultivate in their scholarly treatises either a misleading preciseness, or a painful elaboration of the obvious, or a scholarly emptiness, with all the Alexandrian erudition and all the thoroughness of "trained incapacity." The potential great social thinkers will again increasingly shift to ideational and idealistic social theories. In the fine arts, the place of the Shakespeares and Goethes, Bachs and Beethovens, Raphaels and Rembrandts will be taken by the unions of music-makers, show-makers, fiction-makers, picture-makers, guided mainly by the marketability of their product and by the fancies of their bosses. (In regard to the shift of the best brains, see *Dynamics*, Vol. IV, chap. 7.) In law and ethics, the remnants of the sensate norms of conduct will be more and more "relativized" until they turn into dust; coarse hedonism, together with hypocrisy and rude force, will be rampant. Society will be muzzled, chained, and imprisoned by the monsters begotten and raised by its own nihilism and hedonism.

On the other hand, there will increasingly appear the partisans of the Absolute ethical norms, often becoming stoics, ascetics, and saints. The soul of the society in the transition will be split into the *Carpe diem* on the one hand, and on the other into ideational indifference and negative attitude toward all the sensory pleasures. Society itself will be increasingly divided into open, perfectly cynical sinners with their "Eat, Drink, and Love for tomorrow is uncertain," and into the ascetics and saints who will flee the sensory world into a kind of new refuge, new monasteries, and new deserts. These need not necessarily be physical, but can be mental; and will mean a growth of negative estimation of, and a restraint from, sensory pleasures. Extreme hedonists and cynicists, on the one hand, and extreme ascetics and mystics on the other, whose kingdom is not of this world, will increasingly appear. The chasm between these will grow and society in its soul and members will be split more and more into these two extreme types, until the transition is over and the extreme hedonism of the *Carpe diem* dies out.

On a small or large scale such a split has uniformly occurred in small and great transitions; and especially in the period of the great transitions from one culture to another. Boccaccio's *Decameron* with its hedonistic company, and the medieval flagellants, mystics, and ascetics are the concrete examples of such a split in the transitions of the fourteenth century. Vulgar Roman Epicureans and Petroniuses on the one hand, and Stoics, ascetics, and Christians on the other, are another example of such a split in the transition of the first centuries of our era. A similar split is already appearing and will undoubtedly grow in the future in Western society.

Finally, the deterioration will especially manifest itself in a progressive degeneration of the very standards and criteria of cultural values. The real sensate standards will be more and more replaced by the counterfeit criteria; the competent arbiters by the qualified ignoramuses of the daily press, of radio, of various forums, by writers of best-sellers and of other varieties of cultural chewing gum. The statesmen will be replaced by politicians; the rulers careful about the well-being of the citizens, by the hoary tyrants with a mania for grandeur, indifferent to human life and its values. Quite imperceptibly the standards will change so radically that at the late stages of sensate culture its "machinery of selection" will be picking up mainly pseudo-values and neglecting real values.

As in the declining stage of the Greco-Roman sensate culture, the aridity of thought and sterility of creativeness will increasingly pervade the whole sensate supersystem until Western society awakens to all the hollowness of its streamlined culture. Confronted with this dead shell of what before was a magnificent creation, it will have but one exit from the situation: to leave the hollow corpse for something that lives and creates, for an ideational or idealistic or integral form of culture.

The *disintegration* of the sensate phase means an emergence and multiplication of the conflicts within its systems of meanings and between its human agents and groups. What before, at the full-blooded stage of sensate culture, was one consistent system, with unnoticed rifts, will presently fall apart, disclosing congeries where before there seemed to be unity. A multitude of sensate currents of thought will spring up, each professing its faithfulness to sensate dogma, and each attacking the other sensate currents. As a result, materialism, empiricism, temporalism, humanitarianism, utilitarianism, economism, "scientism," and all the other sensate currents will be more and more undermined, weakened, and split into an ever-increasing number of smaller and smaller currents, each lost in the wilderness of the multitude of congeries. Like the factions of a civil war, the late epigonic opponents will progressively weaken one another and ruin the whole sensate supersystem of meanings and values. Where before there was a great supersystem, there will be a mere conglomeration of congeries, each undermined and discredited.

This disintegration of the systems of meanings and values will be reflected in the mentality of individuals and groups —the bearers and the agents of sensate meanings and values —in a similar disintegration of their mentality. Where before there was a mental and moral order—a reflection of the order of the systems of sensate values and meanings, shortly a mental and moral chaos will arise. The distinction between true and false, right and wrong, beautiful and ugly, positive and negative value will be more and more obliterated. Since no socio-cultural norms—universally accepted and recognized—exist any more in the culture itself, no such norms can be present in the mentality of the individuals and groups. Mental and moral atomism will grow and with it, mental and moral anarchy.

Its consequence must be an increase and a sharpening of antagonisms and conflicts. With these will come an increase of the rule of rude force: wars, revolutions, crimes, and other forms of social struggle stripped of all inhibitions and restraint. These will lead to a further destruction of human lives, material comfort, and material wealth. Such a destruction will deprive sensate culture of its main charm and

THE DISINTEGRATION OF SENSATE CULTURE 305

fascination, defeating its main value, its *raison d'être*, and thereby causing the downfall of its prestige, attraction, and captivation. Hence follows the increasing defection of human agents from it and the shift of their allegiance to different systems of values and meanings.

Consolidating and integrating into innerly consistent systems, these new values and meanings will yield larger and larger systems and finally the supersystem of ideational or idealistic or integral culture. Served increasingly by the increasing number of the most creative minds progressively attracted to it, the new culture will rise in its influence and power until it becomes the dominant supersystem of ideational or idealistic or integral culture. This point achieved, the period of transition from the dying sensate to a new type of culture will end, and with it the chaos and tragedy of the transitional period will terminate. Society can then enter a new, integrated, stable, orderly, and creative phase of its existence.

Persons and groups again will adopt superindividual and even supergroup systems of meanings, norms, and values for making their inner and external lives coherent and filled to the brim, meaningful and rich, creative and valuable. These new systems of values will be the norms controlling and orienting their minds and conduct between the positive and negative values in all fields of socio-cultural life. Therefore the mental, moral, and social anarchy will cease or greatly subside. Man who lost self-control in the overripe stage of sensate culture will again regain it. The reign of rude force will be greatly limited and subjugated to the new values and norms. Might once again will give the way to Right. Social relationships will be reshaped into a new form, less coercive and more noble than in the preceding period of transition. New social, cultural, mental, and moral order will be on the *agenda* of history. If this end of the transition should not be achieved, its absence will signify that the creative history of Western society is ended. In that case it will sink in the morass of endless anarchy and will be removed from the creative stage of history into its morgue or museum.

Such is the meaning of the decline of the sensate phase of our cultural supersystem. It does not mean an end of Western culture, nor the perdition of Western civilization. It means the end of the fundamental phase, and a transition to another phase of the supersystem. In this sense our theory of the decline of the sensate phase has little in common with other theories of the death of Western culture, or of the perdition of the Western population, or of the liquidation of all the material and immaterial values of Western society, or of the doom of the Western culture and society. Based mainly on organic analogies, all such theories are fallacious. Instead of the "death of Western culture and society," our conception embraces only an end to one of the phases of its supersystem and a shift to another phase, fuller and less one-sided; possibly neo-ideational, if not neo-idealistic. Such a conception is free from the morbid pessimism of all the theories of the "death" of culture and society.

Looking beyond the nearest horizon of the decline and transition, we can envisage a new ideational or—what is less probable—an idealistic phase to be entered by our supersystem. In such a phase, the poisonous effects of the declining sensate phase will be greatly eliminated, and new creative forces will be released. As before, these forces will supply their own great and magnificent values, expanding the world of true reality and value, making man again an image of the Absolute on this planet, spiritualizing culture, ennobling society and bringing men nearer to the ever-creative and ever-perfect Absolute. Then, sooner or later, this phase in its turn, will begin to disintegrate, and will again be replaced by a new and different phase; and so the great symphony of human socio-cultural life will continue from phase to phase, from movement to movement, ever new in its creative variations and ever old in the recurrence of the main phases of the supersystem. Viewed in this light, the proposed conception is one of the most optimistic conceptions of socio-cultural change.

On the other hand, the tragic character of the decline and of the transitional period, before the new phase is reached, does not permit our theory to share in any way the shallow optimism of the salesmen of "progress," of the philistine "boosters" of the commercialized "bigger and better." If the Cassandras crying "the death of civilization" are mistaken, they at least do not turn the great tragedy of this historical process into a musical comedy. As for the "salesmen of progress," be they "science managers," scholars, presidents of this or that, journalists, or chamber of commerce speakers, they are not only mistaken but they do not have even the virtue of the misguided Cassandras. They are so deaf that they can never distinguish a tragic "*dies irae, dies illa*" from something "fine and dandy." Whatever happens in the course of time they welcome as a later and therefore bigger and better manifestation of progress. If the "Ninth Symphony" of history is replaced by the most vulgar jazz, they authoritatively declare it to be "streamlined progress." If human blood is shed in overflowing streams, they find it "an exciting and stimulating experiment" as long as it is not their blood. Only when the tragic *"dies irae"* falls upon themselves, then at once they lose their empty optimism and turn into the clownish wailers of the historical circus.

Though the decline of the sensate phase of our culture does not mean the death of Western culture and population, nevertheless the temporary destruction of great cultural values in the transitional period may be too catastrophic; the magnitude of human misery too enormous, the tragedy of these *dies irae* too great, to permit us to join these philistine salesmen of hollow progress. Neither the Cassandras of "death of the Western culture," nor the Candides and Pollyannas of streamlined progress are acceptable company for us. Our path goes between these two fallacious highways of socio-cultural thought. (For the general conception of socio-cultural change, see *Dynamics*, Vol. IV, *passim*)

## 2. THE ROOTS OF THE CRISIS

It is now in order to ask: How has this tragic crisis come about? What are its roots and reasons? Why has contemporary man—so successful in his scientific and technological achievements—not prevented the disintegration of his sensate culture and of his own degradation and tragedy?

Most of the current answers hardly scratch the surface of the problem. They view it as a mere maladjustment of purely economic, or political, or technological, or biological nature. The maladjustment is regarded as something incidental, not inherent in the nature of modern sensate culture. Accordingly, for the elimination of the evil, they prescribe with perfect confidence either an economic readjustment—in money and banking, in prices and wages, in social security and insurance against unemployment, old age, or disease, even to the elimination of private property; or else a modification of the political machinery—from a reconstruction of the League of Nations, a monarchy or a republic, a democracy, or a totalitarian state, to a reform of the civil service or the system of political parties.

Other doctors see salvation in a mild religious therapy: making the churches more comfortable, the services more attractive, and the sermons more entertaining. Still others believe in the magic power of education and expect marvels from changing here and there the curricula of schools; from an increase of Bachelors, Masters, and Doctors of all sciences real and imaginary; from "educational talks" in clubs, forums, town halls, by radio and television, especially of the type of the "Professor Quiz" and the "Information, Please" programs; finally, from the continuous reading of daily papers and magazines, Digests, and Digests of Digests. There are also those doctors who see the root of the evil in a biological deterioration, wrong heredity, wrong race, negative selection, and other biological factors. Respectively they put great faith in such measures as birth-control, the increasing consumption of vitamins, the sterilization of the socially unfit, racial purity, and the like. Finally, some of the experts find the source of the trouble in sunspots, climate and misbehavior of the cosmic factors; these console us, however, by assuring us that the sun soon will be less spotty, the climate less naughty, and that everything will soon be all right.

There is no doubt that some of these measures, when

properly applied, can produce some minor improvements. But there is also no doubt that none of these can stop the crisis. The reason is that none of them reaches the source of the virus. Not touching the source, they cannot eliminate the disease.

The reason for such a statement is quite inductive. All these palliative measures, without any exception whatsoever, have been applied several times. And yet they neither prevented, nor stopped, nor eliminated the crisis. Not infrequently some of them only aggravated the situation. So much for all the economic, political, educational, and other prescriptions. As for the "sunspot" and biological theories, no sunspot or purely climatic theory has been able to account for the historical destinies of any of the great cultures of the past. Still less do they account for the small and great "swings" in the rise of a sensate culture that has lasted for several centuries—regardless of cycles of climate, sunspots, or any other cosmic conditions. Still less do they account for the present crisis. Generally, incessant change of socio-cultural life has very little to do with these factors. Biologically, recent generations appear to be more healthy than past ones: the stature of the present generation has increased; its duration of life has increased also; its diseases have diminished. Biologically we are as good as any previous generation. In spite of all the alarm raised by eugenists, racialists, and hereditarists, the trouble does not lie in biological conditions.

For these reasons one can seriously doubt the adequacy of these diagnoses as well as their remedies. Their error consists in looking for the source of the tragedy in the wrong place, in underestimation of the character of the disease, and especially in viewing it as something incidental, not inherent in the very nature of modern overripe sensate culture. In fact, the roots of the tragedy lie infinitely deeper. They are immanent, go far back, and are inherent in sensate culture. The same forces that determined the growth of its magnificent achievements made unavoidable the growth of the cancer of its disintegration and crisis. The price and the Nemesis of sensate culture is this *alter ego*, the Siamese twin of its growth and magnificence.

*We have seen that modern sensate culture emerged with a major belief that true reality and true value were mainly or exclusively sensory. Anything that was supersensory was either doubtful as a reality or fictitious as a value. It either did not exist or, being unperceivable by the senses, amounted to the nonexistent.* Respectively, the organs of senses, with the secondary help of human reason, were made the main arbiter of the true and false, of the real and unreal, and of the valuable and valueless. Any charismatic-supersensory and superrational revelation, any mystic experience, any truth of faith, began to be denied, as a valid experience, a valid truth, and a genuine value. *The major premise of the sensory nature of the true reality and value is the root from which developed the tree of our sensate culture with its splendid as well as its poisonous fruit. Its* first positive fruit is an *unprecedented development of the natural sciences and technological inventions.* The first poisonous fruit is a *fatal narrowing of the realm of true reality and true value.*

Since true reality and true value were thought to be sensory, anything that was supersensory, from conception of God to the mind of man, anything that was nonmaterial, that could not in the way of daily experience be seen, heard, tasted, touched, or smelled, had to be declared unreal, nonexistent, and of no value. And that is exactly what has happened.

The rude and imperfect human organs of sense were made the supreme arbiter of what was real and what was not, what was value and what was not. As a result, the infinity of the true reality was impoverished and reduced to only one of its aspects—that which our organs of the senses could detect at a given time; all its other aspects which human reason and intuition can comprehend, especially the rare charismatic experience of the few elect, were discarded as nonexistent.

For the same reason, an identical degradation and shortsighted circumscription has affected the world of values generally, and the value of man and his culture particularly. Man himself and all his values were declared to be real only in so far as they were sensory; anything that was in man or in his culture which was imperceptible to the senses of the rank and file of human beings was declared a doubtful or fictitious pseudo-value. In this way man was reduced mainly to anatomy and physiology. Even as the possessor of nonmaterial mind and thought, of consciousness, and of conscience, he was often questioned and denied. In this manner the major premise clipped the wings of man with which he could soar to the vision of more sublime values and the less coarse aspects of reality.

Once the culture entered this path, it had to move along it, toward a greater and greater sensorization of the world of reality and of value. This path led inevitably to the growth of materialism, because nothing can be more sensory than matter; to a more radical mechanisticism, because nothing can be simpler than mechanical motion; to growing hedonism, utilitarianism, and sensuality in the world of the values, because only sensory pleasure and pain, sensory utility and disutility are real from this standpoint. Hence there has been a growth of mechanistic materialism, flat empiricism, superficial positivism, and vulgar utilitarianism bound up with the growth of modern culture.

Man himself and his evaluation of himself could not escape the same trend.

Man as a bearer of the divine ray in the sensory world, as an incarnation of the charismatic grace, was declared a superstitious delusion. His reality and value was reduced to his biological organism, with all its imperfections. No wonder, therefore, that such a conception led to the previously described degradation of man both as a reality and as a value. Certainly there is nothing sacred in an imperfect human organism. In many respects it is more defective than the organisms of other species of creatures. If the value-reality of man is no more and no less than his organism, it is only consistent that he be treated just as other organisms are treated. If he is useful for a given moment, we can care for him, as we care for cows and horses. If he is unserviceable, we can eliminate him, as we eliminate snakes and mosquitoes, parasites and old animals.

This is exactly the treatment man generally gets now especially in those groups where this equation between man and organism is taken most literally. Man as a man has no value whatsoever for most sensate groups at the present time. They do not recognize any charismatic value of man; therefore they treat him exactly as we treat other organisms. Only in so far as man is a Communist or a Nazi, or "New Dealer" or "Old Dealer," or at least, in so far as he obeys and serves the rules of the dominant faction, can he exist, without being deprived of the elementary conditions of decent living. If his "color" is different from the faction's "color," then cold-bloodedly, with scientific efficiency, he is crushed, liquidated, banished, and becomes a nonentity or a negative value. This equation manifests itself in such contemporary phenomena as war, revolutions, crimes, and other forms of brutality discussed earlier. Such a practice is but a logical consequence of the major premise of contemporary culture. These evils are its poisonous growths quite as much as science and technology are its marvelous fruits. Both spring from the same root of the limitation of true reality and value to the reality of the senses.

From the same root have grown the other forms of degradation of man, atomization of values, and disintegration of culture surveyed before: in art and philosophy, in law and ethics, and so on. They are largely the consequence of the major premise for the same reasons. The same root is responsible for present-day society as an enormous number of armed camps, that by direct or indirect application of force and fraud try each to defeat the others. Relationships of employers and employees, bankers and labor unions, of social classes to one another, of rich and poor, of educated and noneducated, of privileged and underprivileged, of political parties, occupational groups, and finally, of nations, are at the present time in an incessant war, controlled mainly by the rude force and trickery which a given group has. He who has greater force triumphs, while the weaker party is pitilessly trampled on and crushed. Such is the root of the crisis of our sensate culture.

### 3. THE WAY OUT AND BEYOND

Since the Western culture is entering the transitional period from its sensate supersystem into either an ideational or an idealistic phase; and since such epoch-making transitions have hitherto been the period of the tragic *dies irae, dies illa,* the greatest task of our time evidently consists, if not in averting tragedy—which is hardly possible—then, at least, in making the transition as painless as possible. What means and ways can help in this task? We leave without further discussion the numerous subsidiary means, like the political, economic, educational, genetic, and other prescriptions which, if they are sound, may somewhat alleviate the tragedy but can in no way prevent it or serve as the "way out" from it. The most important means evidently consists in the correction of the fatal mistake of the sensate phase and in a concerted preparation for the inevitable mental and moral and socio-cultural revolution of Western society. The first step in this direction consists in *as wide, as deep, and as prompt realization as possible of the extraordinary character of the contemporary crisis of our culture and society*. It is high time to realize that this is not one of the ordinary crises which happen almost every decade, but one of the greatest transitions in human history from one of its main forms of culture to another. An adequate realization of the immense magnitude of the change now upon us is a necessary condition for determining the adequacy of measures and means to alleviate the magnitude of the pending catastrophe. He is a poor doctor who treats dangerous pneumonia as a slight cold. Similarly, nothing but harm can ensue from the prevalent treatment of the present crisis as a slight and ordinary maladjustment. Such a blundering diagnosis must be forgotten as soon as possible, together with all the surface rubbing medicines abundantly prescribed by shortsighted socio-cultural physicians.

The second step consists in an unequivocal recognition that the *sensate form of culture, with its major and minor premises, is not the only great form of culture and is not free from many defects and inadequacies*. Ideational and idealistic forms in their own way are as great as the sensate form.

Third, when one of these forms ages and begins to show signs of its creative exhaustion, as they all do after some period of their domination, *a given culture, in order to continue its creative life, must shift to another basic form of culture—in our case, from the agonizing sensate to the ideational or the idealistic or integral*. Only such a shift can save it from a complete disintegration or mummification. This shift should not be opposed, but should be enthusiastically welcomed as the only escape from a mortal agony.

Fourth, the concerted preparation for the shift implies *the deepest reexamination of the main premises and values of sensate culture, rejection of its superannuated pseudovalues and reenthronement of the real values it has discarded*. The general line of such a reexamination and reevaluation lies in the direction of the integralist conception of truth, reality, and values outlined in Chapter III. More specifically, it demands an unequivocal recognition that sensory reality and value are but one of the aspects of the infinitely richer true reality and value; that these have a supersensory aspect of which we get a glimpse through our reason and through charismatic grace or intuition in its sublime forms; that this supersensory side is the supreme aspect of the value-reality, and as such it is absolute; that the same is true in regard to the reality and value of man and of the sublimest flowers of his culture. Man is not only an organism but is also a bearer of absolute value. As such, he is sacred and, regardless of sex, age, race, and social status, cannot be used as a mere means for anything or anybody. Likewise, the great values of his culture—science and technology, religion and philosophy, ethics and art— are a reflection, a realization, of the absolute values in the empirical world. As such, they cannot be degraded to mere instrumentalities for purely sensual enjoyment or utility. They are in themselves ends. Since man and his values are sacred, the relationship of man to man should be guided by sublime love, as the categoric imperative. Since truth, goodness, and beauty are absolute values, any further relativization of these, any further degradation to a mere arbitrary convention, becomes out of place. As absolute values they are all one value. Being one, science cannot claim complete freedom from the control of goodness and beauty, and therefore cannot and should not serve any evil purpose. If and when it does so, it misuses its duty and becomes pseudo-science. The same principle applies to art. When it turns into a mere means for sensual pleasure and declares itself free from any moral and cognitive obligations, it degrades itself to mere entertainment, and becomes a pseudo-value. From *the integralist standpoint, the present antagonism between science, religion, philosophy, ethics, and art is unnecessary, not to mention disastrous. In the light of an adequate theory of true reality and value, they all are one and all serve one purpose: the unfolding of the Absolute in the relative empirical world, to the greater nobility of Man and to the greater glory of God. As such they should and can cooperate in the fulfillment of this greatest task.*

Fifth, such a transformation of the mentality of Western culture must naturally be followed by a *corresponding transformation of social relationships and forms of social organization.* The first step here also consists in an unequivocal recognition that all empirical forms of social organization are not absolute but relative values, positive under one set of conditions and negative under another. The same is particularly true of the forms of social-political, economic, and other organizations of superripe sensate culture. Neither Capitalism, nor Socialism, nor Communism, nor Totalitarianism; neither private, nor corporate property; neither mechanical individualism nor mechanistic collectivism is an absolute value. Neither monarchy nor republic, neither aristocracy nor democracy, neither national state nor international federation can claim to be absolute values. In certain conditions each of these is the best possible form; under other conditions each of these becomes a mere fetish, empty, hollow, even harmful. For instance, such great values as the national state or even private property are at the present time obsolete to a considerable degree. They have outlived the period of their great service to mankind. At the present time they are the sources of social disservice rather than of social well-being. They are the sources of war and revolution, of bloodshed and hatred; even of poverty and misery for the overwhelmingly greater part of mankind—for all except the rulers and the possessors of huge fortunes. Just because man is sacred, no state or its rulers has any right to inflict ruin and misery upon millions for the sake of the aggrandisement of the territory, possession, and power of the state or for that of their own glory. The time of isolated states is past and mankind is already one interacting community. Just because man is sacred, no rich class has a right to enjoy the prodigal life and to hold huge fortunes in its possession while millions of decent, honest, industrious men are jobless, breadless, and devoid of the elementary necessities of life. The interaction and interlocking of the lives and happiness and dignity of all classes of mankind is so close and interdependent at the present time that no such isolation is justifiable or possible any more. This is no recommendation of purely mechanical communistic or totalitarian "socialization and communization" of private property: such mechanical procedures can give only the same disastrous results for society as they have invariably given before. But there must be a change of the whole mentality and attitudes in the direction of the norms prescribed in the Sermon on the Mount. When such a change occurs, to a notable degree the technical ways of remodeling the economic and political structures in this direction become easy. Without this change, no mechanical, politico-economic reconstruction can give the desired results.

And so it is with all the other values that are the means-values for the supreme end-value. Most of these means-values, great at the period of their "spring and summer," are becoming increasingly withered, enfeebled, and sterile. *A transformation of the forms of social relationship, by replacing the present compulsory and contractual relationships with purer and more godly familistic relationships, is the order of the day.* Since coercion expands more and more at the present time, since the contractual relationships have become hollow and decayed, the only way out is a concerted action directed to the introduction of the familistic relationships. Not only are they the noblest of all relationships, but under the circumstances there is no way out of the present triumph of barbarian force but through the realm of familistic relationships. The best methods for making the familistic relationship the foundation of the future society is a purely technical matter not to be discussed here. But for any technical form of social organization to be a way out of the present reign of bloody struggle, it must be a realization of familistic principles. No longer will coercion or the hollow and egotistic contract suffice for the task.

Such, in brief, is the way out of the tragedy. While permitting all the glorious achievements of our sensate culture to live on, such a course will correct the fatal blunders and reestablish the richness, fullness, and manifoldness of true reality and value. In doing so, it will restore the sanctity of man and his social and cultural mission. Through all that, it eradicates the very root of the malignant growth on our social and cultural life.

Such are the conditions without which the disease cannot be stopped and the tragedy of transition alleviated. There is no doubt that the realization of these means is infinitely more difficult than the application of the superficial measures of economic or political or other "readjust-ment." *Our remedy demands a complete change of the contemporary mentality, a fundamental transformation of our system of values, and the profoundest modification of our conduct toward other men, cultural values, and the world at large.* All this cannot be achieved without the incessant, strenuous, active efforts on the part of every individual in that direction. Such efforts are incomparably more difficult than a mechanical tampering with economic, political, biological or other conditions. But easy half-measures will always fail, especially in the conditions of a great crisis. The experience of the last few decades shows clearly all the impotency and often even the harmfulness of a host of easy ways out. The more we tampered with economic conditions, the worse they became. The more we outlawed war, the more disastrous it grew. The more social security we tried to establish, the more insecurity we obtained. It is high time to stop deluding ourselves with these easy measures; they have not stopped and cannot stop the process of disintegration. The remedy suggested here is infinitely more difficult, but it is the only one that will prove helpful.

### 4. CRISIS—ORDEAL—CATHARSIS—CHARISMA—RESURRECTION

The proposed remedy is based not upon wishful think-ing but upon a sound sociological induction: such was the way out during all the comparable crises of the past. It can be reduced to a compact formula: *Crisis—ordeal—cathar-sis—charisma—resurrection.* The process always consisted in a replacement of the withered root of sensate culture by an ideational or idealistic root, and eventually in a substitution of a full-grown and more spiritual culture for the decadent sensate form. Per contra, in crises of outworn ideational or idealistic cultures the replacement was the reverse: a sensate tree supplanted the ideational or idealistic tree. More explicitly, the problem of overripe sensateness was solved by the emergence of a new religion or by the regeneration of an older religion. The essential reorientation of values, spiritualization of mentality, and ennoblement of conduct were regularly achieved in the form of and through a religious revolution. Virtually all the great world religions either first arose or else experienced their most vital renaissance in periods of profound crisis, as in ancient Egypt at the close of the Old Kingdom and at the end of the Middle Kingdom and of the New Empire, or in Babylonia around the year 1200 B.C. The phenomenon is illustrated more than once by the history of Hindu culture, where each notable crisis was met by a regeneration of Hinduism or by the emergence or revival of Buddhism. The same principle is seen in the history of China, where the crisis of the seventh and sixth centuries B.C. was resolved by the advent of Taoism and Confucianism. Again, in the history of Hebrew culture the crises of the ninth to the fourth century B.C. owe their cure or their partial alleviation to the prophetic religions of Elijah and Elisha; Amos, Hosea, and Isaiah; Ezekiel and Jeremiah; and Ezra and his successors. Finally, to cite an additional instance, the crisis of sensate Greco-Roman culture was terminated by the growth of Christianity. The respective societies were preserved from dissolution, be it noted, not so much through the "practical and expert" manipulation of economic, political, genetic, or other factors, but mainly through the transmutation of values, the spiritualization of mentality, and the socialization of conduct and ennoblement of social relations effected through the medium of *religion*. Hence the prescribed formula: Crisis—ordeal—catharsis—charisma—resurrection.

Let us trace the course of the revolution in some detail. As has been pointed out in earlier chapters, at the close of the sensate periods of the past the formerly magnificent edifice began to totter. Material pleasures and comforts, utility, security, safety, and freedom progressively declined. War and other forms of strife, brutality, bloodshed, and destruction became endemic. Efforts to patch up the crumbling system invariably miscarried. Under such circumstances people could not fail to perceive eventually the hollowness of sensate culture, the hopelessness of further allegiance to sensate values, and the impossibility of attempting to preserve an orderly way of life on so rotten a foundation. This realization, in turn, led to a defection from the banner of sensate culture and values and to a transfer of allegiance to ideational or idealistic values which appeared to be eternal, indestructible, and independent of anything material and external. Through this fiery ordeal was the catharsis, or purification, of society from its sensate sins and vices finally achieved.

With this catharsis accomplished, there ensued the next phase—that of grace, or charisma. The destructive phase was followed by one that was constructive. The "atomization" of values was replaced by their universalization and "absolutization"; expediency, pleasure, and utility, by duty; licentious freedom, by the sanctity of norms and justice; coercion and egoistic contract, if not by all-embracing, all-bestowing, and all-forgiving love, at least by more familistic and altruistic relationships. Religion, ethics, and law overcame the unbridled sway of force and fraud. God took the place of materialism; spiritual values, that of sensate values. In brief, all the essential sensate values were replaced by less sensate values, either ideational or idealistic.

Purified and ennobled, society proceeded to erect a new house based on the Absolute, God, love, duty, sacrifice, grace, and justice. The poison of decadent sensate culture eliminated, strife and bloodshed diminished, security and safety of life returned, stable order was reestablished, and fresh creative forces were released. Society and individuals were once more at peace with themselves, with their fellow men, with the world, and with God. Thus was ushered in the phase of resurrection, with its long perspective of new creative life.

Such was the invariable course of the great crises of the past. Such is the way out of our own crisis. There is no other possibility.

If human beings were capable of fully profiting by past experience and the lessons of history, the remedy would have been found easily, without the necessity of any fiery ordeal, or even any serious crisis: as soon as the sensate system showed the first signs of decay, the requisite ideational or idealistic reorientation of values, mentality, and conduct would have been willingly undertaken by the society concerned. Unfortunately, "Homo sapiens" seems to be rather purblind so far as the lessons of historical, socio-cultural experience are concerned. He applies and profits by the experience of other persons in matters concerning his physical health. When he is sick, he gives up various pleasures; makes other necessary sacrifices, such as going to bed and taking the prescribed medicine; and behaves in general in a rational manner. He thus frequently avoids much direr consequences, including possibly death itself. In such matters he does not question the existence of causal relationships and causal consequences. Hence he displays neither recklessness nor stupidity, nor does he expect the impossible.

But from the lessons of history concerning life and death, the blossoming and sickness of society, man learns hardly anything. He behaves either as if past history were non-existent or as if the past presented no situation essentially comparable to that in which his own society finds itself; as if there were no causal relationships and consequences; as if there were no such thing as socio-cultural sickness, and hence no need to sacrifice momentary pleasures and other sensate utilities and values in order to avoid an infinitely greater catastrophe. In this field of experience he remains virtually unteachable.

For instance, in the face of the inexhaustible evidence of the ephemeral character of all hastily built empires resting on coercion, men in their purblindness and folly have repeatedly attempted and still attempt to construct eternal empires by precisely such methods. Notwithstanding the perennial failure of efforts effectually to control prices by a mere fiat of the government, such efforts everywhere persist. How many times men have expected to achieve heavenly bliss through a purely mechanical elimination of private property! Yet these experiments are still repeated in spite of their inevitable futility. In the course of human history several thousand revolutions have been launched with a view to establishing a paradise on earth. And they are still proceeding at full blast, in spite of the fact that practically none of them has ever achieved its purpose. Every page of human history bears witness to wars undertaken in the firm conviction that they would "end war," "abolish despotism," "make the world safe for democracy," overcome injustice, eliminate misery, and the like. And we observe "Homo sapiens" still engrossed in this crazy quest. From this standpoint, the history of human progress is indeed a history of incurable human stupidity!

This unteachableness manifests itself also in the current hope of extricating ourselves from the crisis by means of a variety of facile but shallow artifices, without any fundamental reorientation of values, any thoroughgoing change of mentality and conduct, any persistent personal effort to realize man's divine creative mission on earth instead of acting merely as a "reflex mechanism," or an organism endowed with digestive and sex functions and controlled by its "residues," "drives," and "prepotent reflexes." Hence the crisis itself, and hence the inevitability of a fiery ordeal as the only available means of teaching the otherwise unteachable. *Volentem fata ducunt, nolentem trahunt*. The more unteachable we are, and the less freely and willingly we choose the sole course of salvation open to us, the more inexorable will be the coercion, the more pitiless the ordeal, the more terrible the *dies irae* of the transition. Let us hope that the grace of understanding may be vouchsafed us and that we may choose, before it is too late, the right road—the road that leads not to death but to the further realization of man's unique creative mission on this planet! *Benedictus qui venit in nomine Domini*.

# INDEX

Absolute, norm, 18-20, 135, 144-46
reality, 18-20
truth, 81, 83-4, 102, 111
value, 18-20, 135, 144, 317-18
Absolutism *vs.* relativism, fluctuation of, 143-44
Absolutization, of values, 203, 317, 323
Achilles, 63
Acceleration of social processes, 33, 62, 97, 257
*Adaequatio rei et intellectus*, 98, 117
Adams, Henry, 172, 418, 419, 561, 564
Adaptation, and truth, 104-5, 112-15, 311-12
Aeschylus, 37, 138, 139
Aesthetic. See Arts fine
Agnosticism, 86, 117-18
Albertus Magnus, 307, 459, 490, 648, 654
Alexander, John, 286
Allegiance, shift of population's, 288
Alternation of domination of,
absolutism and relativism, 143-44;
compulsory, contractual, familistic relationships, 169-70;
economic misery and prosperity, 232-37;
empiricism and non-empiricism, 90-91, 103-4;
ethical and law systems, :38, 142-44, 155;
forms of culture, 19-24, 25, 29, 271;
forms of fine arts, 36-37, 45, 47;
idealism and materialism, 94-95;
systems of truth, 83-85;
American and European cultures,
cultural trends of, 280-92;
similarity of, 273-75;
social trends of, 275-80;
unity of, 295-96
Alvorado, F., 291

Amos, 322
Anarchy, in transitional periods, 23, 157-61, 198, 204, 205, 211, 221-23, 321-25. See also, Antagonisms, Brutality, Revolution, War
Anomic suicide, 208
Antagonisms, contemporary, 161-64, 194, 200, 205-6, 242, 247, 314. See also Brutality, Revolution, War
Antihumanitarianism, contemporary, 161, 164, 181, 194, 211, 227-31, 244-47, 313-14. See also Brutality, Revolution, War
Anthropology, creativeness of contemporary, 267
Aquinas, Saint Thomas. See Saint Thomas Aquinas
Archimedes, 109
Architecture, 18, 37, 46, 53, 70, 76, 255, 263, 284
Aristocracy, managerial, 185-87
Aristotle, 102, 127, 137, 139, 261, 263
Arnold, Matthew, 292
Arts fine, as barometer of culture, 30; characteristics of idealistic, ideational, sensate, 31-35; fluctuation of main forms of, 37-43
Arts fine, statistics of genre, paysage, portraits in, 51; of religious and secular topics in, 45, of sensual and spiritual creations in, 50-51; of visual and other styles in, 47
Arts fine contemporary, achievements of, 52-55; decline of, 264-66; maladies of, 55-74; professional character of, 73-4; revolt against, 75-79; similarity of American and European, 284-94
Ascetic, and sensual character of art, 50-51, 58, 62, 66, 293-94
Ascetics, split of population in tran-

sitional periods into sensualists and, 301-2

Associations, compulsory, contractual, familistic, 167-69; decline of contractual, 177-78, 181, 184-88, 192-93, 278; rise of contractual, 169-75, 275-76

Atomization of values, contemporary and in transition periods, 96-97, 116-20, 142-44, 153, 157-63, 192-93, 203-4, 205. See also Absolutism, Relativism

Augustine, Saint. See Saint Augustine

Aurelius, Marcus, 83

Autocratic government, growth of, 177-184, 277-78

Avenarius, Richard, 245, 284

Baader, F. X. von. See Von Baader, F. X.

Bach, J. S., 50, 53, 55, 58, 127, 264, 301

Bacon, F., 268

Bakunin, M., 291

Baldwin, J. M., 283

Balzac, H., 55, 265, 291, 292

Bankruptcy, empirical science, 124-131, sensate culture, 231

Barbarism, contemporary. See Antagonisms, Antihumanitarianism, Brutality, Revolution, War

Basil the Great, 84

Baudelaire, C. P., 291

Beethoven, L., 50, 55, 58, 72, 106, 127, 264, 301

Behavioristic interpretations of man, 93-4, 121, 244, 312

Beissel, C., 282

Bellows, G. W., 286

*Bellum omnium contra omnes*, 160

Berg, 77

Berkeley, G., 266

Berlioz, H., 50

Best brains, shift of allegiance of, 300-1

Best-sellers, contemporary, 59, 70, 302-3

Bierstadt, A., 285, 286

Bigness, curse of. See Colossalism

Biological, factors and remedies of the crisis, 16, 24, 212, 309-10

Bioorganismic theory of culture, 16, 23-24

Biran, M. de. See De Biran

Bird, W., 290

Birthrate, decline of, 188-89

Blindness of contemporary society, 131, 217, 222

Boccaccio, G., 302

Bodin, J., 160

Bois, P. du. See Du Bois, P.

Bonald, L. G. A. de. See De Bonald, L. G. A.

Boyle, R., 268

Bradford, W., 289

Bradstreet, A., 289, 290

Brahms, J., 55, 265

Brown, C. B., 290

Brown, J. G., 285

Brutality contemporary, 227-31

Buckle, H. T., 291

Buddha, 106, 111, 134, 135

Business-leaders, among historical persons, 259-60. See also Economic

Bureaucracy, similarity of corporative and state, 185-6; contemporary increase of, 177-87

Byron, Lord G., 265, 290, 291

Calvin, J., 290

Calvinism, and capitalism, 140; ethics of, 140-41

Capitalism, and corporative economy, 184-87; and private property, 185; as contractual system, 169-70, 275; decline of, 181-87

Carlyle, T., 283, 291

Carnap, R., 80

Carnegie, A., 186

*Carpe diem*, 136, 139, 301

Carpenter, J. A., 289

Carricature, in sensate art, 33, 43, 63-84

Cassandra, 307, 308

Catharsis, in crises, 321-24

Celsus, 83, 84

Charisma, in crises, 321-24
Charismatic intuition, 111
Chase, W., 286
Chateaubriand, F. R., 55, 265, 290
Chekhov, A. P., 66
Childe Hassam, 286
Childless marriages, 188
Christian, art, 39-43;
  culture, 17-18;
  ethics, 134-35, 139-40;
  truth, 83-5
Church, F. E., 286
Churchill, W., 15, 22, 23
Claude, 286
Coercion, contemporary rule of,
  158-61, 163, 206, 227. See also
  Antagonisms, Antihumanitarian-
  ism, Brutality, Coercive, Revo-
  lution, War
Coercive social relationships, defini-
  tion of, 168-69; contemporary
  increase of, 177-88, 192, 193-94
Cognition, integral, 112-14;
  intuitive, 81, 105-112;
  rational, 81-2;
  sensory, 81, 86-101, 112-13. See also
  Truth
Coincidentia oppositorum, 112
Cole, T., 285
Coleridge, S. T., 290
Colossalism vs. quality, in sensate
  culture, 53, 70-72, 252-56
Comedy, in sensate art, 33, 43, 63-4
Commercialization of values, 58-9,
  140-41, 163
Complexity, incoherence and variety
  of, contemporary art, 54, 67-9;
  culture, 247-52; science, 125-27
Compulsion. See Coercion
Comte, A., 127, 266, 267, 283, 291,
  300, 301
Condorcet, M. J. A., 283
Conflict, of Christian and pagan
  truth, 83-5
Conflicts, sociocultural, 241-43, 247.
  See also Antagonisms, Brutality,
  Revolution, War
Constable, J., 286

Contractual social relationships and
  capitalism, 170; and democracy,
  171; and liberty, 171-72; charac-
  teristics of, 167-68; conditions of
  genuine, 176-77; crisis of, 176-95,
  276; growth of, 170-75, 275
Contradictions of our culture, 241-
  43, 247-52
Control, governmental, expansion of,
  176-95, 276
Cooper, J. F., 290
Copeland, G., 289
Copernicus, N., 268, 300
Copley, J. S., 286
Corot, J. B. C., 286
Corporation and trust, bureaucracy,
  185-86; economy, 184-87
Cotton, J., 282, 289
Coulanges, F. de. See De Coulanges,
  F.
Cousin, V., 291
Creation, as discovery, 106-7; role of
  intuition in, 106-112
Creativeness, decline of, in art, 70-
  75, 264-66;
  ethics and law, 157-60, 261-62;
  philosophy and religion, 259-61,
  263;
  science, 127-9, 268-9;
  social sciences and humanities,
  125-8, 130, 266-67
Creativeness, in various fields of culture, statistics of, 258-60
Criminality, increase of, 224-25
Crises, way out of past great, 321-26
Crisis contemporary, diagnoses of,
  15-17, 21-25;
  factors of, 308-15;
  general symptoms of, 21-24, 241-
  42, 247, 252, 256;
  way out of, 308-10, 315-26
Crisis of, contemporary, art, 55-79;
  capitalism, 181-87; contractual
  associations, 176-95; ethics and law, 157-65;
  family, 187-92; international
  order, 192-93; liberty, 176-95;
  philosophy, religion, science,

116-32. See also Creativeness, decline of

Cubism, 76-79

Culture, as a unity, 17-18, 296-97; idealistic, ideational, sensate, mixed types of, 17-21; meaning of disintegration of, 298-308

Culture, similarity of American and European, 295-97

Cycle. See Alternation

Cynicism, contemporary, 157, 163, 164. See also Atomization, Coercion

Dadaism, 76-77

D'Alambert, 268

D'Annunzio, G., 66

Dante, A., 53, 68, 127, 230, 265

Darwin, C. R., 268, 283, 300

Daubigny, C. F., 286

Daudet, L., 292

David, J. L., 286

Davies, A., 287

Da Vinci, L., 265

Davis, C., 286

Death of culture, 16, 24-26, 306-7

Death-rate, recent increase of, 239

De Biran, M., 291

Debussy, C. A., 265

Decay. See Crisis, Decline, Disintegration

Decline of creativeness. See Creativeness, Crisis, Disintegration

De Coulanges, F., 267

De Crevecoeur, M. G., 290

Degradation of man and values in contemporary, art 58, 63-67, 246; culture, 242-44; ethics and law, 157-165, 246-47; philosophy and science, 116-24; 244-45; social life, 206, 229-231

De Maistre, J., 267, 291, 292

Democracy, as contractual system, 170-75; decline of, 176-95; 276; growth of, 170-75, 275

Demoralization, 157-65

Demuth, 287

Depressions economic, in crises, 231-39

De Roberty, E., 127

Descartes, R., 266, 300

De Vigny, A., 291

De Tocqueville, A., 291

Dewey, J., 245, 284

Dickens, C., 55, 265, 292

Dickinson, J., 290

Dictatorships, contemporary growth of, 176-95, 276

Dilthey, W., 127

Discoveries and inventions, decline of, 127-29, 260-69; role of intuition in, 105-11; statistics of movement of, 87-88

Disease mental, increase of, 206, 224

Disintegration of culture, meaning of, 298-307. See also Creativeness, Crisis

Diversity of sensate culture, 54, 67-69, 125-27, 247-52

Divorce, increase of, 188

Domination, alternation of. See Alternation, Rhythm

Dostoevski, T., 55, 265, 291, 292

Dualism of our culture, 241-44

Du Bois, P., 160

Duerhing, 291

Duhem, P., 284

Dupré, J., 286

Dürer, A., 106, 265

Durkheim, E., 127

Duvenac, F., 286

Dynamic nature of sensate culture, 20-21, 33, 43, 58, 62, 96-97, 137, 164-65, 202-3, 206, 212-13, 217-18, 242, 247-49

Eakins, T., 286

Eclectic. See Incoherent

Economic, factors of crisis, 16, 24, 212, 309-10; interpretation of culture, 93-94, 121, 244, 312

Economic misery, in crises, 231-39

Economic values in, Middle Ages, 134-35, 139-40, 149-50; Protestantism, 140-41; sensate culture,

58-59, 135-36, 140-41, 163. See also Utility

Edwards, J., 282, 290

Eliot, G., 292

Eliot, J., 282

Elisha, 322

Elijah, 322

Ellis, W., 121

Emerson, R. W., 283, 291

Emperor William Hohenzollern, 23

Empirical science and truth, 21-22, 81; and illusionism, 43, 81, 99, 116-18; and inventions and discoveries, 87-90; and materialism, 93-96, 120-21; and nihilism, 96-97, 117; and nominalism, 99; and relativism, 96-98, 119-20; and scepticism, 113-18; and temporalism, 96-97, 120; and utility, 99-101, 116, 130-32

Empiricism, bankruptcy of, 124-32; statistics of fluctuation of, 91-92

End-value, substitution of means for, 70-71

Epicurus, 262

Epstein, J., 66

Erigena, J. S., 112, 263

Eroticism, in sensate art, 51, 293

Erskine, C., 121

Eternal vs. temporal values, 32-33, 43, 61, 81-83, 95-97, 120, 133-36, 144, 147, 159, 162, 192-93, 203-5

Ethical atomism, nihilism, relativism. See Atomization, Relativism

Ethics, absolutistic and relativistic, 18-20, 135, 143-46, 317
idealistic, ideational, sensate, 133-38

Expansion of government regimentation, 176-95, 276

Expressionistic style in art, statistics of, 47

Ezekiel, 322

Ezra, 322

Fact-finding science. See Empirical science, Empiricism

Factors of crisis, 16, 24, 212, 308-15

Faith, truth of, 20, 81, 83-85, 105-112

Familistic social relationship, 167-68, 318-30

Family, crisis of contemporary, 187-90

Fechner, G. T., 174

Felix, M., 84

Feuerbach, L. A., 291

Fichte, J. G., 291

Fielding, H., 290

Fine arts. See arts fine

Fidelitas, 169

Fiske, J., 283

Flaubert, G., 292

Fluctuation. See Alternation

Force, contemporary rule of, 158-61, 163, 206, 227. See also Antagonisms, Antihumanitarianism, Brutality, Coercive, Revolution, War

Ford, H., 186

Foster, B., 286

Fourrier, F. C. M., 291, 292

France, A., 141

Franco, Gen., 223

Franklin, B., 141, 282, 290

Freedom. See Liberty

Freneau, P. M., 290

Freud, S., 122, 157, 245

Futurism, 76-79

Gainsborough, T., 286

Galileo, 106, 109, 127, 268, 300

Genius, increasing scarcity of, 127-29, 260-71. See also Creativeness, Historical persons

Genre, statistics of pictures of, 51

Gershwin, G., 289

Gibbon, E., 267

Gioberti, V., 292

God, 18-20, 81, 83-84, 102, 111-12, 135, 144, 317

Godwin, W., 290

Goerro, 291

Goethe, J. W., 55, 72, 265, 290, 291, 301

Gogol, N. V., 291

Gorki, M., 66

Government, contractual, 170-75, 275; dictatorial, 176-95, 276
Government regimentation, increase of, 176-95, 276
Green, T. H., 291
Gregory, Saint. See Saint Gregory

Hakluyt, R., 289
Hamilton, A., 290
Happiness, ethics of, 142; in ideational and sensate ethics, 133-37
Harris, W. T., 283
Hartmann, E. von. See Von Hartmann, E.
Harvey, W., 268
Hawthorne, N., 291, 292
Hector, 63
Hedonism, 51, 135-36, 139-40, 142
Hedonists, split of population into ascetics and, 301-2
Hegel, G. W. F., 127, 263, 266, 267, 283, 291
Hemingway, E., 66
Henri, R., 286
Heraclitus, 263
Herbart, J. F., 291
Herder, J. G. von. See Von Herder, J. G.
Herodotus, 127, 138, 139
Heroes of idealistic, ideational, sensate art, 57, 63, 294
Herzen, A. I., 291
Hesiod, 138
Hill, E. B., 289
Hill, T., 285, 286
Hindemith, P., 77
Historical persons, statistics by periods and fields of activity, 258-60
Historical process, as creative, 24-25, 78-79, 131-32, 203-4, 271, 306-7
History, debunking, 94-95, 121-22
Hitler, A., 15, 16, 22, 23, 117, 211, 223
Hobbes, T., 266
Hoffman, E. T. W., 290
Hogarth, W., 286
Homer, 40, 53
Honegger, A., 77
Hooker, T., 282

Horace, 40
Hosea, 322
Howells, W. D., 292
Hughes, R., 121
Hugo, V., 55, 291, 292
Hume, D., 263, 266, 300, 301
Hutchinson, Mistress A., 282

Ibn-Khaldun, 301
Ibsen, H. J., 291
Idealism vs. materialism, fluctuation of domination of, 93-96
Idealistic art, 33-34, 37-38, 42-43; culture, 20-21; ethics and law, 137, 140, 154; philosophy, 93-96; truth, 81-82, 102
Ideational, art, 30-33, 37, 39-42, 45-50; culture, 18-20; ethics and law, 133-34, 138-39, 147-52; liberty, 172-74; style in art, 47; truth, 81, 83-86
Illusionism, in sensate culture, 33, 43, 81, 98-99, 116-18. See also Blindness
Imitation, in late sensate art, 39, 69, 249-50
Impressionism, in art, 60-61, 75-76
Individualism and contractualism, 171-72, 277; and singularism, in sensate mentality, 33, 73-74, 97, 99, 159, 162
Impoverishment, in crises, 231-39
Incertitude, 125
Incoherence, in sensate culture, 54, 67-69, 125-27, 247-52
Ingham, 285
Inness, G., 286
Insecurity, contemporary, 164-65, 179-80, 194, 202, 205, 226, 231, 234-35, 239-40
Instrumentalism. See Empirical science
Integral truth, 112-14
Integrated art, 30-34; cultures, 17-21, 25, 296-97; systems of truth, 81-82. See also Disintegration, Incoherence, Syncretism

Intuition, as a source of truth, and inventions, 81, 105-12

Inventions and discoveries, decline of, 127-29, 268-69; movement of, 87-88; role of intuition in, 105-11

Irrational, in man, 324-26

Irving, W., 290

Isaiah, 322

Jacobi, H., 291

James, H., 292

James, W., 117, 245, 284

Janus, 243

Jefferson, T., 282

Jeremiah, 322

Jesus Christ, 80, 84, 150

Job, 173

Judgment of God, in law, 148

Juridical systems, ideational, 146-52; sensate, 152-56

Kant, I., 106, 107, 118, 127, 263, 266, 283, 291, 300, 301

Keithe, 285

Kent, R., 287

Kepler, J., 268

King Arthur, 63

Kropotkin, P., 291

Lamarque, J. B., 268

Lammenais, 291

Lao-Tse, 111, 119

Laplace, P. S., 268

Lassalle, F., 223

Lavoisier, A. L., 107, 268

Law, characteristics of ideational, 146-52; sensate, 152-56; crisis of contemporary, 157-63

Leibnitz, G. W., 266, 268, 300

Lenin, V., 211, 223

Leopardi, G., 291

Le Play, F., 127

Lermontov, M. Y., 291

Lessing, G. E., 283

Leutze, E., 285

Lewis, P., 284

Liberty, definition of, 172; ideational and sensate forms of, 172-74;

misuse of, 198-99; rise and decline of, 174-75, 177-84

Linear progress, belief into, 175, 232-34, 307

Locke, J., 86, 266, 290, 300, 301

Lombroso, G., 291

Lomonosoff, M. V., 107

Lotze, R. H., 291

Love, in Christian ethics, 133, 139; in fine arts, 50-51, 66

Lovejoy, A., 284

Lucian, 262

Ludwig, E., 121

Luks, G., 286

Lulli, J. B., 50

MacDowell, E., 289

Mach, E., 80, 117, 245, 284

Machiavelli, N., 160

Mahavira, 111

Mahler, G., 50

Maistre, J. de. See De Maistre, J.

Major premise of, idealistic, ideational, sensate cultures, 20-21

Maladies of contemporary culture. See Crisis, Degradation

Man, degradation of. See Degradation

Man, as unteachable, 324-26

Marriage, crises of contemporary, 187-90

Marsilio of Padua, 160

Marx, K., 122, 127, 157, 223, 245, 267, 291, 301

Materialism in contemporary, art, 33, 43, 58, 63-67, 70-72, 78; ethics and law, 135-36, 140-42, 152, 157-58, 163; philosophy and science, 93-96, 118-19

Materialism vs. idealism, fluctuation of, 94-95

Mathematics, discoveries in, 129; intuition in, 107-8

Mather, C., 282, 289, 290

Mather, I., 282, 289, 290

Matthew, Saint. See Saint Matthew

Maupassant, H., 291

Maurois, A., 121

Mayer, R., 106, 107, 109, 268
Melchers, G., 286
Melville, H., 283, 290
Mental disease, increase of, 206, 224
Metcalf, W., 286
Michelangelo, 53, 265
Michelet, J., 291
Might as right. See Coercion, Co-
    ercive
Mill, J. S., 291
Millar, R., 121
Millet, F. D., 286
Millet, J. F., 286
Mizkiewicz, 292
Mohammed, 111
Mommsen, T., 267
Montesquieux, C. L., 267, 301
Monteverde, C., 50
Moran, T., 286
Morgan, J. P., 186
Mo-Ti, 262
Mozart, W. A., 50, 55, 68, 106, 110,
    264
Muck-raking, in contemporary cul-
    ture, 294. See also Degradation,
    Pathological
Music, 18, 40, 45, 49, 65, 77, 159; de-
    cline of creativeness in, 255-56,
    264-65; intuition in, 110
Mussolini, B., 15, 23, 211, 223
Mystic intuition, 111

Napoleon, 251
Narcissus, 122
Natural sciences, movement of dis-
    coveries in, 87-88, 127-29, 268-69.
    See also Empirical science
Naturalistic style, of sensate art, 33;
    statistics of, 47
Newman, F. W., 291
Newton, I., 106, 107, 108, 127, 268,
    290, 300
Nicholas of Cusa, 112
Nietzsche, F., 266, 283, 291
Nihilism, 96. See Atomization, Co-
    ercion, Cynicism
Nobel, A. B., 265
Nominalistic mentality, 99

Nordau, M. S., 291
Norms. See Ethics
Nudity in art, 51

Occam, William of, 263
Oedipus, 63, 121, 138
O'Neill, E. G., 66, 289
Ordeal, as evidence in law, 148
Ordeal, catharsis by, 321-24
Organismic theories. See Bioorgan-
    ismic
Origen, 84
Ovid, 40

Paine, T., 282, 290
Palestrina, 50, 53, 68, 264
Pareto, V., 122, 127, 157, 245
Pascal, B., 109
Pasteur, L., 268
Paul, Saint. See Saint Paul
Pathétique in sensate art, 33, 42
Pathological, emphasis on, in art, 33,
    63-67, 294. See also Degradation,
    Heroes
Pavlov, I., 113
Paysage, 31, 32; statistics of pictures
    of, 51
Pearson, K., 117, 245, 284
Penn, W., 282
Pepys, S., 289
Perry, R. B., 284
Petronius, 302
Petzold, 245
Phidias, 37, 38, 52, 72, 106, 127, 263
Philosophy, decline of creativeness
    in, 259-61, 263; degradation of
    man and values in, 116-24, 244-45
Philosophy, movement of, empirical
    and non-empirical, 91-92; ideal-
    istic and materialistic, 94-95;
    sceptical, 117-18. See also Em-
    pirical science, Empiricism,
    Truth
Picasso, P., 69
Picton, 289
Pierce, C. S., 284
Pindar, 37, 138, 139

Plato, 57, 102, 106, 127, 137, 139, 261, 263
Pliny, 83, 254
Poe, E. A., 283, 290
Poincaré, H., 106, 107, 111, 117, 245, 284
Political regime, contractual, 170-75; dictatorial, 176-95. See also Contractual, Dictatorship
Polycletus, 38
Polygnotus, 38, 52
Pontius Pilate, 81
Portraits, percentage of, among paintings, 51
Poussin, N., 286
Praxiteles, 127
Present, overestimation of the, 96-97
Pressure groups, 162
Priestly, J., 282
Professional artists, 73-75
Progress, belief in, 175; salesmen of, 307
Prokofieff, S., 77
Prometheus, 63
Protestantism, ethics of, 140-41
Proudhon, P. J., 291
Psychoanalytical interpretation of man, 93-94, 121, 244, 312
Psychology, contemporary, 267
Punishment, increase of severity of, 226-29

Quantitative colossalism vs. quality, 53, 70-72, 252-56

Radcliffe, A., 290
Raphael, 53, 106, 127, 265, 301
Realistic style, of sensate art, 33, 47
Reality, as infinite manifold, 18-20, 81, 83-84, 102, 111-12, 135, 144, 317; rational, sensory, superrational and supersensory aspects of, 20-21, 81-83, 86, 102, 105-15, 308-13, 317-18
Reason, truth of, 20, 81-82, 103-6, 112-15
Reclus, E., 291
Relativism vs. absolutism, 143-44

Relativistic nature, of sensate, ethics and law, 137, 144, 152-53, 159-63; mentality, science and truth, 96-97, 116, 119. See also Atomization
Relationships social, forms of, 167-69
Religion, as adjunct to police, 160; as system of revealed truth, 17-19, 81, 83-85, 111-12; decline of creativeness in, 259-61; sensate pseudo, 111, 160, 251. See also God, Ideational
Religious, art, 30-33, 37, 39-42, 45-50; culture, 18-20; ethics and law, 133-34, 138-39, 147-52; liberty, 172-74; topics in art, 45
Religious leaders, per cent among historical persons, 259-60
Rembrandt, 127, 265, 301
Renan, E., 291
Renouvier, C., 291
Resurrection of culture, 321-25
Revolt, against sensate art, 76-79
Revolutions, brutality in, 227-31; increase in crisis periods, 206-7; movement and statistics of, 217-24
Revolutions, in systems of truth, 83-85
Rey, A., 284
Reynolds, Sir Joshua, 286
Rhodes, C., 186
Rhythm. See Alternation
Ricardo, D., 267
Richardson, S., 290
Rickert, H., 284
Riehl, 284
Roberty, E. de. See De Roberty, E.
Robinson, T., 286
Rockefeller, J. D., 186
Roosevelt, F. D., 15, 23, 187
Rosenkranz, K., 292
Rosmini-Serbati, A., 292
Rothschild, 186
Rousseau, J. J., 223, 267, 283, 286, 290
Ruskin, J., 292

Saint-Simon, C. H., 283

Saint Augustine, 80, 84, 85, 111, 112, 263, 300

Saint Gregory, 49

Saint Matthew, 134, 147

Saint Paul, 80, 84, 106, 111, 256, 300

Saint Thomas Aquinas, 80, 102, 117, 127, 137, 263, 266, 300

Santayana, G., 284

Sargent, J. S., 285, 286, 287

Savoir pour prévoir, 100-1; failure of, 130-32, 217, 222

Schelling, F. W. J. von. See Von Schelling, F. W. J.

Schiller, F. C. S., 55, 265, 291

Schleiermacher, F. D. E., 291, 292

Schönberg, A., 77

Schopenhauer, A., 263, 266, 291, 292

Science. See Empirical science, Empiricism, Truth

Science leaders, per cent among historical persons, 259-60

Scientific discoveries. See Discoveries

Scott, W., 290

Secretan, 292

Secular and religious topics in art, statistics of, 45

Selectivity of culture, 248-49

Sensate, art, 32-33, 43-52, 53-79; culture, 20-21; ethics and law, 135-37, 152-65; liberty, 172-74; science and truth, 81, 86-102, 116-32

Senses, truth of, 81, 86-102, 116-32

Sensuality. See Eroticism, Sensate

Sewall, S., 289

Shaftsbury, A. A. C., 290

Shakespeare, W., 55, 68, 72, 106, 127, 265, 301

Shelley, P. B., 292

Shift. See Alternation

Shift of allegiance. See Allegiance

Shostakovitch, 77

Simmel, G., 127

Singularism, 99

Scepticism, 86, 117-18

Smith, A., 301

Smith, J., 289

Smollett, T. G., 290

Social classes, antagonisms of, 161-64, 196, 200, 205-6, 242, 247, 314; cheated, 195-96

Social relationships, forms of, 167-68. See also Coercive, Contractual, Familistic

Socrates, 139

Solovieff, 291, 292

Sophocles, 37, 38, 127, 138

Sorokin, P. A., 13, 36, 40, 51, 79, 102, 146, 156, 169, 181, 187, 193, 217, 224, 231, 239, 252, 259, 271, 277, 280, 301, 308

Spencer, H., 127, 266, 267, 283, 291, 301

Spengler, O., 16

Spinoza, 266

Spiritual, and sensual in art, 50-51, 58, 62, 66, 293-94

Stalin, J., 15, 23, 117, 211, 223

Stamitz, J. W. A., 50

Statesmen, per cent among historical persons, 259-60

Static character of, ideational, art, 32; ethical norms, 133-35, 138-40; revealed truth, 81, 83, 84

Steinbeck, J., 66

Stirner, 283, 291

Strachey, L., 121

Strauss, R., 50

Stravinsky, I., 50, 68, 77

Stuart, G., 286

Suetonius, 83

Suicide, anomic and egotistic, 208; factors of, 208-9; increase of, 224

Sully, T., 285, 286

Superficiality of sensate art, 60-63; science, 116-19, 125-27

Symbolism of ideational art, 31-32, 39

Symptoms of culture disintegration, 241

Syncretism, in art, 54-55, 68-69; in culture, 247-52

Tacitus, 83

Taine, H., 267, 291

Tarde, G., 127

Taylor, D., 289

Technique *vs.* genius, 70-73, 119

Technological Inventions. See Inventions

Tempo of social processes, accelerating, 33, 62, 97, 257. See also Dynamic, Static

Temporalism *vs.* eternalism, 32-33, 43, 61, 81-83, 95-97, 120, 133-36, 144, 147, 159, 162, 192-93, 203

Terpander, 127

Tertullian, 84

Theology, 261. See also Christian, Religion

Theophilus, 40

Thoreau, H. D., 283, 291

Thucydides, 127

Time, importance in sensate culture, 96-97; overemphasis of the present, 96-97. See also Temporalism

Tocqueville, A. H. C. de. See De Tocqueville, A. H. C.

Tolstoi, L., 55, 265, 283, 291, 292

Totalitarianism, contemporary growth of, 176-95, 276

Transitional periods. See Crisis

Trumbull, J., 286

Truth, conflict of different systems of, 83-85; forms of, 81-83; integral, 112-14; intuitive, 81, 105-12; of faith, 20, 81, 83-85, 105-12; rational, 20, 81-82, 103-6, 112-15; sensory, 81, 86-102, 116-32; shift of domination of systems of, 83-85. See also Empirical science

Tschaikovsky, P. I., 55, 265

Turgenev, I. S., 291, 292

Turgot, 283

Turner, W., 286

Twain, M., 291, 292, 293

Unions of artists, 73-75

United States, similarity of, cultural trends in Europe and in the, 280-92; social trends, 273-80; indivisibility of culture of Europe and that of the, 295-96

Unity of culture, 17-18, 296-97

Universalization of values, 203, 316-17. See also Absolute, Atomization

Utilitarianism, ethical, 135-36, 138, 140-42, 152-53, 159-64

Utility, as criteria of beauty, 33, 58-59; goodness, 135-36, 138, 140-42, 152-53, 159-64; truth, 87, 93, 99-101, 116-17, 130-31

Vaihinger, H., 284

Value, absolute, 18-20, 135, 144, 317-18; relative, 96-97, 116-20, 142-44, 153, 157-63, 192-93, 203, 205. See also Absolute, Atomization, Degradation, Universalization

Vico, G., 301

Vigny, A. de. See De Vigny, A.

Virgil, 40

Virgin Mary, 84

Voltaire, F., 223

Von Baader, F. X., 291, 292

Von Hartmann, E., 291, 292

Von Herder, J. G., 283

Von Schelling, F. W. J., 266, 291

Wagner, R., 50, 55, 68, 265, 291, 292

Walpole, H., 290

War, increase in crisis periods, 205-6; movement in history, 212-17

Ward, L., 283

Wealth, Christian, Protestant, and modern attitude towards, 133-38, 139-42, 159-63

Weber, M., 127, 174

Weir, J., 286

Wesley, J., 141

Whistler, J., 285, 286

Whitehead, A. H., 284

Whitman, W., 283

Wigglesworth, M., 289, 290

Williams, R., 282, 289

Willkie, W., 187

Windebrandt, W., 284
Winthrop, J., 289
Wisdom. See Truth
Wollaston, W. H., 290
Wollstonecraft, M., 290
Woolman, J., 282, 290
Wordsworth, H., 290

Wronsky, 292

Zeller, E., 291
Zeno, 263
Zola, E., 68
Zorach, 287
Zoroaster, 111, 134

## DUTTON EVERYMAN PAPERBACKS

SHAKESPEARE OF LONDON, Marchette Chute     D-1

THE PROPER BOSTONIANS, Cleveland Amory     D-2

THE FLOWERING OF NEW ENGLAND,
Van Wyck Brooks     D-3

THE REPUBLIC OF PLATO     D-4

THE STORY OF SAN MICHELE, Axel Munthe     D-5

NAKED MASKS: Five Plays by Luigi Pirandello     D-6

OF THE NATURE OF THINGS, Lucretius     D-7

LETTERS FROM AN AMERICAN FARMER,
J. Hector St. John de Crèvecoeur     D-8

THE ENGLISH NOVEL, Walter Allen     D-9

THE CRISIS OF OUR AGE, P. A. Sorokin     D-10

# Theme of Book

I. Progressive decay of sensate culture

II Emergence of new idealistic culture

Manifested In:

A) Science
   1. Increasing distructiveness of sensate scientific achievements.
   2. Transformation of basic theories in a morally responsible (idealistic) direction

B) Philosophy
   1. Increasing decline of materialistic "positivic" philosophies
   2. Emergence and growth of epistential & neo-Thomist philosophy

C) Religion (double process)
   1. Militant atheism
   2. Religious Revival

D) Ethics (double process)
   1. Utter bestiality (e.g. WW II) and increasing criminality
   2. Moral heroism & sublime altruism

E) Politics
   1. proliferation of all kinds of tyrannical dictatorships
   2. Swelling grass-roots movement for establishment of a competent, honest, & morally responsible government by the people.

# Three Diagnoses of World Situation

I Sharp form of economic or political crisis
   A. Prescribe readjustment of economic conditions
     or modification of political conditions
       1. Probably most prevalent theory

       2. Ex. of its falsity:
         Kaiser eliminated & Germany defeated
         yet it neither prevented nor weakened
         subsequent development of crises


II Crisis is the death agony of western civilization
  and culture
     A. No remedy can avert this destiny
       1. Ex. of its falsity:
         Western society at end of M. Ages
         underwent a similar shift and
         yet such a shift neither put
         an end to their existence nor
         paralyzed their creative force
       2. Alleged death is but the
         birth pangs of a new form
         of culture


III Crisis not merely political or economic
  maladjustment but involves Western
  society in all its main factors. It
  consists in the disintegration of a
  fundamental form of Western
  culture dominant for the last 4 centuries.

Three Major Principles of Distinctive West. Culture

I Ideational - supersensory & superrational
    God as the only true reality & value (M. A)

II Idealistic - mixture of supersensory & sensory
                    (13th & 14th centuries)

III Sensate - predominantly secular & utilitarian
                    (16th century to present.

Evolution of Fine Arts
    Crete - mycenean - sensate
    Greek 8 - 6 BC - ideational
    Greek 6 - 5 B C - idealistic
                    (par excellence)
    Greek 3 BC - 4 AD - sensate with
        transition ideational
    6 AD - 12 AD - ideational predominate
    12 AD (13th Cent) - idealistic
    16 AD to Present - sensate

Comparison of Types of Art

I Ideational
    Topic - supersensory kingdom of God
    Objective - bring believer in closer union with Δ
    Content & Form - sacred, no comedy etc.
    Emotional Tone - pious, ethereal
        Style - symbolic & wholly internal; simple

II Sensate
    Topic - emperical men, events, & adventures
    Objective - refined sensual enjoyment, relaxation
                    amusement etc.
    Content Form - voluptuous nudity, voluptuousness

Emotional Tone - sensational, sensual, incessantly new

Style - naturalistic, realistic, visual

## III Idealistic

Topic - partly supersensory, partly sensory
(only in sublimest & noblest aspects)

Objective - instructive, moralizing, civic

Content, Form - blind to everything vulgar,
debasing, ugly

Emotional Tone - calm, serene

Style - partly symbolic, allegoric & partly
realistic & naturalistic

## Achievements & Maladies of Sensate Art

### I Achievements

1. Unexampled in volume
2. Unexampled in size
3. Infinite diversity & variety
4. Superb inner value in much of it

### II Maladies

1. Function of giving enjoyment leads to
mere means of sensual enjoyment

2. Endeavor to portray reality as it appears to
senses causes it to become the art of
progressively thinner & more illusory surface

3. In quest for sensory & sensational it becomes
increasing & fatally deflected from positive
to negative phenomena

4. Diversity impels it to seek ever greater variety
until harmony, unity & balance are submerged
in an ocean of incoherence

5. Diversity leads to increasing complication of
technical means & tends to make these
instrumentalities, ends in themselves

6. Sensate is the art of professional artists. Such
specialization results in the separation of the
artists from the community & ...